# THE
# ARCHITECTURAL HERITAGE
## OF BRITAIN AND IRELAND

## An Illustrated A–Z
of
Terms and Styles

A SHELL BOOK

written and photographed by
## MICHAEL JENNER

MICHAEL JOSEPH
LONDON

*For Diana who has accompanied me to so many of the places
featured in this book.*

*Also by Michael Jenner*

YEMEN REDISCOVERED
BAHRAIN – GULF HERITAGE IN TRANSITION
SYRIA IN VIEW
SCOTLAND THROUGH THE AGES
LONDON HERITAGE
A TRAVELLER'S COMPANION TO THE WEST COUNTRY
JOURNEYS INTO MEDIEVAL ENGLAND
IRELAND THROUGH THE AGES


MICHAEL JOSEPH LTD

Published by the Penguin Group
27 Wrights Lane, London W8 5TZ
Viking Penguin Inc., 375 Hudson Street, New York, New York 10014, USA
Penguin Books Australia Ltd, Ringwood, Victoria, Australia
Penguin Books Canada Ltd, 10 Alcorn Avenue, Toronto, Ontario, Canada M4V 3B2
Penguin Books (NZ) Ltd, 182–190 Wairau Road, Auckland 10, New Zealand

Penguin Books Ltd, Registered Offices: Harmondsworth, Middlesex, England

First published in Great Britain 1993

A CIP catalogue record for this book is available from the British Library

ISBN 0 7181 3517 2

The moral right of the author has been asserted

The information contained in this book is believed correct at the time of printing. While
every care has been taken to ensure that the information is accurate, Shell UK cannot accept
responsibility for any errors, omissions or changes in the details given.

The name Shell and the Shell emblem are registered trademarks.

Line drawings by Gillie Newman
Designed by Penny Mills

Typeset in Monophoto Walbaum 11½ x 12½
Printed and bound in Hong Kong by Imago Publishing Ltd.

# Contents

**1** St Paul's Cathedral, London, is a familiar sight, but how familiar are we really with the individual features of the composition? And how many can we name? Most obvious in this view of the west front are the **columns** which form the upper part of a two-storey **portico**. They belong to the **composite order**, a Roman invention combining the attributes of the **Ionic** and **Corinthian** orders. The Ionic contributed the scroll-like elements on the capital known as **volutes**, and the Corinthian influence may be seen in the **acanthus** leaf decoration that surrounds them. The **shaft** of each column has **fluting**, i.e. vertical grooves which are separated by narrow, flat bands or **fillets**. The columns have been arranged in pairs, a device known as **accouplement**.

The horizontal element supported by the capitals is the **entablature**, and this in turn consists of an **architrave**, and a **frieze**. A series of small brackets known as **modillions** supports the **cornice**, above which there is a triangular structure known as the **pediment**. To finish off the composition, there are three statues or **acroteria** perched on the points of the triangular pediment.

The list of features can be extended, but what is the point of the exercise? Quite simply this: although St Paul's is obviously much more than the sum of its parts, an awareness of its individual parts enhances beyond measure our appreciation of the composition as a whole, which was intended to be read in its small print as well as to be taken in at a glance. Knowledge of the basic vocabulary of architecture thus allows us to understand more fully the language of the buildings that surround us.

# INTRODUCTION

If there was a single moment when my eyes were opened to the potential beauties of buildings it was almost certainly at Norwich Cathedral when I first looked into a mirror mounted on a trolley and was able to explore the glories of a Gothic vault without getting a crick in my neck. It was strange to be in effect looking up when I was actually looking down, but even stranger to view isolated parts of a great building conveniently framed within a mirror. As a disembodied image the structure was mysteriously transformed into an abstract pattern of ribs and bosses. It was still a vault but one which seemed to float upside down, defying the law of gravity. It had somehow become pure form. Since then I have relived that experience on many occasions when looking at other buildings through the viewfinder of a camera while trying to frame a picture that would convey the essence of a complex structure through a single vista or a even a simple detail.

But if my eyes had been opened by mirrors and photographic lenses, there was another aspect to architecture which needed no artificial contrivances: the human dimension. To take an extreme case, Hawker's Hut, perched on the cliffs of north Cornwall was built essentially as a shelter for one person, an eccentric parson. The perfect snugness of this tiny retreat, commanding a panoramic view out to sea, taught me that a building does not have to be high and noble, nor designed by an architect, to be impressive.

Indeed, the attraction of a building may be its very absence of architectural design. A modest residence such as a Hebridian black house conveys most eloquently the simple domestic routine of countless generations past. Then again, a stylish decorative detail can give us an insight into the taste and ambitions of a particular individual at a specific moment in history: for example, Cardinal Wolsey's Italianate medallions at Hampton Court Palace. Such fingerprints from the past are so often the magical mystery ingredient which gives a building its human interest and true fascination.

Growing familiarity with buildings in all parts of the British Isles brought with it the bonus of being able to compare and contrast. Then I began to delve, somewhat hesitantly at first, into thick tomes of architectural history. The benefits were not slow in coming. My visual delight in the fan-vaulted cloister of Gloucester Cathedral broadened into a much deeper appreciation when I learned that this was the earliest example of that technique in these islands and was, so to speak, a native invention, since until that time most of our Gothic architecture had been largely an imitation of French achievements.

Soon I was hooked on the subject of buildings and an ardent sampler of the best examples of the various styles. If I happened to come across a comment in an architectural book, such as one of the Pevsner guides to the buildings of England, that a particular country house was the most splendid piece of Greek Revival in Wiltshire or Norfolk or the comeliest Tudor manor house in Kent or Cumbria, then I would make a mental note to see it for myself. I have had the good fortune to be able to indulge my curiosity to the full over the past ten years in the course of a series of books and articles, and this present work has gradually evolved alongside them.

Then there was the formidable technical jargon of the architectural trade, those ogees, purlins, shaped gables, flushwork and so forth. To my surprise, browsing through the architectural lexicon brought entertainment as well as enlightenment. The naming of the parts brought my eye to focus on countless tiny details which hitherto had escaped my attention. So that elegant spiral flourish on an Ionic capital was a volute; and the abacus of the Greek Doric order was an uncompromising square slab contrasting effectively with those fluted columns rising from the floor without any form of ornamental base.

Soon I was taking a connoisseur's delight in crockets on pinnacles, acroteria on pediments and chevrons on chancel arches. I could see the difference between a serious piece of Palladianism and a run-of-the-mill pastiche. And without taking sides in the Battle of the Styles I could appreciate the contrasting visions of the Gothic Revivalists and the Neo-Classicists. Architecture gradually became fun and part of my everyday experience.

This book is an attempt to convey to the general reader all the basic ingredients that have fed and sustained my own passion for buildings. It is on the one hand a practical dictionary defining details, identifying styles and classifying types. It also contains an historical perspective by including many structures which date from a time long before architecture became the business of professional architects; for example, the prehistoric buildings at Knap of Howar on the remote Orkney island of Papa Westray which mark the birth of our domestic housing and link us, of the semi-detached culture of the twentieth century, with our Neolithic ancestors of the fourth millennium BC. Likewise, the mighty earthworks of the Iron Age hillforts are deemed worthy of consideration as examples of landscape architecture even if they were never conceived as anything more than communal defenses.

On the other hand, this book is intended as a forthright celebration of architecture in the British Isles. The numerous photographs aim to present physical evidence of the splendid achievements of masons, carpenters, bricklayers, decorators, designers and architects through the ages. I hope that this visual testimony will encourage many people to find much lasting pleasure in a truly remarkable architectural heritage as they embark on their own voyages of discovery.

Michael Jenner
London, 1992

# HOW TO USE THIS BOOK

While the alphabetical ordering of the material makes it straightforward to locate individual entries, every effort has been made to open up alternative avenues for the reader to explore the contents of the book. Cross-references are used not only to point out where an entry is defined elsewhere under a different name, e.g. PILLAR [see PIER], but they may also indicate where an entry is dealt with in the course of a larger entry, e.g. LINENFOLD [see PANELLING]. Where a subject is so vast, e.g. CHURCH, that its constituent parts occur in many places throughout the book, then a multitude of cross-references are given. The reader with a special interest in ecclesiastical architecture will thus be directed at the end of the concise general entry on CHURCH to a host of relevant entries from AISLE and ALTAR to VESTRY and WAGON ROOF. Occasionally, cross-references are used in a more oblique manner to direct the reader's attention to related items of interest, e.g. after the entry on GREEK REVIVAL the following are given for further consideration: BATTLE OF THE STYLES, CARYATID, CLASSICAL, ORDER, TEMPLE.

Whilst every care has been taken to place photographs and line drawings next to the appropriate entry, it has not always been possible to include an illustration for reasons of the restricted space available. The expedient of the picture cross-reference has thus been devised in order to overcome this limitation. For example, although there is no picture illustrating POLYCHROMY under that entry, the reader is directed by illustration numbers at the end of the entry to the examples of that phenomenon located elsewhere. These cross-references to pictures are not exhaustive and merely serve to point out to the reader the most telling examples. The index provides a quick reference to enable the reader to check which buildings are mentioned in the book. These examples have been printed in bold in the text to make for easy location.

With these various possibilities for retrieving information, it is hoped that both enlightenment and diversion will result. However, given the basic nature of cross-references, it is inevitable that the reader will sometimes end up after a while right back where he or she started out. As in real life, when exploring a country rich in historic architecture, it is as much a part of the total experience to get sidetracked along the way as it is to arrive directly at one's destination. So although this book operates at one level as a simple A to Z, it is also intended as a complex map on which the reader can roam in any direction; and the landscape it portrays bristles with signposts to the remotest corners of the British Isles as well as back in time more than five thousand years to the beginnings of prehistoric architecture.

# A

## ABACUS

Uppermost element of a Classical capital. In the Greek Doric order this consists of a flat, square slab; but in Ionic, Tuscan and Roman Doric the lower edge has a moulding. The square abacus also occurs in Saxon and Norman architecture, but the Gothic style produced circular and polygonal forms, in which the abacus was usually merged into the main part of the capital. [see CAPITAL, ECHINUS, ORDER, **83**]

## ABBEY

Monastic establishment under the juris-

**2** OPPOSITE *Chapter-house of Valle Crucis Abbey*, Clwyd.
**3** *The great west range at Fountains Abbey*, N Yorks.

diction of an abbot or abbess. The term often refers to the church of an abbey; and it may apply long after the disappearance of the monastic complex as a whole, e.g. **Sherborne Abbey**, *Dorset*; **Selby Abbey**, *N Yorks*. The name adheres to many country houses which occupy the site and sometimes the buildings of previous abbeys, e.g. **Lacock Abbey**, *Wilts*; **Hartland Abbey**, *Devon*. [see MONASTERY, **85, 159, 311, 351**]

## ABUTMENT

Mass of masonry which gives lateral support to an arch or vault. [see BUTTRESS]

## ACANTHUS

Mediterranean plant with large, deeply cleft leaves with sharp points, adapted for the design of Corinthian and Composite capitals. [see ORDER]

4 *Accouplement in the Ionic colonnade of Park Crescent, London, part of Nash's Regent's Park scheme.*

## ACCOUPLEMENT
Grouping in pairs of columns or pilasters.

## ACHIEVEMENT
Heraldic display of armorial bearings, e.g. escutcheon, crest etc., or the armour of a nobleman which was placed on or above his tomb, e.g. that of the Black Prince in **Canterbury Cathedral**, *Kent*. [see ESCUTCHEON, HATCHMENT, TROPHY]

## ADAM STYLE

The achievement of the Adam brothers, John (1721–92), Robert (1728–92) and James (1732–94) may be measured by the fact that they imprinted their name on a style which remains a landmark in the history of design.

The real genius behind the Adam Style was Robert, who was greatly influenced by what he had seen during a four-year stay in Italy. He declared that the austere formality practised by the Palladian school was a flat and insipid rendering of ancient artistry. He resolved to bring about 'a revolution in the whole system of this useful and elegant art'. The essential ingredients of the Adam Style were later defined in *The Works of Robert and James Adam Esquires* of 1773 as 'a beautiful variety of light mouldings, gracefully formed, delicately enriched, and arranged with propriety and skill'. To which might be added a bold use of colour and motifs such as festoons, urns, chimeras and anthemions. New ideas were freely evolved and given fanciful historic names such as Pompeian and Etruscan. The Adam Style pioneered the concept of total design which co-ordinated ceilings, walls, fireplaces

5 *The stately vestibule at Osterley Park House, London, bears the hallmark of the Adam Style.*

and furniture right down to details such as doorknobs and keyholes.

During the 1760s and 1770s the Adam Style was the epitome of fashion. Commissions flooded in for the remodelling of country houses and town mansions. The most dazzling Adam interiors in London include **Kenwood House, Osterley Park House, Syon House** and **20 Portman Square**; and elsewhere in England, **Harewood House** and **Nostell Priory**, *W Yorks*; **Audley End**, *Essex*; **Bowood House**,

## ACROTERIA

Plinths or pedestals for statuary positioned on the apex and lower angles of a Classical pediment. The term also refers to the statues. Acroteria create a dramatic skyline on the **Four Courts**, Dublin, Ireland, of 1786 by James Gandon; and the façade of 1709–36 at the **Queen's College, Oxford**, *Oxon*. [see **263, 298**]

## ACUTE ARCH [see ARCH, LANCET]

## AEDICULE

Niche flanked by columns or colonnettes

to form a recess for a statue. [see **37, 317**]

## AGGER

Foundation of a Roman road which sometimes survives as a raised embankment, e.g. **Ackling Dyke** on Oakley Down, *Dorset*. [see ROMAN]

## AGGREGATE

Hard material used in fragments and combined with mortar to make concrete. The remains of demolished structures have traditionally been recycled as aggregate, e.g. Roman tiles by the Saxons and

*Wilts*; **Saltram House**, *Devon*; and **Kedleston Hall**, *Derbys*. In their native Scotland the Adams left their mark on **Hopetoun House**, *Lothian*; **Mellerstain** House, *Borders*; and **Culzean Castle**, *S'clyde*, as well as in **Charlotte Square, Edinburgh**. Grandiose urban ideas are still in evidence in what little now remains of the Adams' ill-fated **Adelphi** project in London.

While the Adam Style was in vogue its effect was potent. A happy client boasted: 'He has made me a ceiling and chimney-piece, and doors, which are pretty enough to make me a thousand enemies; Envy turns livid at the first glimpsing of them.' But the fickleness of fashion was to turn against Robert Adam, whose designs were dismissed by Horace Walpole as 'gingerbread and snippets of embroidery'. Posterity has been kinder; and the consistency of purpose behind the Adam Style and all its delicate refinements has been widely acknowledged. [see CEILING, ETRUSCAN, PLASTERWORK, **113, 206, 281**]

*6 Neo-Classical Adam stairwell at 20 Portman Square, London.*

Normans, Gothic masonry by the Tudors. [see CONCRETE]

## AISLE

Originally a part of a church running parallel to the nave and divided from it by an arcade. Often this was an extension to the original church, e.g. the **Lane Aisle** at **St Andrew, Cullompton,** *Devon*. Early medieval halls, e.g. at **Oakham Castle**, *Leics*, were aisled, i.e. supported by one or more arcades, before roofing techniques such as the hammerbeam enabled wide spaces to be spanned. Today the term aisle commonly refers to the passage between rows of seats in a church or auditorium. [see BASILICA, **147, 383**]

## ALABASTER

Pale, translucent form of gypsum, easily carved to produce fine detail. When cut very thin, it once served as a primitive form of glazing. It was much favoured for sculptured tomb effigies from the Middle Ages onwards. It was also used in the eighteenth century for stately interiors, e.g. at **Kedleston Hall**, *Derbys*, by Robert Adam, and at **Holkham Hall**, *Norfolk*, by William Kent. [see TOMB SCULPTURE]

## ALCOVE

Niche or recess in a room.

## ALIEN HOUSE

Monastic establishment founded by a foreign (usually French) mother house. Since its revenues remained under foreign control, it was potentially a drain on the national economy.

## ALLEY

Narrow passage between buildings. In older townscapes, e.g. **Tewkesbury**, *Glos*, alleys provided access to back plots.

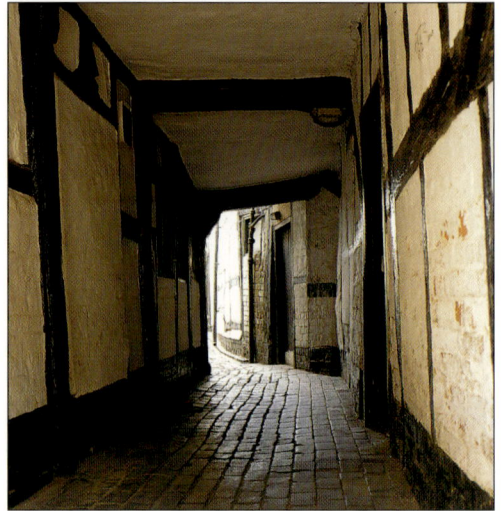

*7 One of the many ancient alleys which lead off the main street of Tewkesbury, Glos.*

## ALMONRY

Room or separate building, usually in a monastery, where alms were distributed.

## ALMSHOUSE

Group of dwellings, often arranged around a courtyard, which provided accommodation for the poor and needy. Medieval almshouses were usually founded by the wealthy both as an act of public charity and for the salvation of the souls of the benefactors. Many ancient almshouses have survived intact, e.g. the **Hospital of St Cross** at **Winchester**, *Hants*, of 1136 reckoned to be the oldest in the country. The **Great Hospital, Norwich**, *Norfolk*, was founded in 1246. An impressive range of medieval almshouses, mentioned by Chaucer, is located at **Ewelme**, *Oxon*. Tudor examples abound in town and country, e.g. the **Lord Leycester Hospital, Warwick**, *Warw*; and the **Whitgift Hospital, Croydon**, *Surrey*. In the latter half of the seventeenth century, the idea of the almshouse evolved under royal patronage when a new style of retirement home for the armed forces came into being, e.g.

8 *Courtyard of medieval almshouses at Ewelme,* Oxon.

the **Royal Hospital** at **Kilmainham, Dublin,** Ireland, in 1679. This was followed three years later in London by Christopher Wren's **Chelsea Hospital**, and from 1695 by his **Royal Naval Hospital, Greenwich**. [see BEDEHOUSE, **174, 242**]

## ALTAR

Table-like structure of stone in a church serving as the focal point for Christian worship and for the celebration of the Mass. In medieval churches saints' relics were sometimes deposited inside an altar. Larger churches and especially cathedrals contained many individual altars set up in the various chantry chapels, aisles and transepts; in the twelfth century **Canterbury Cathedral,** *Kent,* had as many as twenty-five altars. After the Reformation in the 1530s many stone altars were replaced by wooden communion tables; and in the chapels and meeting houses of the Nonconformists they disappeared altogether. The Victorian revival of ritual restored the altar as the focal point of church planning. [see SHRINE]

## ALTAR SCREEN [see REREDOS, RETABLE]

## ALTAR TOMB

Tomb resembling a stone altar, often with an effigy of the deceased placed on top. In Ireland, the side panels of such tombs were the object of elaborate carving of great artistry, e.g. at **Jerpoint Abbey,** *Kilkenny*; **Ennis Friary,** *Clare*; and **Strade Friary,** *Mayo*. [see TOMB SCULPTURE]

9 *The richly embellished altar tomb of Piers Fitz Oge Butler at Kilcooly Abbey,* Tipperary, *Ireland.*

10 *The Roman amphitheatre at Caerleon,* Gwent, *Wales, is the best preserved part of the legionary fortress.*

## ALURE
Parapet or wall-walk along a battlement. [see PARAPET]

## AMBULATORY
Extension of the aisles of a church to meet behind the high altar, and thus to form a semicircular walk through the apse. The ambulatory is one of the main distinguishing features of cathedrals and abbey churches, e.g. **Norwich Cathedral,** *Norfolk*, and **St Bartholomew-the-Great, London.** The term also denotes the covered walk of a cloister. [see APSE, CHEVET]

## AMPHITHEATRE
Circular or elliptical arena for sports, games and other spectacles, enclosed within banks of seats. The Romans introduced this class of structure to Britain, e.g. at **Cirencester,** *Glos*, and at **Caerleon,** *Gwent*, Wales. The Roman amphitheatre at **Chester,** *Cheshire*, is the largest in Britain; it was used for entertainment and military training by the 20th Legion. An ornamental turf amphitheatre of early eighteenth-century date is a feature of the

**Claremont Landscape Garden,** *Surrey*. **Gwennap Pit,** *Cornwall*, is an amphitheatre created in the early nineteenth century out of a hollow where John Wesley used to preach to the local people. A modern version of an amphitheatre was built in 1990 at the **Broadgate Circle, London**; it serves in winter as an ice rink. [see ROMAN, THEATRE]

## ANCONES [see CONSOLE]

## ANDIRONS [see FIRE-DOGS]

## ANGEL LIGHT
Small triangular opening formed between the arches in the tracery of a Perpendicular Gothic window.

## ANGEL ROOF
Carved angels with wings spread were a favourite device of medieval carpenters for embellishing the open-timbered roofs of parish churches, e.g. at **All Saints, Martock,** and **St Mary, Westonzoyland,** *Somerset*; **St Wendreda, March,** *Cambs*; and **Holy Trinity, Blythburgh,** *Suffolk*.

11 *Magnificent angel roof of carved oak in the church of St Mary, Westonzoyland,* Somerset.

[see TIMBER-TRUSSED ROOF, 372]

**ANGLO-SAXON** [see SAXON]

**ANNULET** [see SHAFT RING]

## ANTAE

Pilasters at the corners of a Classical building whose base and capital do not follow the same order as that of the façade. Antae usually occur in pairs at either end of a portico. They also feature in a different guise in non-Classical architecture as a slight extension of the side walls in the early stone churches of Ireland, e.g.

15

**Temple Macdara, St Macdara's Island**, *Galway*, where the antae extend up the gable and intersect at the apex.

## ANTECHAMBER
Room of lesser importance leading to a grander reception room or royal bedchamber. Often the anteroom itself was very imposing, designed to reflect the status of the owner.

## ANTHEMION
Decorative Classical motif derived from the honeysuckle.

## APARTMENT HOUSE
The concept of accommodating a number of self-contained units of habitation behind a shared front door and served by a common staircase did not become socially acceptable in England until the late nineteenth century. Even then, it was necessary to employ a noble architecture expressing class, tradition and respectability. The resulting formula of the mansion block enjoyed its heyday in the Edwardian era. Among the most baronial of London's early prototypes was **Albert Hall Mansions, Kensington**, of 1879–81 by Norman Shaw. In the 1920s and 1930s a sleek Modernism provided fresh inspiration, e.g. the **Isokon flats, Hampstead,** by Wells Coates and the **Highpoint flats, Highgate,** by Tecton. In the 1950s and 1960s the stylish apartment house gave way to the anonymous tower-block. Since the 1980s there has been a marked tendency to disguise apartment houses with all manner of features more appropriate

12 *Albert Court, Kensington, London: a fine Victorian apartment house in the mansion-block style.*

to traditional houses, e.g. pitched roofs and gable ends. [see COUNCIL HOUSING, PEABODY BUILDINGS, TENEMENT, 26]

## APSE

Semicircular or polygonal extension to a building, especially the east end of a church or cathedral. [see AMBULATORY, CHEVET, 113]

## AQUEDUCT

Channel or conduit constructed to convey water, usually on an elevated bridge-like structure. Outside **Dorchester**, *Dorset*, traces remain in the hillside of a Roman aqueduct in the form of a canal which follows the contour of the landscape. Most spectacular is the **Pont-Cysyllte Aqueduct** near **Llangollen**, *Clwyd*, Wales, built by Thomas Telford from 1795 to carry the Shropshire Union Canal at a height of over 120 feet (36·6m) over the River Dee. The noble **Dundas Aqueduct, Bath**, *Avon*, is in the Classical manner; it carries the Kennet and Avon Canal over the River Avon. [see BRIDGE, CONDUIT, CULVERT, VIADUCT]

13 *Pont-Cysyllte Aqueduct near Llangollen*, Clwyd, *Wales, represents a major achievement of the canal era.*

## ARABESQUE

Abstract decorative pattern, much used in Islamic design, forming an intricate network of repeated shapes.

## ARCADE

1) Two or more linked arches, often used to form a covered walkway in a cloister. As a decorative motif carved in relief on a solid wall, it is known as a blank or blind arcade. [see 147, 262]

14 *The Royal Opera Arcade, London, of 1816–18, a prototype imitated in other commercial developments.*

2) The term was later applied to the covered shopping galleries developed in the early nineteenth century, e.g. **London's Royal Opera Arcade** of 1816–18 and the **Burlington Arcade** of 1819. With the spread of the technology of glass and iron in the Victorian era many shopping arcades were built throughout the country, e.g. the **Royal Arcade, Norwich**, *Norfolk*, of 1899 by the local architect George Skipper, a

# ARCH

1) Load-bearing struc-
ture which forms an
opening of pointed or
semicircular shape. The
elements composing an
arch are most com-
monly wedge-shaped
blocks of masonry, but
some of the earliest
Saxon arches were built
with flat Roman bricks
with mortar in between.
The.round or semicircu-
lar type of arch, as originally pioneered by the
Romans, became the
dominant characteristic
of the eleventh-century
Romanesque or Norman
style in Britain. The
move to the pointed
arch in the late twelfth
century marked the
beginning of an entirely
new chapter in architec-
tural history and the
birth of the Gothic
style; it revolutionized
building design,

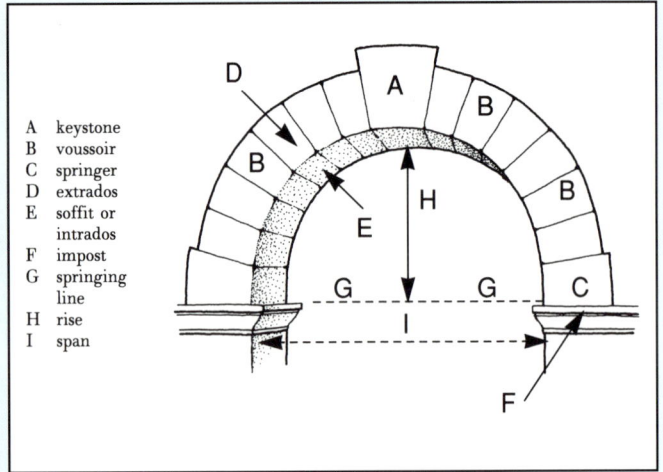

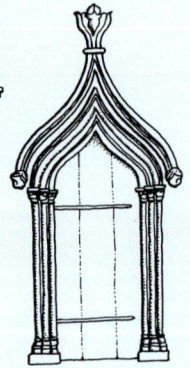

A   keystone
B   voussoir
C   springer
D   extrados
E   soffit or
    intrados
F   impost
G   springing
    line
H   rise
I   span

Norman

Saxon

Ogee

striking hybrid of Art Nouveau and
Orientalism. [see GALLERIA]

## ARCHITRAVE

1) Lowest of the three principal elements
of the Classical entablature. [see ENTABLA-
TURE, ORDER]

2) Moulded surround of a door or window.

## ARCHIVOLT

Decorative moulding which follows the
contour of an arch on its face or underside. [see ARCH, 110]

## ARCUATED

Describes the construction method based
on the principle of supporting arches, by
contrast to the post-and-lintel principle.
[see ARCH, TRABEATED]

## AREA

Sunken space between the street pavement and the basement of a town house.
[see 99, 332]

## ARMOURY

Strongroom of a castle or barracks for the
storage of weapons and armour.

Four-centred arch           Lancet arches           Tudor arch

enabling lighter and more graceful structures to be devised. As Gothic evolved in the course of the Middle Ages, it was the form of the pointed arch which showed the most significant changes and variations. The acute slender shape of the Early English lancet arch evolved gradually through a series of flatter forms, culminating in the squarish Tudor arch of the sixteenth century. [see GOTHIC, NORMAN]

2) As a free-standing structure the triumphal arch of Roman antiquity was used as a prestigious public monument. This concept was revived in the early nineteenth century in London, e.g. **Constitution Arch** of 1828 at **Hyde Park Corner** by Decimus Burton and **Marble Arch** of 1827 by John Nash, which originally stood outside Buckingham Palace and was removed to its present location at the top of Park Lane in 1851; and the **Admiralty Arch** of 1910 by Aston Webb which provided a triumphal entrance from Trafalgar Square into the Mall. [see QUADRIGA, **216, 297**]

## ARRAS
Hanging screen of tapestry used to decorate a medieval hall or chamber. The arras was usually carried along with other portable furnishings from castle to castle. The name derives from Arras in northern France, renowned for its rich tapestries.

## ARRIS [see FLUTING]

## ARROW LOOP or SLIT
Narrow opening in a castle wall to enable an archer to fire at assailants. [see BALISTRARIA, OEILLET]

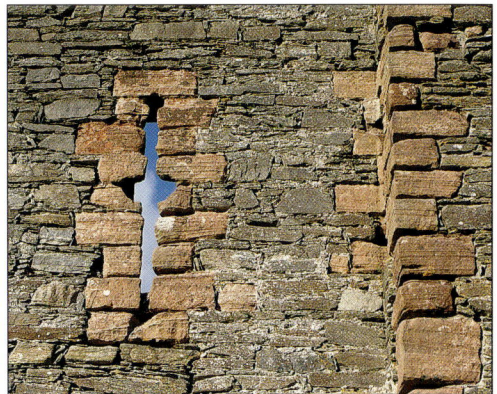

**15** *An attractive arrow loop of contrasting sandstone at Skipness Castle, S'clyde, Scotland.*

19

## ARSENAL

Establishment for the manufacture and/or storage of weapons and ammunition, e.g. the **Royal Arsenal, Woolwich,** London.

## ART DECO

A style of the 1920s and 1930s which may be traced back to the 1925 Exposition des Arts Décoratifs in Paris.

Art Deco delighted in bold shapes and smooth surfaces and was imbued with a spirit of adventure which owed as much to Hollywood as to any European source. Art Deco was usually associated with leisure and entertainment in buildings such as the **Odeon Cinema** and the **Savoy Hotel, London**; and the **Midland**

*16 The Art Deco Hoover Factory, Perivale, London, projects an optimistic image of industry.*

**Hotel, Morecambe,** *Lancs.* The style also had an impact on industrial architecture, e.g. the **Hoover Factory, Perivale,** London. The outbreak of the Second World War in 1939 marked the demise of Art Deco. [see MODERNISM]

## ART GALLERY

The idea of a purpose-built structure for the permanent display of paintings originated with the Tudor long gallery, e.g. at **Barrington Court,** *Somerset.* The **Dulwich Picture Gallery, London,** ranks as the oldest public collection in the British Isles, dating back to 1626, but the building itself, designed by John Soane, was not completed until 1814. The **Waterloo Gallery** of 1828–9, added to **Apsley House, London**, by the Duke of Wellington, was typical of the gallery

17 *The Waterloo Gallery, Apsley House, London, shows the favoured style of nineteenth-century art gallery.*

design that remained in favour for the rest of the nineteenth century. Similar Classical interiors with skylights to provide diffused illumination of the paintings were created in the **National Gallery** of 1832–8 and the **Tate Gallery** of 1897, London.

It was not until the middle of the twentieth century that any radically new concept of the art gallery began to emerge. The concrete bunker of the **Hayward Gallery, London**, symbolized the Brutalism of the 1950s and 60s. The **Sainsbury Centre for Visual Arts** at the **University of East Anglia, Norwich, Norfolk**, of 1977 by Norman Foster represented a sleeker, more aesthetic response which employed the latest in modern technology. Significant designs of the 1980s were the Post-Modernist extensions to the **Tate Gallery, London**, by James Stirling and to the **National Gallery, London**, by Robert Venturi. Increasingly, art galleries are being housed in converted buildings such as the new **Tate Gallery** in a disused Victorian dockside warehouse in **Liverpool**, *Mers*, and the **Irish Museum of Modern Art** in the old **Royal Hospital** at **Kilmainham, Dublin**, Ireland. [see GALLERY, MUSEUM]

**18** *A novel English variation on the theme of Art Nouveau at the Horniman Museum in south London.*

## ART NOUVEAU

This late nineteenth-century movement in art, architecture and design was particularly strong in Austria, Belgium and France. Its chief characteristic was the use of sinuous, plant-like shapes based principally on the water lily to create a powerfully sensual style. Art Nouveau was generally not held in high esteem in Britain by the patrons of architecture who preferred the robust bravado of Edwardian Baroque. Hence, there are only isolated examples of British Art Nouveau, e.g. the **Whitechapel Art Gallery** of 1899–1901 and the **Horniman Museum** of 1896–1901 in **London** by Charles Harrison Townsend; but these buildings are closer to the native ideals of the Arts and Crafts movement. The architect who did the most in Britain to carry forward the spirit of Art Nouveau was Charles Rennie Mackintosh; but his work was more widely appreciated on the Continent than at home. [see GLASGOW STYLE]

## ARTS AND CRAFTS

A movement, formally initiated in 1867, in which the design principles of William Morris (1834–96) played the leading role. Genuine craftsmanship by traditional methods and the pursuit of beauty through direct inspiration from nature were the guiding lights of Morris and his followers in their campaign against industrialized mass production. Morris was not an architect, but his ideas are implicitly expressed in the home he commissioned in 1859 from Philip Webb: the **Red House, Bexleyheath**, *Kent*, though retaining many features of the Gothic Revival, does show a move towards a more home-spun intimacy of scale. As the name suggests, the Arts and Crafts movement was greatly concerned with a natural vision of the home, as exemplified by Morris's own floral designs for wallpaper and tex-tiles. The **William Morris Gallery, Walthamstow**, London, contains many samples of his work.

19 *The Black Friar* (ABOVE) *described as 'the best pub in the Arts and Crafts fashion in London'.*
20 *Morris's Red House, Bexleyheath*, Kent (BELOW).

## ASHLAR

Masonry cut into square blocks, hewn to a smooth finish and generally laid in regular courses with tight joints. Ashlar represents the highest quality of masonry.

## ASSEMBLY ROOM

Type of ballroom, used for the social gatherings of fashionable society, which evolved in the eighteenth century as the most favoured venue for occasions of all sorts, but mainly dances and concerts. Assembly rooms were a special feature of spa towns, e.g. the **Pump Room, Bath**, *Avon*; and the **Pittville Pump Room, Cheltenham**, *Glos*. The **Assembly Rooms, York**, *N Yorks*, were designed by the 3rd Earl of Burlington. [see CONCERT HALL]

## ASTRAGAL

Moulding, usually consisting of a bead and reel motif, to be found on an entablature. [see ORDER]

## ASTYLAR

Denotes a façade without columns or pilasters.

## ATHENAEUM

The original Athenaeum was a university founded by the Emperor Hadrian in ancient Rome. The name was borrowed in the nineteenth century for grand Classical buildings with a claim to embody cultural values. The **Athenaeum Club, London,** designed in 1829 by Decimus Burton, was an élite establishment for artists, writers and scientists. Its architecture was copied from the Italian *palazzo* rather than from anything specifically Greek, as the name might suggest, although the frieze around the building was based on that of the Parthenon in Athens. Charles Barry's **Athenaeum, Manchester,** of 1837–9, also of the *palazzo* type, was founded as an adult

21 *The Athenaeum Club, London, evokes the Classical spirit with an elegant Grecian frieze.*

education institute, but it is now part of the City Art Gallery. [see PALAZZO]

## ATLANTES (plural of ATLAS)

Sculptures of massive male figures devised by the ancient Greeks as supports of an entablature, and known to the Romans as telamones. Variants of the form were applied to the façades of grand public and commercial buildings, especially in the Baroque revival of the Edwardian era. [see CARYATID, HERM, **144**]

## ATRIUM

In Roman architecture this was the entrance court of a villa, enclosed but open to the sky. The term has been revived in recent times to denote the arrangement of a multi-storey building around an internal courtyard or foyer which receives natural light through a glass roof or wall, e.g. the new buildings in London for **Lloyd's** and **ITN**.

22 OPPOSITE *A seated atlas joins forces with a caryatid at 82 Mortimer Street, London.*

## ATTIC

In Classical architecture this was the storey above the entablature, but the word has come to denote the uppermost storey of virtually any building, especially when used for storage.

## AUDITORY CHURCH

As the reformed Church of England gradually distanced itself from the customs of Rome, so in the new churches of the seventeenth century a break was eventually made with the old layout which focused on the sanctuary. Instead, a squarish plan was adopted, in which the altar lost out in importance to the

23 *The seventeenth-century chapel at Littlecote House,* Wilts, *is a perfect example of an auditory church.*

24 *This prehistoric stone alignment at Avebury,* Wilts, *is known as the West Kennet Avenue.*

25 *Sicilian Avenue is a stylish Edwardian shopping mall in Holborn, London.*

lectern and pulpit. Essentially a religious auditorium, the new type first appeared in Cromwellian times, e.g. the private chapel of **Littlecote House,** *Wilts.* The auditory church was perfected by Christopher Wren who defined its purpose:

> In our reformed Religion, it should seem vain to make a Parish Church larger, than that all who are present can both hear and see. The Romanists, indeed, may build larger churches, it is enough if they hear the Murmur of the Mass, and see the Elevation of the Host, but ours are to be fitted for Auditories ... with Pews and Galleries ... and all to hear distinctly, and see the Preacher.

Most of Wren's churches in the City of London are of the auditory type. The auditory church was further evolved in the eighteenth and nineteenth centuries by the Nonconformist sects. [see CHAPEL, MEETING HOUSE]

## AUMBRY
Medieval term for a small cupboard or closed recess in a wall of a church where the chalice was kept.

## AVENUE
The word originates from the French *'avenir'* meaning 'to come to'. In the context of Baroque urbanism the avenue was a principal thoroughfare linking important street junctions. The name is applied to some prehistoric stone alignments, e.g. **West Kennet Avenue** at **Avebury,** *Wilts.* Nowadays the term can also denote an ordinary street, or even a pedestrian shopping mall, e.g. **Sicilian Avenue, London.**

## AVIARY
As an item of garden architecture, the aviary or bird house may be given rather grand treatment, e.g. at **Waddesdon Manor,** *Bucks,* built in the late nineteenth century. Its designer is unknown, but the fanciful metalwork has echoes of French Rococo. By contrast, the **Snowdon Aviary, London Zoo,** of 1963 is a heavy and ungainly structure of massive poles at awkward angles supporting a tent-like wire mesh.

# B

## BACK-TO-BACK

Primitive type of urban housing of the late eighteenth and early nineteenth centuries consisting of a row of terraced houses backing directly on to a similar row facing in the opposite direction. The absence of backyards allowed the builders to cram in more houses per acre; but the resulting lack of through ventilation created unhygienic living conditions. The back-to-back is associated with the worst excesses of the Industrial Revolution in the cities of northern England.

## BAILEY

Courtyard or enclosed forecourt of a castle. Also known as a ward. [see CASTLE]

## BALCONY

Projecting platform, enclosed by a railing or balustrade, attached to an upper storey, e.g. the ceremonial balcony at **Buckingham Palace, London**. The wet British climate did not encourage the balcony as a feature of native architecture, but it was occasionally used from the seventeenth century, along with other features borrowed from Italy. Ornamental iron balconies were popular in the terrace architecture of the late Georgian era, e.g. the east side of **Mecklenburgh Square, London**. As a purely functional item, the balcony came into its own in blocks of flats in the twentieth century, when it served as a sort of elevated street to provide access to individual front doors. Internal balconies are to be found in

26 OPPOSITE *Balconies are a strong feature of the façade of this apartment house in central London. Note the cupolas with their extravagant finials.*

opera houses, theatres and cinemas. [see LOGGIA, VERANDA]

## BALDACHIN [see CANOPY]

## BALISTRARIA

Cross-shaped aperture in a fortified wall, designed for firing crossbows. [see ARROW LOOP, OEILLET]

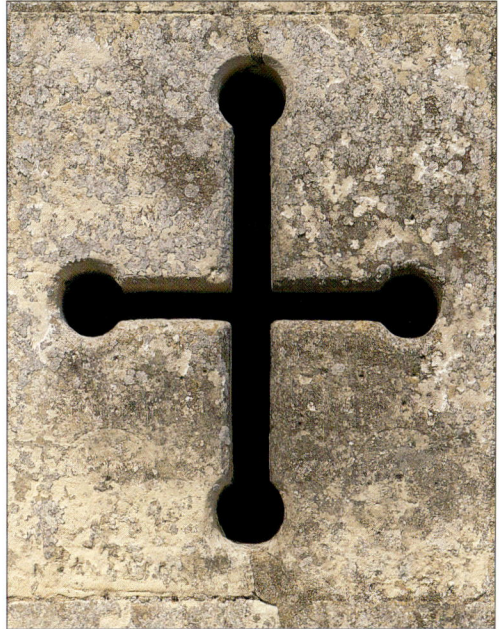

27 *A stylish balistraria at Titchfield Abbey, Hants, suggests that design was as important as defence.*

## BALL FLOWER

Spherical stone ornament carved with a three- or four-leafed pattern. It was a popular motif of Decorated Gothic, e.g. in **Hereford Cathedral**, *Heref & Worcs*; but it also occurs as a feature of Early English Gothic, e.g. in **Salisbury Cathedral**, *Wilts*.

Ballflower

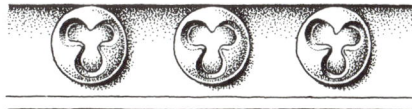

# BALUSTER

Post or pillar, usually arranged in a series beneath a handrail to form a balustrade. [see BANISTER, **83**]

# BALUSTRADE [see BALUSTER]

# BANISTER

Used mostly in the plural, to denote the vertical supports of a stair handrail, and by extension, the handrail as well. The word is a corruption of 'baluster'. [see STAIR]

# BANK

It was not until the late eighteenth century that a specific style of commercial architecture for banks evolved, namely the Neo-Classical. Most influential were Robert Taylor's original Palladian designs for the **Bank of England, London**; but from 1788 John Soane carried out extensive alterations in his distinctive style inspired more by Greece than by Rome. The Neo-Classical lead given by the Bank of England was widely followed since the style expressed the desired values of permanence, prudence and tradition. Bank architecture has since become more varied, and the styles employed now range from Gothic Revival to High Tech; but one of the masterpieces of the genre remains the headquarters of the **Midland Bank, London,** of 1924–39 by Edwin Lutyens, which is firmly in the Classical mould.

# BANQUETING HOUSE

Palatial building for hosting receptions, court masques and banquets. A banqueting house was often a fantasy building or folly used for occasional junketing in the park of a country house, e.g. the Gothic structure at **Wardour Old Castle**, *Wilts.* The early seventeenth century **Banqueting House, London,** by Inigo Jones was once part of Whitehall Palace. [see PINEAPPLE]

# BAPTISTERY

Special building housing the font of a church or cathedral. As such, its usage was largely confined to the Continent. The term is sometimes applied to that part of a large church where the font is located, e.g. in the **Metropolitan Cathedral of Liverpool**, *Mers*, and **Coventry Cathedral**, *W Mids.* [see FONT]

# BAR TRACERY [see TRACERY]

# BARBICAN

Defensive outwork protecting the gate or entrance to a castle or fortified town. Because of its exposed position the barbican is usually not a well preserved feature, but several have survived, e.g. at **Lewes Castle**, *E Sussex*; **Goodrich Castle**, *Heref & Worcs*; **Prudhoe Castle**, *Northum*; **Warwick Castle**, *Warw.* The Welsh castles of **Beaumaris, Conway** and **Harlech,**

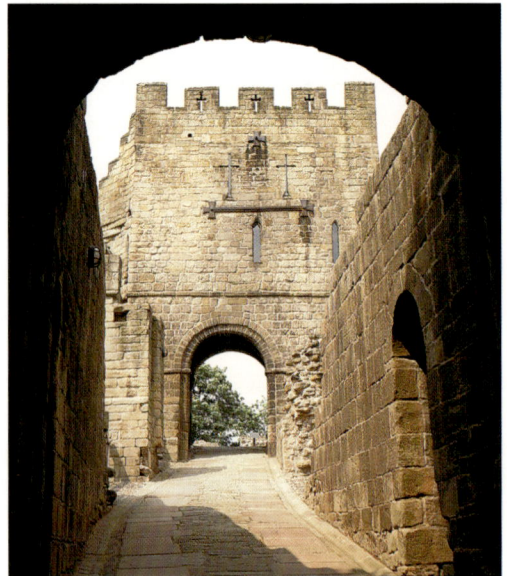

28 *A sense of confinement is conveyed on entering the barbican at Prudhoe Castle*, Northum.

*Gwynedd*, preserve remains of their barbicans. The barbican at **Walmgate Bar, York**, *N Yorks*, is intact. [see GATEHOUSE]

## BARGEBOARD
Wooden panel mounted on the gable end of a pitched roof to prevent penetration by rainwater. This functional feature of medieval architecture was often embellished with decorative carving, e.g.at **Ford's Hospital, Coventry**, *W Mids.* [see HALF-TIMBERING]

## BARLEY-SUGAR COLUMN
Name familiarly used to describe a twisted or spiral column, e.g. on the south porch of **St Mary the Virgin, Oxford**, *Oxon.* Also known as a Solomonic column on account of the legendary use of such columns in Solomon's Temple in Jerusalem.

## BARMKIN
Scottish term for a walled enclosure around a tower house which served for the protection of livestock, e.g. at **Loch Leven Castle**, *Tayside*, Scotland. The contrivance is known in Ireland as a bawn, e.g. at **Aughnanure Castle**, *Galway*, which has an impressive double bawn. [see TOWER HOUSE]

## BARN
Building for the storage of grain or other agricultural produce, known as tithe barn when built to store the tithe (originally one tenth of the harvest in lieu of a fixed rent). Some fine medieval barns survive, e.g. timber barns at **Cressing** and **Widdington**, *Essex.* Stone barns are generally better preserved, e.g. at **Bradford-on-Avon**, *Wilts*, and **Glastonbury**, *Somerset.* The most highly acclaimed is the thirteenth-century barn at **Great Coxwell**, *Oxon*, built by the Cistercians and often described as a miniature cathedral of the countryside. [see GRANGE, **135**]

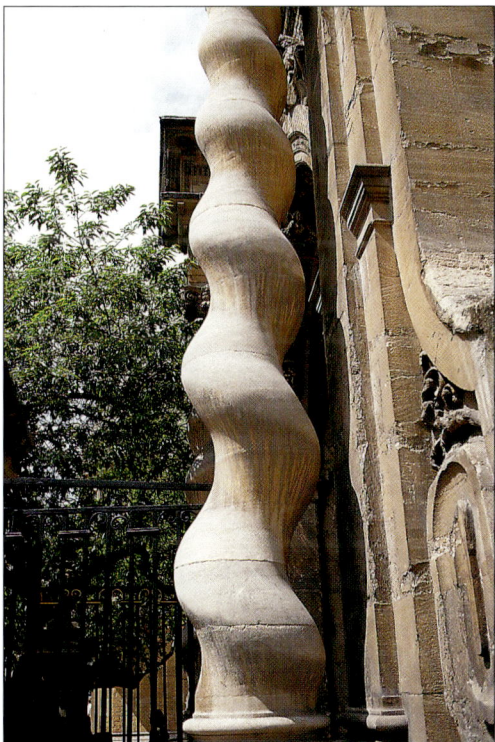

29 *Barley-sugar columns flank the porch at the church of St Mary the Virgin, Oxford, Oxon.*

30 *This noble stone barn at Great Coxwell, Oxon, incorporates a dovecote in the gable end.*

## BARONIAL

A revivalist style of the nineteenth century which drew its inspiration from the outward trappings of medieval castles and manors such as towers, battlements and gatehouses. Baronial was particularly favoured for the country houses of wealthy industrialists, financiers and noblemen who wished to convey an impression of feudal magnificence, e.g. **Peckforton Castle**, *Cheshire*, of 1844; **Knightshayes Court**, *Devon*, of 1869; and **Castell Coch** near **Cardiff**, *S Glam*, Wales of 1871. In Ireland, the style was taken up with enthusiasm by the great landowners for an entire gen-

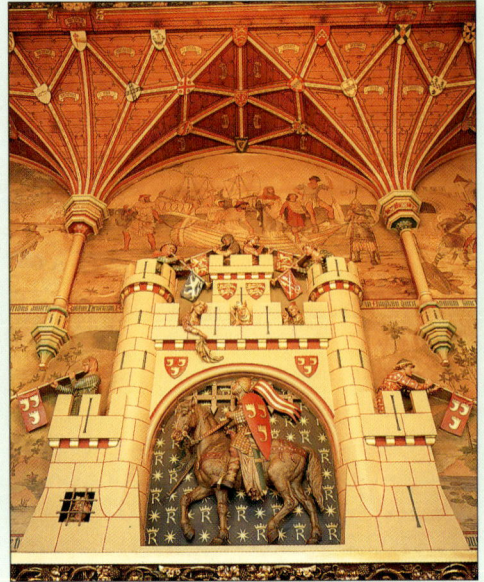

32 *Upper part of the Baronial chimneypiece in the banqueting hall of Cardiff Castle*, S Glam, *Wales.*

eration of imposing country houses, e.g. **Ashford Castle**, *Mayo* of 1870; **Kylemore Abbey**, *Galway* of 1864; and **Dromore Castle**, *Limerick* of 1867. Scottish Baronial took its lead from the highly influential house of Sir Walter Scott at **Abbotsford**, *Borders* of 1822, and the rebuilding in 1852–5 of **Balmoral Castle**, *Grampian*, for Queen Victoria and Prince Albert. The Baronial style was also applied to commercial buildings such as insurance companies. Baronial remained a potent attraction as a style for the country house well into the twentieth century, e.g. **Castle Drogo**, *Devon*, of 1910–30 by Edwin Lutyens. [see BARTIZAN, GOTHIC REVIVAL, NORMAN REVIVAL]

31 *The Scottish Baronial style in the grand manner: Dunrobin Castle*, Highland, *Scotland.*

## BARRACK

Accommodation for soldiers or militia, e.g. the **Royal Citadel, Plymouth**, *Devon*, of 1661–71. The ruins of **Ruthven Barracks**, *Highland*, Scotland, date back to 1716. Some of the most impressive ranges of eighteenth-century barracks are at **Fort George**, near **Inverness**, *Highland*, Scotland. Modern barrack design may be seen in London at the

## BAROQUE

In its purest form, the Baroque style was essentially a product of southern Europe in the seventeenth and eighteenth centuries. It derived its vocabulary from Classical architecture, but used it in a more dramatic manner, delighting in a bold massing of structures. The theatrical effect was heightened by a flamboyant use of lofty domes, projecting pediments, external statuary, balustrades and ornate pilasters. The Baroque interior gave even freer rein to invention with sinuous curves and spectacular painted ceilings. It is thought that the term Baroque originated from the Portuguese '*barocco*', signifying a misshapen pearl; hence it carried a derogatory meaning.

Within the British context, Baroque was largely confined to England. It made a brief appearance in the closing decades of the seventeenth century and lasted until about 1730. It was pioneered in London by Christopher Wren, most notably in **St Paul's Cathedral** and the **Royal Naval Hospital**, Greenwich; but this was a more restrained English type of Baroque than the full-blooded version popular on the Continent. The style was applied with greater force by John Vanbrugh at **Castle Howard**, *N Yorks*, from about 1700, and even more spectacularly at **Blenheim Palace**, *Oxon*, from 1705. Baroque also made a powerful impact on church architecture in London, e.g. **Christ Church, Spitalfields**, of 1714–29 and **St Anne, Limehouse**, of 1712–24 by Nicholas Hawksmoor; and **St John,**

**Smith Square, Westminster**, of 1714–28 by Thomas Archer. However, the more modest Palladian style was generally preferred for country houses great and small throughout the eighteenth century. It was not until the end of the nineteenth century that the grandiloquent qualities of Baroque were rediscovered and revived to express the bombastic mood of the high noon of British imperialism. [see EDWARDIAN, RESTORATION, ROCOCO, 239]

**33** *The painted dome in the great hall of Castle Howard*, N Yorks, *is a fine example of Baroque.*

Chelsea Barracks and the Knightsbridge Barracks of the Household Cavalry. [see CASEMATE]

## BARREL ROOF [see WAGON ROOF]

## BARREL VAULT [see GROIN VAULT, TUNNEL VAULT, VAULT]

## BARROW

Long mound or tumulus covering burials

or containing a chambered tomb. The phenomenon, also known as the long barrow, is most frequently associated with the New Stone Age and Bronze Age cultures of southern England. Some barrows were later re-used. More modest barrows of Saxon date occur, e.g. in **Greenwich Park**, London. [see CAIRN, CHAMBERED TOMB, PREHISTORIC]

## BARTIZAN
Round turret projecting out on a corbel from the corner of a tower, e.g. at **Cawdor Castle**, *Highland*, Scotland. Bartizans were a favourite feature of the Scottish tower house and were widely imitated in buildings in the Scottish Baronial style.

**34** *A profusion of bartizans adorn the clocktower of the Town House, Aberdeen,* Grampian, *Scotland.*

## BASE
In Classical architecture, the lowest part of a column, i.e. between the shaft and the pavement. The Greek Doric order is unique in that it dispenses with a base. The bases of Norman columns display great variety, e.g. those in the crypt of **Rochester Cathedral**, *Kent*. The bases of Gothic columns show increasing complexity, especially those of the Decorated phase. [see COLUMN, ORDER, PEDESTAL]

## BASEMENT
Lowest storey of a building, either wholly or partly below ground level. A basement may even be a few steps above pavement level when it serves as the substructure for the *piano nobile* or principal storey of a Palladian mansion. [see **263**]

## BASILICA
A Roman building for the dispensation of justice and regulation of commerce, rectangular in shape and with an apse at one or both ends. Longitudinal arcades provided access to aisles on either side of the central area. The basilican plan with a round apse at the eastern end was adopted for the first Christian churches in England. However, this form was later rejected in favour of the square-ended nave-and-chancel type which was ultimately of Celtic origin. The basilica was revived for church architecture in the late nineteenth century. [see BYZANTINE REVIVAL, CHURCH, ROMAN, SAXON]

## BAS-RELIEF
Sculptural work which protrudes by less than half of its contour from the surface on which it is carved. The French term means literally 'low relief'. [see SCULPTURE]

## BASTION
Defensive projection of a castle or city

**35** *Medieval bastions keep watch along the defences of Kildrummy Castle,* Grampian, Scotland.

wall to permit the garrison a clear aim at any besieging force. [see CASTLE, FORT]

## BASTLE HOUSE

Farmhouse designed for defence like a small tower with a vaulted ground floor for livestock and accommodation for the family above. This type of dwelling, e.g. **Black Middens,** near **Bellingham,** *Northum,* is characteristic of the border country between England and Scotland. [see PELE TOWER]

## BATH HOUSE, BATHROOM

The idea of a room or building for the purpose of taking a bath was introduced to Britain by the Romans. The splendid **Roman Bath** of Aquae Sulis at **Bath,** *Avon,* is fed by a natural hot spring, but elsewhere it was necessary to heat the water. Sumptuous domestic bath houses have been discovered at a number of Roman villas, e.g. **Lullingstone,** *Kent;* **Chedworth** and **Great Witcombe,** *Glos.* The latter occupied three rooms and was decorated with fine mosaics illustrating

marine life. After the withdrawal of the Romans, bath houses went out of use for many centuries. Norman barons took their baths in wooden tubs, which remained the custom throughout the Middle Ages. Edward III had cisterns installed at Westminster in 1351 for the luxury of hot and cold running water. London's public bath houses were closed down by Henry VIII on the grounds that they served primarily as brothels. The rising cost of wood made hot baths expensive, while cold baths were considered a danger to health.

Attitudes changed only gradually in the seventeenth century, but the demands of hygiene could no longer be ignored by elegant society. At **Chatsworth,** *Derbys,* a stately bathroom was installed prior to 1700 with a grand sunken bath of white marble. The occupant of the **Georgian House, Bristol,** *Avon,* had a cold plunge bath in the cellar. Lead plumbing was slowly introduced, but portable tubs continued to be used even in the best houses. The general provision of bathrooms had

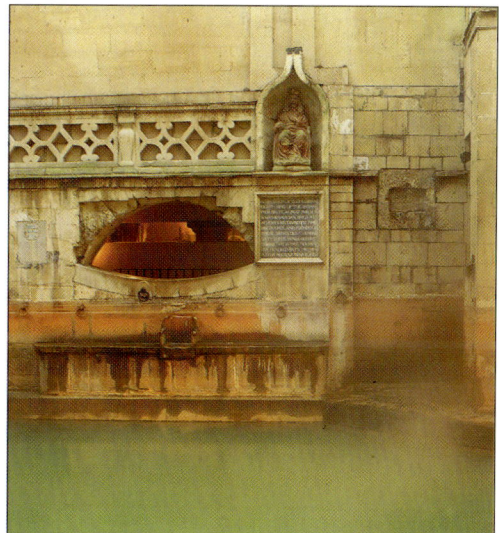

**36** *The King's Bath at Bath,* Avon, *occupies the site of its Roman predecessor.*

35

to await the plumbing genius of the Victorians, whose elaborate devices for showers and water jets rank among the engineering achievements of the age. [see HYPOCAUST, LAVABO]

## BATH STONE [see LIMESTONE]

## BATTEN
Long, thin length of timber mainly used in roofing for anchoring slates; also for fixing the laths to support plasterwork.

## BATTER
Inclined slope of a wall which enhances the stability of a structure and serves in a castle as a defensive device at the base of a tower. Missiles dropped from the battlements would rebound off the batter into the faces of the enemy.

## BATTLEMENT
Indented parapet wall of a medieval castle or city wall. The openings are known as crenelles or embrasures; the solid parts are merlons. Mock battlements became a favourite feature of the Baronial style. [see BRATTICE, CASTLE, CRENELLATION, MACHICOLATION, 78]

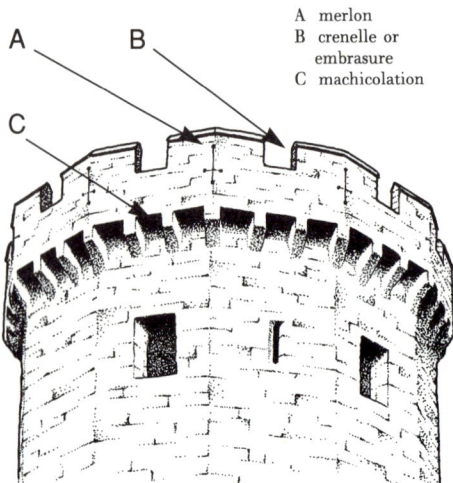

A  merlon
B  crenelle or embrasure
C  machicolation

## BATTLE OF THE STYLES

Name given to the conflict between the inherited Classical style of the eighteenth century and the Gothic Revival, which emerged in the early nineteenth century. The cause of the Gothic Revival was forcefully promoted by Augustus Welby Northmore Pugin (1812–52) in pamphlets such as *An Apology for the Revival of Christian Architecture in England*. Pugin inveighed against the architecture of the Greek temple as an unsuitable model for houses of Christian worship, and he championed Gothic for buildings of all types. The project for the reconstruction of the **Houses of Parliament, London**, after the fire of 1834, marked a decisive shift in favour of the Gothic cause, since it was

**37** *Italianate façade of the Foreign Office, London. Note the aedicules occupied by statues.*

**38** *The Houses of Parliament, London: a Gothic triumph.*

laid down that the new building should harmonize with the Gothic fabric of Westminster Abbey.

However, the stylistic debate raged on for many years; and architects were divided into opposing camps in the Battle of the Styles. Eventually, the Gothic Revival emerged as the dominant trend. By the middle of the nineteenth century Francis Cross could report:

> We have Gothic Houses of Parliament, libraries, halls, churches, aye, even the very Methodist body have been vaccinated into a furor for Gothic ... The almshouses, hospitals, workhouses, schools, villages, houses, cottages – everything now is Gothic.

But Lord Palmerston fought a vigorous rearguard action on behalf of the Classical side by insisting that the design for the **Foreign Office, London**, of 1861 be in an Italianate style. Rather than lose the commission, the dedicated Gothic Revivalist, George Gilbert Scott, conceded the point; and – in his own words – he 'bought some costly books on Italian architecture and set vigorously to work to rub up'. Afterwards Scott promptly reverted to his preferred Gothic Revival style. [see CLASSICISM, GOTHIC REVIVAL, GREEK REVIVAL]

## BAWN [see BARMKIN]

## BAY
Vertical division of a building marked by arches, buttresses, columns or ranges of windows. A façade may be described as having a number of bays. [see 280, 377]

## BAY WINDOW
Window projecting from a building, and often rising the full height of a room such as a medieval hall where it was located at the dais end by the lord's table, e.g. at **Crosby Hall, London**. Bay windows again became popular from the early nineteenth century, not only to provide an attractive feature on a house facade, but also to admit more light and to afford a panoramic view from within. [see BOW WINDOW, ORIEL, WINDOW]

## BEAD
Round moulding like a string of beads. [see MOULDING]

## BEAD AND REEL [see ASTRAGAL]

## BEAKHEAD
Carved motif of Norse origin consisting of a mythological head with a beak-like protrusion, commonly found in Norman buildings, e.g. at the churches of **St Morwenna, Morwenstow**, *Cornwall*, and **St Mary, Iffley**, *Oxon*. [see NORMAN]

## BEAM
Transverse, horizontal timber supporting a floor or roof truss. [see SLEEPER, TIE BEAM, TIMBER-TRUSSED ROOF]

## BEDEHOUSE
From Old English 'gebed', meaning 'to

**39** OPPOSITE *Two bays of bow windows dominate this façade of the Elizabethan mansion of Kirby Hall,* Northants. *Note the symmetry of the fenestration.*

pray', bedehouse denotes an almshouse where the inmates were duty bound to offer prayers for the soul of the benefactor, e.g. at **Higham Ferrers**, *Northants*, founded in 1428 by Henry Chichele. [see ALMSHOUSE]

## BEEHIVE CELL
Round structure of unhewn drystone masonry in which the stones are laid in oversailing courses to create a domical form, e.g. in the early Christian monasteries of Ireland such as **Skellig Michael**, *Kerry*. Also known as a clochan.

40 *Beehive cells at the island monastery of Skellig Michael,* Kerry, *Ireland.*

## BELFRY
Bell tower or place where bells are hung. This is usually an integral part of the church, but at **St Mary the Virgin, Berkeley**, *Glos*, and at **St Michael and All Angels, Ledbury**, *Heref & Worcs*, the belfry is a detached structure. The bell tower at **Chichester Cathedral**, *W Sussex*, is also a separate building, and is known by the Italian term '*campanile*'. The word 'belfry' is actually derived from Old French '*berfrei*' meaning 'tower' and has no linguistic connection with 'bell'. [see ROUND TOWER, 130]

## BELLCOTE, BELL GABLE
Framework mounted externally on the roof of a church which accommodates a bell or set of bells. Sometimes, this may be a vertical extension of the gable end, e.g. at **All Saints, Little Casterton**, *Leics*; or a turret-like structure, e.g. at **St Peter & St Paul, Long Compton**, *Warw*.

## BELL TOWER [see BELFRY]

## BELVEDERE
Derived from Italian, *'bel'* – beautiful' and *'vedere'* – to see', signifying a place which commands a fine view. This can be a lantern or turret on the roof of a house, a scenic terrace or a special building located at a spot enjoying a panorama. [see GAZEBO]

## BENCH END
Carved panel affixed to the end of a wooden pew. In the late Middle Ages these were given special treatment by

41 *Novel decoration of a bench end in the church of St Sennen, Zennor, Cornwall.*

carpenters to portray a variety of themes ranging from the religious to the secular and profane. The church of **St Nonna, Altarnun**, *Cornwall*, possesses some seventy-nine bench ends illustrating subjects as diverse as a jester, a fiddler, a bagpipe player, local dignitaries, St Michael and the Instruments of the Passion. The church of **St Sennen, Zennor**, *Cornwall*, has a bench end of a lascivious mermaid holding a comb and mirror. Bench ends were also carved to display patterns imitating the stone tracery of Gothic windows and heraldic devices, e.g. at **St Peter & St Paul, Fressingfield**, *Suffolk*. [see PEW, POPPYHEAD]

## BERM
Part of an earthwork between ditch and bank. [see EARTHWORK]

## BILLET
Moulding, especially in Romanesque or Norman architecture, of raised cubes or cylindrical shapes interspersed with corresponding voids. [see MOULDING]

## BISHOP'S PALACE
In the Middle Ages bishops were equal in rank and prestige to the feudal magnates; and their mighty houses of state were styled as palaces, e.g. those at **Wolvesey** and **Bishop's Waltham**, *Hants*. A fragment remains of the Bishop of Winchester's London palace in **Southwark**; and at **Lincoln**, *Lincs*, there is an impressive undercroft. The **Bishop's Palace** at **St David's**, *Dyfed*, Wales, is a powerful thirteenth-century structure. Security was a concern of medieval bishops, as may be seen at the **Bishop's Palace, Wells**, *Somerset*, where Ralph of Shrewsbury built a formidable defensive wall and moat in the fourteenth century. **Lambeth Palace, London**, the official residence of the Archbishop of Canterbury,

has parts dating back to the Middle Ages. [see **47, 103, 114, 137**]

**BISHOP'S THRONE** [see CATHEDRA]

**BIVALLATE** [see HILLFORT]

**BLACK AND WHITE WORK**
Practice of painting the exposed beams and studs of a half-timbered house jet black and whitewashing the plaster infill in order to create a striking contrast. Many medieval buildings were subjected to this treatment in the nineteenth century; and it is also characteristic of the mock-Tudor houses built by the Victorians and Edwardians. The Midlands are particularly noted for this 'magpie' effect, e.g. at **Gawsworth Hall**, *Cheshire*. [see HALF-TIMBERING, MOCK TUDOR]

43 *The Black House at Arnol, Isle of Lewis, Scotland: a small gem of rural domestic architecture.*

**BLACK HOUSE**
Modest dwelling of the longhouse type found in the Hebrides and western Highlands of Scotland. As the name suggests, the black house is usually dark and smoke-stained inside; but the name came about as a way of distinguishing this traditional type, built with rough stones, from the new whitewashed houses which appeared from the mid-nineteenth cen-

42 *Hall-i'-th'-Wood, Bolton,* Greater Manchester: *the black and white work makes a strong visual impact.*

tury. A few remain in their original form, e.g. at **Arnol, Isle of Lewis**, and at **Colbost, Isle of Skye**, Scotland. Despite its primitive appearance, the black house was not without sophistication: it was doublewalled and the cavity was filled with turf for effective insulation against winter gales. [see LONGHOUSE]

## BLANK or BLIND
Terms to describe an arcade or tracery carved on a solid wall purely for decorative purposes, i.e. with no actual opening. Blank windows serve to create symmetry in a façade. Blank arcading, both external and internal, is a common feature in Gothic churches. [see **187**]

44 *Blank arcading adorns the exterior stonework of St Margaret, King's Lynn*, Norfolk.

## BLINDSTORY [see TRIFORIUM]

## BLOCKED COLUMN [see COLUMN]

## BOASTED WORK
Roughly tooled masonry which has not been given a detailed finish.

## BOISERIE [see PANELLING]

## BOLECTION
Moulding which serves to conceal the joint between two elements of differing thickness, e.g. a panel and its frame. [see MOULDING]

## BOND [see BRICKWORK]

## BONNET TILE
Curved tile used to bridge rows of flat tiles where they meet along the angles of a hipped roof. [see PANTILE, ROOF]

## BOSS
Decorative projection of wood or stone usually located at the intersection of ribs in a stone vault or of beams in a timber roof. The use of elaborately carved bosses is particularly associated with the Decorated and Perpendicular phases of Gothic, e.g. in the nave vaults of **Exeter Cathedral**, *Devon*; **Norwich Cathedral**, *Norfolk*; and **St Mary Redcliffe, Bristol**, *Avon*. Some impressive wooden bosses are

45 *A profusion of bosses and ribs in the vault of the Percy Chantry, Tynemouth Priory*, Tyne & Wear.

on display in **Southwark Cathedral**, London. [see LABEL STOP, VAULT, 157]

## BOTHIE or BOTHY
Scottish word for a simple hut or shelter in the hills used by a shepherd.

## BOTTLE-OVEN [see KILN]

## BOUDOIR
The word is French, meaning 'a place to sulk', originally an ironical description of the intimate chamber of a noble lady. The term is occasionally used in stately homes, e.g. Lady Ward's **Gothick Boudoir** at **Castle Ward**, *Down*, N. Ireland; and the **Blue Boudoir** at **Warwick Castle**, *Warw.*

## BOW WINDOW
Convex window, a popular feature of Regency architecture, especially for shopfronts, e.g. **Goodwin's Court, London**. [see BAY WINDOW, 328]

## BOWTELL
Convex moulding, also known as an edge roll. [see MOULDING]

## BOX
Small house in the country, most commonly used for accommodating sporting guests, e.g. a shooting box.

## BOX-FRAME
Concrete structure composed of a framework of box-like compartments.

## BOX PEW [see PEW]

## BRACE
Diagonal timber supporting a frame. [see HALF-TIMBERING, TIMBER-TRUSSED ROOF]

## BRACKET
In Gothic architecture, an ornamental stone projection designed to carry a statue. The term also denotes a structural element to support a balcony or gallery. [see CONSOLE, CORBEL]

## BRASSES
Brass plaques fixed to the top of a tomb or the floor of a church to commemorate the persons buried beneath. Brasses were made from an alloy of copper, zinc, tin and lead, known as latten. The images on the brasses are generally linear portraits of the deceased. The church of **St Mary, Stoke d'Abernon**, *Surrey*, contains the earliest brass in England, dated to 1277, showing Sir John d'Abernon kitted out in full knightly equipment. Other early brasses include that of Sir Roger de Trumpington of 1289 at **St Mary & St Michael, Trumpington**, *Cambs*; and of Sir Robert de Septvans of 1306 at **St Mary, Chartham**, *Kent*. A most impressive collection of brasses, ranging from 1329 to 1539, has survived at **St Mary Magdalene, Cobham**, *Kent*. Rich clothiers of the medieval period are depicted on the brasses in the wool churches of East Anglia and the Cotswolds. [see INDENT, TOMB SCULPTURE]

## BRATTICE
Wooden gallery projecting from the battlement of a medieval castle.

## BRATTISHING
Carved decoration in the form of a cresting along the top of a screen or cornice, often resembling a miniature battlement. [see CRESTING]

## BRESSUMER or BREASTSUMMER
Horizontal beam or lintel supporting a wall, e.g. above a fireplace. [see HALF-TIMBERING]

## BRICK TILE [see MATHEMATICAL TILE]

# BRICK, BRICKWORK

The brick, which is a tablet of clay fired in a kiln, is the most common building material in the British Isles. The technology was first brought to Britain by the Romans, who used a much flatter brick than that favoured today, being only 1–1½ in (2·5–3·8cm) thick and more accurately described by the old term of wall tile. In Saxon times, the only bricks used were those plundered from the ruins of Roman structures, as may be seen in several ancient churches, e.g. **All Saints, Brixworth**, *Northants*. Recycled Roman bricks were also used by the Normans, e.g. at **Colchester Castle**, *Essex* and **St Albans Abbey**, *Herts*. New brick made an appearance *c.* 1260 at **Little Wenham Hall**, *Suffolk*, but it was not until the later Middle Ages that it became widespread, e.g. at **Tattershall Castle**, *Lincs*, of *c.* 1440, **Herstmonceux Castle**,

46 *Late medieval brickwork at Tattershall Castle,* Lincs. *Note the collegiate church beyond.*

*E Sussex*, of 1440 and **Oxburgh Hall**, *Norfolk*, of 1482. During the Tudor period (1485–1603) brick became increasingly fashionable for the most prestigious of buildings, e.g. **Hampton Court Palace, London**, from 1514, and **Layer Marney Tower**, *Essex*, of 1520, as well as for Cambridge colleges such as **Queens'** and **St John's**. During the Elizabethan era brickwork reached new heights of ingenuity and versatility, most obviously in lofty and fanciful chimney stacks, e.g. at **Penshurst Place**, *Kent*. The commencement in 1636 of the unfinished mansion of **Jigginstown**, *Kildare*, introduced the use of brick in the grand manner to Ireland. Brick's resistance to fire made it a natural choice in the tightly knit towns and cities of that time, e.g. for the rebuilding of London after the Great Fire of 1666.

The easy availability and convenience of brick boosted the urban boom of the Georgian period, although the brickwork was not always of the best quality and was sometimes concealed behind a façade of stone or stucco. In the Victorian era, increased technical proficiency led to improvements in the regularity of the size of bricks and greater control over a variety of colours. The taste for polychrome brickwork was given dramatic expression by architects such as William Butterfield, e.g. at **Keble College, Oxford**, *Oxon*, of 1870. Bricks were also used in vast quantities for works of engineering such as railway tunnels and viaducts. In domestic architecture, fine quality red brick became the hallmark of Norman Shaw's 'Queen Anne' houses. It was even taken up as a worthy material for churches great and small, e.g. **Westminster Cathedral, London,** of 1895–1903 by John Bentley. One of the most spectacular brick buildings of the twentieth century was **Battersea Power Station** from 1929 by Giles Gilbert Scott. In recent years, there has been a marked revival of traditional craftsmanship; quality brickwork is once again much in demand

47 *Tudor brickwork on display at Fulham Palace, London, showing the diaper work that was characteristic of the period.*

**English bond**

**Flemish bond**

stretcher      header

for prestige projects, e.g. the new **British Library** at **St Pancras, London**.

The techniques of bonding or laying bricks in their courses, cemented by mortar, have changed very little over the centuries. Bricks may be laid so that either the short end or the long side is left exposed to view. These are known respectively as 'headers' and 'stretchers'. English Bond consists of alternating courses of headers and stretchers, whereas Flemish Bond has alternating headers and stretchers in each course. Many other variations are possible. Diagonal crosses in brickwork are formed by the positioning of darker, burnt bricks in the desired pattern; this technique, known as diapering, was extremely popular in the Tudor period and later revived by Victorian architects. [see NOGGING, POINTING, POLYCHROMY]

## BRIDGE

It is doubtful whether permanent bridges were a feature of the prehistoric landscape, and it is to be assumed that ferries and fords provided the necessary access over streams and rivers. The first record of a bridge in Britain was that built across the River Thames in London by the Romans in the first century AD near the present London Bridge. At **Piercebridge**, *N Yorks*, may be seen the remains of the southern abutment and portions of the piers which carried a Roman timber bridge across the River Tees in the second century AD. The most ancient bridges still in existence are probably the rough structures made from blocks of moorstone at **Postbridge** and **Dartmeet** on Dartmoor, *Devon*. The actual antiquity of these clapper-bridges is uncertain, but it is likely that they date back to the early Middle Ages and were used by packhorse traffic. At **Monmouth**, *Gwent*, Wales, there is an imposing fortified bridge-gatehouse from the thirteenth century. Significant four-teenth-century bridges are still in use at **Newbridge**, *Oxon*; **Huntingdon**, *Cambs*; **East Farleigh**, *Kent*. Fifteenth- and six-teenth-century examples include **Bakewell Bridge**, *Derbys*; **Clopton Bridge, Stratford-upon-Avon**, *Warw*; the **Stopham Bridge** across the River Arun, *W Sussex*; and the **Bridge of Dee, Aberdeen**, *Grampian*, Scotland. The advent of the Classical style is marked by **Clare Bridge, Cambridge**, *Cambs*, of 1639 and the **Edensor Bridge, Chatsworth**, *Derbys*. Some eighteenth-century bridges were conceived mainly as aesthetic objects in the landscape, e.g. John Vanbrugh's creation of 1711 at **Blenheim Palace**, *Oxon*, and the **Palladian Bridge** at **Wilton House**, *Wilts*. Robert Adam's elegant work survives at **Kedleston Hall**, *Derbys*, and in **Pulteney Bridge, Bath**, *Avon*.

In 1779 the epoch-making **Iron Bridge** over the River Severn at **Coalbrookdale,** *Shrops*, was built: this was the world's first iron bridge. In the course of the nineteenth century the technique of iron construction was developed by engineers such as Thomas Telford and Isambard Kingdom Brunel, who took over the business of bridge design from conventional

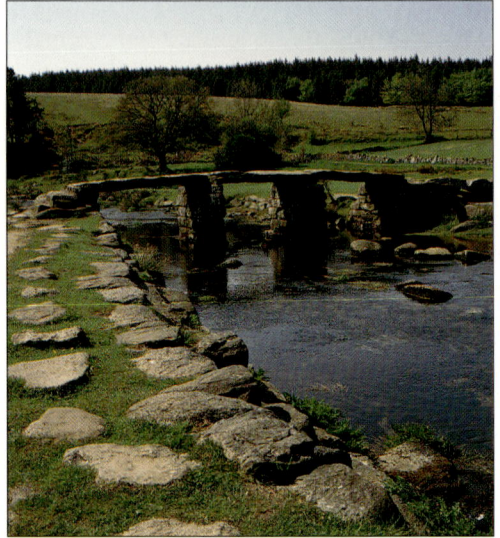

48 *Clapper-bridge at Postbridge on Dartmoor*, Devon, *made of blocks of moorstone.*

49 *The Palladian Bridge at Wilton House*, Wilts, *is essentially an ornamental addition to the landscape.*

50 *The stone bridge at Stopham,* W Sussex, *dates back to the fourteenth century.*

architects. Telford built an iron bridge at **Buildwas**, *Shrops*, another at **Craigellachie**, *Grampian*, Scotland; and in Wales the suspension bridge at **Conway**, *Gwynedd*, complete with castellated stone entrance towers as a tribute to the medieval castle close by. Brunel's bridge-building genius can be seen in the **Clifton Suspension Bridge, Bristol**, *Avon*, and the **Royal Albert Bridge** for the Great Western Railway over the River Tamar, linking Devon and Cornwall.

Robert Stephenson was responsible for several fine railway bridges. The **Forth Railway Bridge** of 1890 by John Fowler and Benjamin Baker, linking Fife and Lothian in Scotland, represented the crowning achievement of the railway era. The 1890s also witnessed the construction of **Tower Bridge, London,** a joint effort of the architect Horace Jones and the engineer John Wolfe-Barry, which is an intriguing blend of advanced technology

and blatant historicism. Major bridges of the twentieth century include the steel **Tyne Bridge, Newcastle**, *Tyne & Wear*, and several suspension bridges, e.g. the **Severn Road Bridge** of the 1960s between Avon in England and Gwent in Wales. [see AQUEDUCT, DRAWBRIDGE, VIADUCT, **186**]

51 *Tower Bridge, London: a late manifestation of the Gothic Revival.*

## BROACH SPIRE [see SPIRE]

## BROCH

Distinctly Scottish phenomenon dating back to around the first century BC, consisting of a cavity-walled round structure with a gracefully tapering profile, which seems to anticipate the shape of a modern cooling tower. Scotland possesses the remains of some 500 brochs, mostly in the Northern and Western Isles. **Dun Carloway, Isle of Lewis**, and the **Glenelg Brochs** in the western Highlands are typical of these modest single-entrance structures which were probably built as strongholds against attacks by sea-borne raiders. The **Broch of Mousa, Shetland**, is the largest, surviving to a height of 40 feet (12·2m). Orkney was a major centre of the broch builders.

52 *One of the surviving brochs at Glenelg in the western Highlands of Scotland.*

## BROKEN PEDIMENT [see PEDIMENT]

## BRUTALISM

Architectural movement of the 1950s and 1960s associated with the monumental deployment of massive elements of reinforced concrete. The design logic was the belief that structure and materials should be openly and powerfully expressed. Though inspired by an idealistic vision, Brutalism has not been judged an aesthetic success. The ability to shape concrete virtually at will led to the abandonment of proper scale and proportion. The rejection of ornament left buildings with large, unattractive expanses of naked concrete, which have weathered badly. The resulting ugliness has blighted many an urban centre, nowhere more prominently than in the **South Bank** complex, **London**. Architects of the 1990s still make extensive use of concrete but attempt to handle it in a more sensitive manner. [see CONCRETE]

## BULL'S EYE WINDOW

Small round or oval window, also known by the French, '*oeil de boeuf*'. [see 262]

## BUNGALOW

Term derived from the Hindustani '*bangla*', i.e. from Bengal. It denotes a single-storey house, usually with pitched roof, which imitates original structures first built in India. The bungalow boomed in the 1920s and 1930s in seaside resorts and suburbs. Its popularity continues, most notably in Ireland.

## BUNKER

Fortified shelter, often subterranean, with a superstructure of reinforced concrete. Many were constructed during the Second World War (1939–45); a prominent survivor in the centre of London is the Citadel, built to house Admiralty communications.

53 OPPOSITE *The raw power of bare concrete is expressed in no uncertain fashion in the Brutalism of London's massive South Bank complex.*

## BURGH

Borough or chartered town in Scotland. Many date back to the twelfth century when David I implemented a policy of urban development. The authentic atmosphere of the burgh is best conveyed by **Culross**, *Fife*, Scotland, whose streetscape, buildings and a fine mercat cross remain essentially as they appeared in the seventeenth century. A notable piece of burgh architecture in Scotland is the stone house known as **Provand's Lordship, Glasgow**, of 1471.

54 *The traditional streetscape of the Scottish burgh is well preserved at Culross,* Fife.

## BURH

Fortified Saxon town of a type pioneered by Alfred the Great in the ninth century to defend Wessex against the Danes. Stout earthworks were built around towns such as **Cricklade**, *Wilts*; **Wareham**, *Dorset*; and **Wallingford**, *Oxon*. Some burhs, notably **Shaftesbury**, *Dorset*, enjoyed the natural defence of a hilltop location. The burh was a decisive force in urban development in England prior to the Norman Conquest.

## BUTTERY

Room in a medieval residence used for the storage of wine and provisions.

## BUTTRESS

Projecting mass of masonry or brickwork which gives lateral support to the walls of a building. Gothic buttressing became an architectural feature of artistic merit. The most spectacular variant was the flying buttress, which conveys the outward pressure of a wall by means of a graceful stone arch connecting with a solid pier, e.g. at **York Minster**, *N Yorks*; and **Westminster Abbey, London**. [see ABUTMENT, SPIRE, 78, 292]

## BYRE

Cowshed, often attached to a simple rural dwelling, e.g. a longhouse or black house. [see BLACK HOUSE, LONGHOUSE]

## BYZANTINE REVIVAL

The Byzantine style of northern Italy, where it is known as the Italian Romanesque, made an appearance in Britain in the late nineteenth and early twentieth centuries in churches such as **St Mary & St Nicholas, Wilton**, *Wilts*; **St Alphege, Bath**, *Avon*; the chapel of **Lady Margaret Hall, Oxford**, *Oxon*; and **Westminster Cathedral, London**. The style is noted for features such as the basilican plan, domes, round arches, lavish mosaics and the Italian campanile. [see BASILICA, CAMPANILE, DOME]

55 OPPOSITE *Flying buttresses and ornate pinnacles feature strongly at York Minster,* N Yorks.

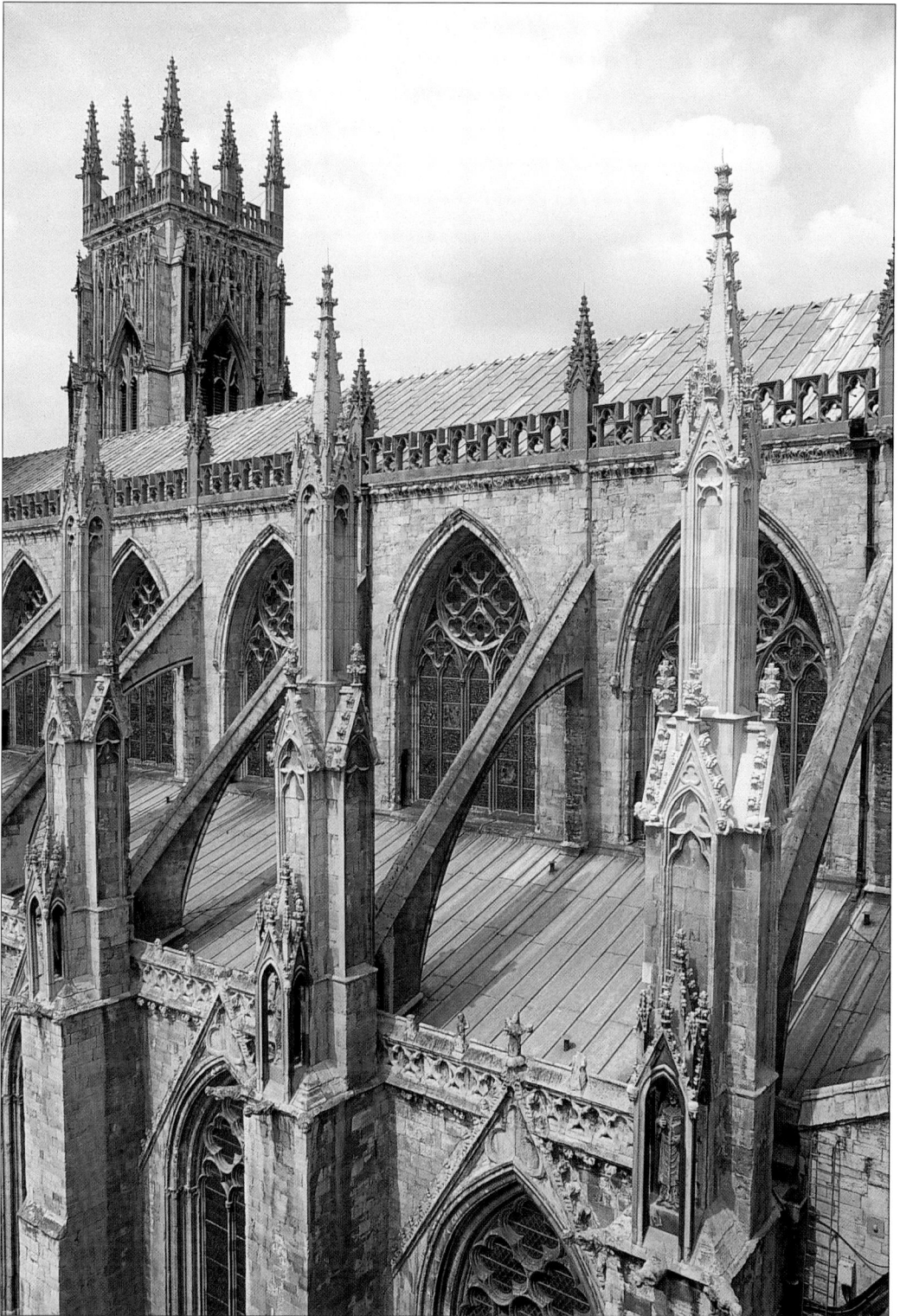

# C

## CABIN
Small primitive dwelling in a rural area.

## CABLE
Moulding resembling a twisted rope or cable. [see MOULDING]

## CABMEN'S SHELTER
Small wooden structure built as a product of Victorian philanthropy to provide cabmen, who were notoriously heavy drinkers, with convenient refuges where they could obtain a hot meal and non-alcoholic refreshment. Some sixty-four were built in London alone, but their number is now much reduced. These characteristic green huts with pitched roof may be seen at several locations in central **London**, e.g. **Russell Square** and **Hanover Square**.

## CAEN STONE
Cream-coloured limestone quarried near Caen in Normandy, France, which was shipped over by the Normans on account of its fine carving quality; it was particularly valued for prestige work. Ease of shipment ensured its widespread use in south-east England throughout the Middle Ages, e.g. at **Westminster Abbey, London**; **Canterbury Cathedral**, *Kent*; **Winchester Cathedral**, *Hants*; the keep of **Dover Castle**, *Kent*; and the **White Tower** in the **Tower of London**. However, Caen stone does not weather well; and Christopher Wren described it as 'more beautiful than durable'. [see LIMESTONE]

## CAHER [see CASHEL]

## CAIRN
Pile of rough stones, usually of prehistoric date, set up as a marker or memorial covering a grave. [see BARROW]

## CAISSON or COFFER
1) Panel of a compartmental ceiling.

2) Water-tight compartment used for construction work on a submerged foundation, e.g. the pier of a bridge.

## CALEFACTORY
Heated room in a monastery.

## CAMBER
Horizontal timber, e.g. a beam, which has a convex profile.

## CAME
Lead strip, used like a glazing bar, to retain a window pane. [see LEADED LIGHT, 380]

## CAMERA OBSCURA
Meaning in Latin a 'dark room', this structure contains a windowless room having a small aperture to admit an image of the view outside which is projected on to a wall or screen, e.g. at the **Outlook Tower, Edinburgh**, and the **Observatory, Dumfries**, *Dumfr & Gall*, Scotland. [see OBSERVATORY]

## CAMP [see CASTRUM]

## CAMPANILE [see BELFRY, 130]

## CANOPY
Hood or covering which is projected or suspended above a door, window, pulpit, tomb, throne or statue niche. A canopy supported on four columns above an altar may be described as a baldachin or ciborium, e.g. in **St Paul's Cathedral** and **Westminster Cathedral, London**. [see 293]

**56** *This tomb canopy in Beverley Minster,* Humbs, *contains an ornate ogee within a triangular arch.*

## CANTILEVER
Horizontal element, i.e. a beam or girder, which is counterbalanced by its own weight behind a fulcrum. The cantilever principle is used in structures such as bridges, balconies and staircases.

## CAPSTONE
Stone laid horizontally on two or more upright stones to form a dolmen or portal tomb. [see DOLMEN]

## CARPENTER'S GOTHIC
Alternative name for Gothic Revival as used in the eighteenth century. [see GOTHIC REVIVAL]

## CARREL or CAROL
Small recess or niche in a library or cloister, used for reading and writing in relative privacy. [see LIBRARY]

## CARTOUCHE
Ornamental display of motto or coat of arms enclosed within a scroll-like panel.

## CAPITAL
Uppermost, crowning feature of a column or pilaster. Capital types are the major distinguishing features of the various Classical orders. There are also a number of generic types which occur in Norman and Gothic architecture. [see ORDER]

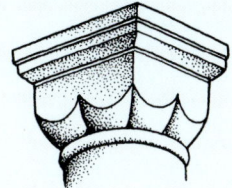

Scalloped capital

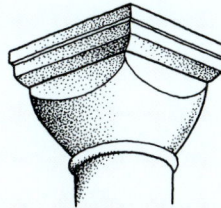

Cushion or Block capital

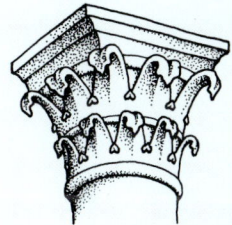

Crocket capital

Water-leaf capital

Stiff-leaf capital

57 *These stately caryatids at St Pancras New Church, London, present a Georgian vision of ancient Greece.*

## CARYATID

In ancient Greek architecture, a column in the form of a colossal female figure supporting an entablature. The caryatids from the Erechtheum in Athens provided the model for the porches of **St Pancras New Church, London**, a masterpiece of the Greek Revival. [see ATLANTES, GREEK REVIVAL, HERM]

## CASEMATE

Vaulted room built into the thickness of a fortified wall, serving as a battery or barrack. [see BARRACK]

## CASEMENT

1) Window frame with hinges on the vertical side.

2) Concave Gothic moulding in the jamb of a door or window.

## CASHEL

Irish ringfort of drystone masonry which remained in use from the Iron Age until the early Middle Ages, e.g. **Drumena Cashel**, *Down*, N. Ireland. Also known as caher. [see DUN, RATH]

58 *Drumena Cashel*, Down, *N Ireland: a drystone enclosure that would have contained a few simple dwellings.*

## CASINO

Italian, meaning 'small house'. The term was first applied in the eighteenth century to an ornamental pavilion in the park of a grander residence, e.g. the **Casino** at **Marino, Dublin**, Ireland, designed by William Chambers. The term was later extended to denote a music salon or ballroom; and it is now generally understood to mean a building used exclusively for gambling.

## CAST IRON [see IRONWORK]

## CASTELLATED

Built in the manner of a castle, i.e. with towers and battlements.

## CASTLE

The combined function of the castle as a fortified residence and a stronghold for a military garrison was essentially a product of the Middle Ages. The first generation of castles to be built by the Normans after 1066 were of the motte and bailey type, i.e. consisting of an artificial motte or mound with a bailey or forecourt enclosing a larger area in front. The castle itself was usually a wooden structure surrounded by a palisade on top of the motte. Usually all that remains of an early Norman castle is the mound e.g. at **Barnstaple**, *Devon*; **Oxford**, *Oxon*; the **Bass of Inverurie**, *Grampian*, Scotland; **Dromore**, *Down*, N. Ireland. The more important Norman castles were built from the outset in stone, e.g. **Colchester Castle**, *Essex*; **Rochester Castle**, *Kent*; and the **White Tower**, nucleus of the future **Tower of London,** which was built 'against the restlessness of the large and fierce populace'.

The general switch from wood to stone occurred in the twelfth century as the Norman barons consolidated their hold on the land. Most castles followed the principle of a central keep in the form of a tower, but another variant was the shell-keep in which the stronghold was contained within a stout defensive circular wall, e.g. at **Restormel Castle**, *Cornwall.* It was also discovered that a round keep was less susceptible to mining than the rectangular type; the circular plan was adopted for the royal castles at **Orford**, *Suffolk*, and **Conisbrough**, *S Yorks*. Edward I's military campaigns in the last decades of the thirteenth century

**59** *The original Norman motte with a stone shell-keep has survived at Cardiff Castle, S Glam, Wales.*

introduced the concentric castle, comprising one or more rings of fortification around the nucleus of a central keep, e.g. at **Beaumaris**, **Caernarvon**, **Conway** and **Harlech**, *Gwynedd*, Wales.

With the waning of the Middle Ages came more settled conditions, and consequently less need for defence and a greater demand for comfort. In the Tudor era many medieval castles were abandoned, but some attempts were

made to convert them into more elegant homes, e.g. at **Kenilworth Castle**, *Warw*. The present ruinous condition of so many ancient castles is due to their destruction during the Civil War of the 1640s. However, a number of castles continued to be occupied and were extended and improved by their owners over successive generations, e.g. **Berkeley Castle**, *Glos*; **Hever Castle**, *Kent*; **Arundel Castle**, *W Sussex*; **Warwick Castle**, *Warw*. In Scotland and Ireland the castle continued to serve its essential defensive purpose – mainly in

60 *Stylish defences at Dover Castle,* Kent (ABOVE).
61 *Ditch and curtain wall form the outer defences of Framlingham Castle,* Suffolk (BELOW).

the form of the tower house – until well into the seventeenth century. Throughout the British Isles there occurred in the nineteenth century a revival of interest in the medieval castle which resulted in the building of many country houses with mock battlements and towers in the the Baronial style. The rebuilding in 1903 of **Lindisfarne Castle**, *Northum*, by Edwin Lutyens

62 *Pembroke Castle*, Dyfed, *Wales: an early medieval structure containing an impressive round keep.*

came uncannily close to the real thing. [see ALURE, ARMOURY, ARROW LOOP, BARBICAN, BARMKIN, BARONIAL, BARTIZAN, BASTION, BASTLE HOUSE, BATTER, BATTLEMENT, CRENELLATION, CURTAIN WALL, DONJON, DRAWBRIDGE, DRUM TOWER, DUNGEON, ENCEINTE, FORT, KEEP, MACHICOLATION, MARTELLO TOWER, MOAT, MURDER HOLE, NORMAN REVIVAL, OUBLIETTE, PARAPET, PELE TOWER, PORTCULLIS, SALLY-PORT, TOWER HOUSE, WALL-STAIR, YETT]

## CASTRUM

Latin name for a military fort or camp. Many of these typically square Roman enclosures based on a gridiron layout later evolved as towns, e.g. **Chester**, *Cheshire*, and **Exeter**, *Devon*. The presence of a Roman settlement underlying a modern town is often indicated by the suffix -caster or -chester, derived from castrum, e.g. **Cirencester**, *Glos*; and **Dorchester**, *Dorset*. Roman camps in open countryside include **Ardoch** and **Inchtuthil**, *Highland*, Scotland; and **Richborough**, *Kent*. The legionary fortress at **Caerleon**, *Gwent*, Wales, is occupied by a modern town. [see FORT, ROMAN]

## CATACOMB

The Continental custom of burials in underground cemeteries predates the Christian Era, but the chambered tomb was preferred in the British Isles. In the Middle Ages, however, subterranean crypts beneath churches and cathedrals were used for burying the dead. The crypt of **St Michan, Dublin**, Ireland, is a rare type of catacomb in which many of the corpses have been mummified by the moisture-absorbing properties of the magnesian limestone vaults. The new cemeteries of the Victorian era introduced their own updated version of the catacomb, e.g. at **Highgate Cemetery** and **Brompton Cemetery**, London. [see CEMETERY, CHAMBERED TOMB, CRYPT, MAUSOLEUM]

**63** *Victorian catacombs in the Circle of Lebanon, Highgate Cemetery, London.*

## CATHEDRA

The Latin word '*cathedra*', denoting the throne of a bishop, is at the origin of 'cathedral', signifying the church containing the seat of the bishop's authority. The bishop's throne was once located on a prominent platform behind the high altar and enjoyed a commanding outlook directly through the choir and nave. **Norwich Cathedral**, *Norfolk*, is the only example in the British Isles where the bishop's throne occupies this original position. The throne of a medieval bishop was often a prestigious item, e.g. at **Exeter Cathedral**, *Devon*, where it is a towering Gothic structure of carved oak, which reaches a height of 57 feet (17·4m). Nowadays, most bishops' thrones are relatively modest in size and design.

## CATHEDRAL

Since the status of a cathedral derives from its being the seat of a bishop, it is a title which can come and go according to changes in diocesan organization. Some cathedrals, although ancient buildings, only acquired that status in recent times, e.g. **St Albans**, *Herts*, in 1877; and **Ripon**, *N Yorks*, in 1836. By the same token, others have forfeited their status, e.g. **St Germans**, *Cornwall*, in 1043; **Crediton**, *Devon*, in 1050; **Sherborne**, *Dorset*, in 1075; and at **North Elmham**, *Norfolk*, are the scant remains of a small Saxon cathedral which once served the whole of East Anglia. At **Old Sarum**, *Wilts*, there remain only the foundations of a great cathedral which endured from 1075 until 1220 when the bishop's seat was moved to the new town of **Salisbury**, *Wilts*. However, most of the great cathedrals of the Middle Ages have survived as such. These mighty buildings were constructed over several centuries and reflect the various changes in architecture over a lengthy period. Some stand out as clear

64 *St David's Cathedral*, Dyfed, *Wales, has a cruci-form plan with a square tower over the crossing.*

examples of a particular style: **Durham**, *Durham*; **Rochester**, *Kent*; and **Southwell**, *Notts*, are strikingly Norman, as are the interiors of **Gloucester**, *Glos*, and **Ely**, *Cambs*. **Salisbury**, *Wilts*, ranks as the purest expression of the Early English style in the thirteenth century. Fine Early English work is also in evidence at **Lincoln**, *Lincs*; **Ripon**, *N Yorks*; and **Wells**, *Somerset*. The Decorated Gothic style is best represented at **Exeter**, *Devon*,

65 OPPOSITE *Norwich Cathedral*, Norfolk: *the grand Gothic composition is dominated by the graceful spire.*

and **York Minster**, *N Yorks*; and Perpendicular Gothic at **Canterbury**, *Kent*; **Gloucester**, *Glos*; and **Winchester**, *Hants*. No new cathedrals were built in the sixteenth century, though some were created from former abbeys in the aftermath of the Dissolution of the Monasteries, e.g. at **Bristol**, *Avon*. Christopher Wren's **St Paul's, London**, of the late seventeenth century stands out as a grand cathedral in the Baroque style. Although there was a dearth of cathedral building in the eighteenth century, the nineteenth century witnessed renewed activity, e.g. **Truro**, *Cornwall*, of 1881 by J.L. Pearson. Ireland produced a new series of Roman Catholic cathedrals ranging from the Gothic Revival **St Patrick's, Armagh**, *Armagh*, of 1840 to the Baroque monumentality of **Mullingar**, *Meath*, in the 1930s.

The Anglican cathedral at **Liverpool**, *Mers*, commenced in 1903 and still under construction at the death of its architect Giles Gilbert Scott in 1960, was the last of the great Gothic designs. More typical of the early twentieth century was the modest brick cathedral at **Guildford**, *Surrey*, of the 1930s. A revolutionary break with the past was heralded by the new **Coventry Cathedral**, *W Mids*, in the 1950s by Basil Spence. This building showed a bold use of sculpture, stained glass and tapestry by modern artists such as John Piper, Jacob Epstein and Graham Sutherland. Equally remarkable is the Roman Catholic **Metropolitan Cathedral** at **Liverpool**, *Mers*, built in the 1960s to a novel design by Frederick Gibberd: a circular, concrete structure crowned by a sixteen-sided lantern filled with coloured glass. The sanctuary is located directly beneath it, representing a complete departure from the longitudinal alignment of the Gothic cathedrals of the Middle Ages. [see ABBEY, ALTAR, AMBULATORY, APSE, BAPTISTERY, BELFRY, BUTTRESS, CATHEDRA, CHANTRY, CHAPTER-HOUSE, CHOIR, CHURCH, CLOSE, CRYPT, GALILEE, GOTHIC, HALL CHURCH, LADY CHAPEL, MASON'S MARK, MINSTER, MISERICORD, NAVE, NORMAN, PRESBYTERY, PULPITUM, RADIATING CHAPELS, REREDOS, SCULPTURE, SPIRE, STAINED GLASS, TRACERY, TRANSEPT, TRIFORIUM, VAULT]

## CAUSEWAYED CAMP

Prehistoric enclosure from the Neolithic period (*c.* 4000 BC–2000 BC). This type of monument owes its name to the openings in the encircling rings of ditch and rampart which were thought to be entrances for causeways. Although this is uncertain, it is generally accepted that these camps were used for ritualistic gatherings by peoples from the surrounding area. The causewayed camps are mainly restricted to southern England; the most famous example is **Windmill Hill** near **Avebury**, *Wilts*. [see HENGE, PREHISTORIC]

## CAVALIER

Raised platform of earth, used in a fortification either as a look-out or as an emplacement for artillery. The Tudor ramparts at **Berwick-upon-Tweed**, *Northum*, contain several cavaliers. They are also a feature at the coastal forts built by Henry VIII. [see FORT]

## CAVETTO

Concave moulding. [see MOULDING]

## CEILING

It was not until the sixteenth century that the exposed timbers of medieval buildings were generally modified by the insertion of an intermediate layer of wood and plaster. This flat surface not

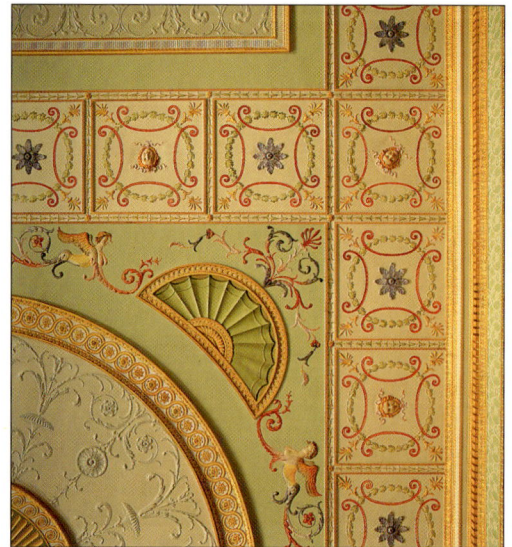

66 *Colourful ceiling by Robert Adam in the library of Osterley Park House, London.*

only made for snugger accommodation, but also provided fresh opportunities for decorative work. Early ceilings consisted of a series of squares formed by beams and rafters which could be covered by wooden panels or plasterwork. Expertise in plasterwork soon progressed to the extent that elaborately moulded ceilings could be suspended from concealed beams. Even Gothic features such as pendants could be imitated in plaster, e.g. at **Trerice**, *Cornwall*. A wide range of motifs such as heraldic devices and monograms could be deployed within a strapwork pattern. Plaster ceilings of the Tudor and Jacobean period are particularly exuberant, e.g. at **Athelhampton House**, *Dorset*; **Lanhydrock House**, *Cornwall*; **Prince Henry's Room, London**; and **Craigievar Castle**, *Grampian*, Scotland. Grandiose ideas were introduced in the early seventeenth century by Inigo Jones at the **Banqueting House, London**, where the ceiling was designed to accommodate a series of paintings by Peter Paul Rubens. The **Painted Hall** of Christopher Wren's **Royal Naval College, Greenwich, London**, boasts a splendid Baroque ceiling by James Thornhill. The Palladian taste for coffered ceilings based on Classical originals set the tone for most of the eighteenth century. Inset panels depicting scenes from Greek and Roman antiquity were also popular. There was a measure of uniformity in such ceilings until Robert Adam introduced a greater degree of invention and imagination in the latter half of the eighteenth century. The Victorian era mechanized the traditional craft techniques through the use of prefabricated mouldings; and it was partly the lack of skilled craftsmen which brought about a simpler approach to ceiling decoration in the twentieth century. [see ADAM STYLE, CAISSON, PLASTERWORK, STRAPWORK, **196**]

67 *Entrance to a monastic cell at Mount Grace Priory,* N Yorks. *Note the hood-mould.*

## CELL

The individual unit of accommodation in a monastery or prison. A monastic cell could be substantially more than a single room, e.g. at **Mount Grace Priory**, *N Yorks*, where the Carthusian brethren were lodged in detached two-storey stone houses, each with a private garden. [see MONASTERY, PRISON]

## CELLA

The main body of a Classical temple. [see TEMPLE]

## CELLAR

Room or space, generally subterranean, used for the storage of wine, coal etc. Medieval cellars were usually vaulted. [see CRYPT, UNDERCROFT]

## CELTIC CROSS [see HIGH CROSS]

## CELTIC

The exact origins of the Celtic tribes and the circumstances surrounding their

68 *Typical swirling motifs of Celtic design on the sculptured Turoe Stone,* Galway, *Ireland.*

appearance in the British Isles are the subject of much controversy. The definition of Celtic is partly linguistic, since it denotes the speakers of one of the Celtic languages, of which today's Gaelic in Ireland and Scotland and Welsh in Wales are the direct descendants. In terms of architecture and archaeology, the Celts are identified with the great hillforts of Britain and the raths or ringforts of Ireland which belong chiefly to the Iron Age (c. 700 BC–AD 43). Enigmatic examples of Celtic sculpture of the pre-Christian period in the form of decorated stones survive at **Castlestrange**, *Roscommon*, and the **Turoe Stone**, *Galway*, Ireland. The later Celtic period in Ireland (from c. AD 500–1100) has bequeathed an impressive legacy of beautifully carved high crosses, and dazzling manuscript illuminations which testify to the vivid artistic imagination of the Celts. The art of the high cross also made an impact in Wales, Scotland and Cornwall. The Celtic churches of Ireland adopted the round-arched Romanesque of continental Europe in the twelfth century; and the Irish variant of the style is known as Hiberno-Romanesque, the equivalent of the Norman style in England at the same

time. The seminal building of the Hiberno-Romanesque was **Cormac's Chapel, Rock of Cashel**, *Tipperary*, from 1127. Also of significance is the **Nun's Church, Clonmacnoise**, *Offaly*, Ireland. [see CHURCH, HIGH CROSS, HILLFORT, RATH]

## CELTIC REVIVAL

Late nineteenth- and early twentieth-century movement inspired by the art and architecture of ancient Ireland. It manifested itself chiefly in an enthusiasm for the intricate designs of the Celtic cross and Hiberno-Romanesque architecture. The chapel of the **University College of Cork**, Ireland, offers one of the richest expressions of the Celtic Revival.

## CELURE

That part of a wagon roof above a church altar, usually panelled and decorated. [see WAGON ROOF]

## CEMENT [see CONCRETE, MORTAR]

## CEMETERY

Any grouping of graves, however informal, may be referred to as a cemetery. It was not until the nineteenth century, when churchyards in the large cities became overcrowded with corpses and posed a threat to the health of the living, that steps were taken to create spacious garden cemeteries. Some of the most famous Victorian cemeteries in London were set up as profit-making enterprises. **Highgate, Brompton, Kensal Green** and **West Norwood** are veritable 'cities of the dead' with streets and avenues, and some tombs resembling miniature houses. **Glasnevin Cemetery, Dublin**, Ireland, belongs to the same tradition. The burghers of **Glasgow** laid out their

69 OPPOSITE *Brompton Cemetery, London: a burial ground of the Victorian era.*

**Necropolis** ('city of the dead' in Greek) on a hill facing the cathedral. It was visited by Albert, the Prince Consort in 1849, and it soon became a tourist attraction. The guidebook encouraged visitors with the rhetorical question: 'Who is not made better by occasional intercourse with the tomb?' [see CATACOMB, CHAMBERED TOMB, CHARNEL HOUSE, CRYPT, MAUSOLEUM, OSSUARY, TOMB SCULPTURE]

## CENOTAPH

Monument erected to commemorate a person or persons buried elsewhere, e.g. the **Cenotaph, Whitehall,** London, of 1919 by Edwin Lutyens. [see MEMORIAL, MONUMENT, TOMB SCULPTURE, WAR MEMORIAL]

## CHAINED LIBRARY [see LIBRARY]

## CHAIR RAIL

Moulding around the wall of a room to prevent damage by chairs and other furniture. [see DADO]

## CHALK

Soft form of limestone, sometimes used in combination with other material to make a durable building material. [see CLUNCH]

## CHAMBERED TOMB

General term to describe a prehistoric structure for collective burials consisting of a megalithic chamber contained within a mound of earth or rubble. A variety of different types of chambered tomb have been identified by archaeologists, and some broad regional similarities have been established. In practice, however, such classifications may be misleading since the common features of chambered tombs are probably more significant than their perceived differences. They all reflect a shared preoccupation with the fact of death and rites of passage into an

70 *Central chamber of the passage grave at Maes Howe, Orkney, Scotland: a masterpiece of drystone masonry.*

afterlife which are often associated with the idea of fertility. Their collective burials are in marked contrast to the subsequent practice of individual interment.

The phenomenon of the chambered tomb dates back to the end of the fourth millennium BC during the New Stone Age and continued into the Bronze Age. The most common general type, known as the gallery grave, consists in its simplest form of a gallery inside a long barrow with side chambers for the various burials. It is best represented by the monuments classified as the Severn-Cotswold group, e.g. **Hetty Pegler's Tump,** *Glos;* **Wayland's Smithy,** *Oxon;* and **West Kennet,** *Wilts.* **Belas Knap,** *Glos,* is famous for its false entrance, which is thought to have been intended as a defence against grave-robbers. A similar

71 *The reconstructed entrance to the passage grave at Newgrange*, Meath, *Ireland.*

type, defined as the Clyde-Solway and Carlingford groups, is found in south-west Scotland, northern Ireland, west Wales and the Isle of Man. Irish gallery graves are divided into two broad categories: the wedge-tomb (so called because the chamber is narrower at one end), e.g. at **Labbacallee**, *Cork*; and the court cairn which has a small forecourt, e.g. at **Creevykeel**, *Sligo*. The passage grave is the other main type of chambered tomb, in which the chamber generally lies at the centre of a circular mound and is reached by a long, narrow passage, e.g. **Bryn Celli Ddu, Anglesey**, *Gwynedd*, Wales. **Maes Howe, Orkney**, Scotland, is remarkable both for the architectural quality of its stonework and the alignment of its passage on the sunset of the winter solstice.

**Newgrange**, *Meath*, Ireland, is aligned on the sunrise of the winter solstice. The artistic vitality and enigmatic symbolism of its carvings, notably the powerful triple spirals on the enormous kerbstone guarding the entrance, combine to make Newgrange the most intriguing megalithic monument in the British Isles. [see BARROW, DOLMEN, MEGALITHIC, PREHISTORIC]

## CHAMFER

The resulting oblique surface when the right angle of a block of stone or piece of timber is cut diagonally. [see SPLAY]

## CHANCEL

Part of a church to the east of the crossing which contains the choir and the main altar. The word is derived from Latin '*cancellus*', denoting the screen which separated the chancel from the nave. [see CHOIR, PRESBYTERY, RETRO-CHOIR]

## CHANCEL ARCH

Internal arch of a church, marking the westerly entrance to the chancel. A

72 *A round Norman chancel arch commands the nave of the church of St Andrew, Stogursey*, Somerset.

67

powerfully decorated chancel arch was a feature of Norman churches, e.g. at **St Peter, Tickencote**, *Leics.*

## CHANTRY

Privately endowed shrine or chapel in a church or cathedral, where prayers were offered for the soul of the founder. In the Middle Ages it was a popular custom among the rich to build chantries in order to promote their own salvation, e.g. the **Percy Chantry** at **Tynemouth Priory**, *Tyne & Wear.* The interiors of cathedrals became increasingly congested with chantries containing imposing tombs; and the competition for available space near the shrines of saints was particularly intense. Some chantries amounted to major architectural extensions, e.g. the **Henry VII Chapel** in **Westminster Abbey, London.** The **Beauchamp Chapel** at **St Mary,**

**Warwick,** *Warw,* is the most magnificent non-royal chantry in the country. [see COLLEGIATE CHURCH, TOMB SCULPTURE, 45, 329]

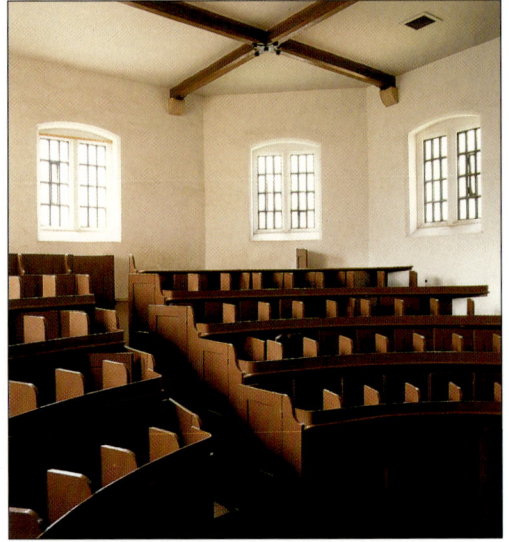

74 *The layout of the prison chapel in Lincoln Castle,* Lincs, *reflects the regime of solitary confinement.*

## CHAPEL

Separate building or space within a church for Christian worship. A chapel of ease was one by the roadside for the convenience of travellers. Private chapels are found in castles and stately homes, e.g. **St George's Chapel, Windsor Castle**, *Berks*, and at **Audley End**, *Essex.* Medieval colleges contain chapels of great architectural importance, e.g. **King's College Chapel, Cambridge**, *Cambs.* Institutions such as schools, hospitals and prisons possess chapels for their inmates. The Victorian prison chapel at **Lincoln Castle**, *Lincs*, was designed to maintain the strict regime of solitary confinement even during religious services: prisoners were led, wearing hoods, into individual wooden box pews, from which they could see only the minister and not the other prisoners.

73 *The Speke Chantry in Exeter Cathedral,* Devon, *dates back to 1517.*

The designation of chapel also applies to the houses of worship of the Nonconformist sects. [see CHANTRY, CHURCH, CORONA, GALILEE, LADY CHAPEL, MEETING HOUSE]

## CHAPTER-HOUSE

Building or room in a monastery or cathedral used for the discussion and regulation of administrative matters. It could be polygonal or square in shape, with canopied stone seats lining the walls. A Gothic chapter-house often has a central column supporting radiating vaults, e.g. at **Wells Cathedral**, *Somerset*, and at **Lincoln Cathedral**, *Lincs*. At **Southwell Minster**, *Notts*, the chapter-house displays some magnificent medieval carvings portraying the leaves of the forest. A square chapter-house has survived at **Bristol Cathedral**, *Avon*; and there are the remains of another in the romantic ruins of **Jervaulx Abbey**, *N Yorks*. [see MONASTERY, **2, 338**]

## CHARNEL HOUSE

Medieval structure for the storage of bones or bodies, usually with a chapel attached. [see CRYPT, OSSUARY]

## CHEQUER-WORK

Decoration of wall or pavement with alternating squares of light and dark colour. [see FLINT, **344**]

## CHERT

Like flint, this stone is composed of silica and occurs in hard nodules of a brittle quality. There are plentiful deposits of chert on the borders of Devon, Dorset and Somerset; and it is widely used in local buildings, e.g. the **Grammar School, Chard**, *Somerset*. [see FLINT]

## CHEVAUX DE FRISE

Defensive arrangement of sharp obstacles

75 *The formidable* chevaux de frise *at Dun Aengus in the Aran Islands, Ireland.*

driven into the ground in front of a fortification in order to deter a frontal assault, e.g. the array of jagged stones which protect the landward approach to the clifftop fort of **Dun Aengus, Inishmore, Aran Islands**, Ireland.

## CHEVET

From French '*chef*' meaning 'head'. Apse with ambulatory, off which there are chapels.

## CHEVRON

Zig-zag moulding, a distinctive feature of Norman architecture, often carved on a chancel arch or doorway. At **Durham Cathedral**, *Durham*, some of the massive round columns in the nave are adorned with boldly incised chevrons. [see NORMAN, **110, 147**]

## CHIMNEY, CHIMNEYPIECE

The meaning of chimney (from French '*cheminée*') has been extended from its original sense of 'fireplace' to denote the flues through which the smoke is extracted. 'Chimneypiece' describes the decorative surround of the fireplace. Early medieval halls had open fireplaces in the

76 *Elegant Neo-Classical chimneypiece with flanking herms at Hopetoun House,* Lothian, *Scotland.*

middle of the room, and the smoke would disperse through a louvre in the roof, e.g. at **Penshurst Place**, *Kent.* Once the fireplace became a built-in fixture against a wall, its surround received special architectural treatment. As the dominant physical feature of a room the chimneypiece was adorned to reflect the status of the owner, and it often displayed the appro-

priate armorial bearings, e.g. at **Donegal Castle**, Donegal, Ireland. The Classical chimneypiece of the eighteenth century, also known as mantelpiece, imitated an entablature supported by attached columns or pilasters. Such elegant compositions, sometimes in white marble, could be completed with a mirror or ornate plasterwork above. In the Victorian era chimneypieces were often made of cast iron with a surround of glazed tiles. [see INGLENOOK, **113, 344**]

## CHIMNEYSTACK

Rooftop structure housing one or more flues for the extraction of smoke. The chimneystack was already embellished as a design feature in the Middle Ages, but Tudor builders turned it into an art form with fanciful compositions in brick which created many a roofline full of dramatic incident, e.g. at **Compton Wynates**, *Warw*. By contrast, Palladian architects of the eighteenth century concealed chimneystacks or disguised them as urns or obelisks, e.g. at **Chiswick House, London**. [see **130, 265, 345**]

## CHINOISERIE

The taste for things Chinese manifested itself in the eighteenth century as merchant ships returned with cargoes of silk, porcelain and prints which illustrated the buildings and landscapes of China. Original Chinese wallpaper was hung in many a country house; and pagodas were built as eye-catching novelties in parks and gardens. But all pales before the Chinese enthusiasms of the Prince Regent from about 1811 at the **Royal Pavilion, Brighton**, *E Sussex*. Its **Banqueting Room** seethes with Chinese dragons; and the **Music Room** is adorned with portraits

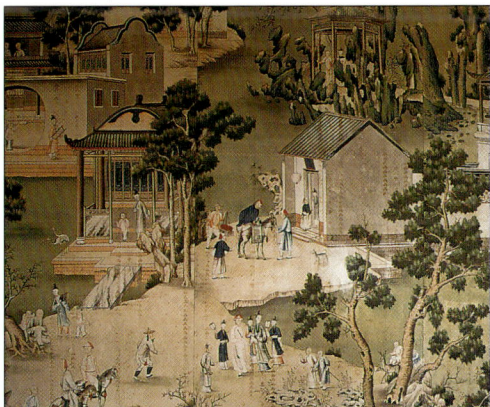

77 *Original eighteenth-century Chinese wallpaper at Westport House*, Mayo, *Ireland.*

of Chinese warriors and musicians. Other notable specimens of Chinoiserie include the **Chinese Dairy** at **Woburn Abbey**, *Beds*, and the **Chinese Room** at **Claydon House**, *Bucks*. [see ORIENTALISM, PAGODA]

## CHOIR

Part of a church or cathedral to the east of the crossing. Also spelled as 'quire'. [see MISERICORD, STALLS]

## CHURCH

The evolution of a specific building for Christian worship commenced soon after AD 325 when Christianity became the official religion of the Roman Empire. The earliest places of Christian worship in the British Isles were probably small rooms or private chapels within larger villas, e.g. at the **Roman Villa** at **Lullingstone**, *Kent*. However, the widespread promotion of Christianity in the fourth century called for an architectural prototype for houses of Christian worship. For this the practical shape of the rectangular Roman basilica was chosen. It was this basilican plan, with an apse at the east end, which was widely adopted in southern England when church building began in earnest after St Augustine's mission of AD 597.

In the north of England, by contrast, the Celtic tradition of a simple nave and chancel with a square east end was followed. The early Saxon churches of England were made of wood and were subsequently rebuilt in stone. There is a unique survival at **St Andrew, Greensted**, *Essex*, of a Saxon church whose nave was constructed from split oak trunks. In Ireland, the early wooden churches have entirely disappeared, but the first stone churches imitated the architecture of their wooden predecessors, e.g. **Temple Macdara, St Macdara's Island**, *Galway*.

The round-arched Romanesque style of

**78** *Church tower of St Nicholas, Abbotsbury*, Dorset, *showing battlements, buttresses and string courses.*

continental Europe reached England just in advance of the Norman Conquest, but it was really after 1066 that the style became widespread throughout the country as a whole. The simple churches of the Saxons were almost all entirely rebuilt in the typically solid Norman style and became enduring symbols of the permanence of the Norman presence. This great rebuilding of the twelfth century extended into Wales and Scotland. Ireland's first Romanesque buildings were constructed in advance of the Anglo-Norman invasion of the 1170s. In England, several churches with round naves were built in imitation of the Church of the Holy Sepulchre in Jerusalem, but in general a rectangular nave with a square chancel was preferred.

79 *Church of St Mary, East Lulworth,* Dorset, *is disguised as a garden temple. Note the sash windows.*

Further rebuilding of parish churches continued at intervals throughout the Middle Ages, although the Black Death of 1348–9 brought most projects to a halt.

The successive phases of Gothic, pioneered by the cathedrals, were applied in turn to the parish churches. As funds became available, so aisles were added, towers and spires erected, and windows enlarged and beautified. Thus most parish churches display an amalgam of Gothic styles. The busiest period of building activity, from c. 1375 to c. 1550, coincided with the Perpendicular phase of Gothic. Many of the new churches of this time were financed by the wealth of the wool merchants, and are known for this reason as wool churches, e.g. **St Peter & St Paul, Lavenham**, *Suffolk*, and **St Mary the Virgin, Fairford**, *Glos*. It was during the Middle Ages that the cruciform plan, based on the Latin Cross, became standard.

After the frenetic burst of church building in the fifteenth century, there was a long lull in the sixteenth century. The energies of the Tudor period were directed towards secular rather than ecclesiastical projects. The new attitudes which emerged after the Reformation of the 1530s led to a reduction in ritual and an increasing emphasis on the sermon and readings from the Bible. A new generation of post-Reformation churches followed the auditory principle, in which the pulpit and the lectern assumed a greater importance in the layout than the altar.

This process of demystification of the Christian church was maintained by the Georgians who largely abandoned the Gothic tradition in favour of Classical models based on Greek and Roman temples, a trend which culminated in the nineteenth century with lavish creations such as **St Pancras New Church, London**, of 1819, complete with Grecian caryatids. The question of the appropriate form for churches lay at the centre of the debate between the rival promoters of Gothic and Classical architecture, known as the Battle of the Styles. By the middle of the nineteenth century, the Gothic cause emerged triumphant, and the latter half of the century witnessed a veritable outpouring of Gothic Revival churches of sometimes spectacular ambition, e.g. **St James, Kingston**, *Dorset*, of 1873–80 by G.E. Street. There also occurred a minor Byzantine Revival and a return to the basilican plan, e.g. at **St Mary and St Nicholas, Wilton**, *Wilts* of 1841–5. Modern church architecture in the twentieth century has not yet managed to establish a convincing tradition of its own. [for the style and forms of churches see ABBEY, AUDITORY CHURCH, BASILICA, BYZANTINE REVIVAL, CATHEDRAL, CELTIC, CHAPEL, COLLEGIATE CHURCH, GOTHIC, GOTHIC REVIVAL, GREEK REVIVAL, HALL CHURCH, MEETING HOUSE, MINSTER, MONASTERY, NORMAN, ORATORY, PARLIAMENTARY CHURCH, PRECEPTORY, ROUND CHURCH, SAXON, WOOL CHURCH] [for the parts

and features of churches see AISLE, ALTAR, AMBU-
LATORY, ANGEL ROOF, APSE, BAPTISTERY,
BELFRY, BELL COTE, BELL GABLE, BENCH
END, BRASSES, CAMPANILE, CHANCEL, CHAN-
CEL ARCH, CHANTRY, CHOIR, CLERESTORY,
CROSSING, CRUCIFORM, CRYPT, FLÈCHE,
FONT, GALILEE, GALLERY, GREEK CROSS,
JESSE WINDOW, LADY CHAPEL, LATIN CROSS,
LOWSIDE WINDOW, LYCHGATE, MISERICORD,
NAVE, PARVIS, PEW, PISCINA, POPPY-HEAD,
PORTICUS, PRESBYTERY, PULPIT, PULPITUM,
REREDOS, RETABLE, RETRO-CHOIR, ROOD,
ROSE WINDOW, SACRISTY, SANCTUARY,
SAXON, SEDILIA, SEPULCHRE, SHRINE, SPIRE,
STEEPLE, STOUP, TOMB SCULPTURE, TOWER,
TRANSEPT, STAINED GLASS, TRACERY, TRIFO-
RIUM, VESTRY, WAGON ROOF]

**CIBORIUM** [see CANOPY]

**CILL or SILL** [see HALF TIMBERING]

**CINQUEFOIL** [see FOIL]

**CIRCUS**
John Wood the Elder brought to the
planning of the Georgian city of Bath,
*Avon*, the novel concept of outlining in
the streetplan the oval shape of a Roman
amphitheatre. Strictly speaking, however,
the Roman circus – as used for chariot
races – was composed of two semicircular
ends joined by straight sides. Wood's

80 *The church of St John, Cirencester, Glos, sports a*
*proliferation of chapels at its east end.*

81 *Drystone dwelling with basic thatched roof at the Scottish clachan of Auchindrain, S'clyde.*

**Circus, Bath,** of 1754 was, in fact, a circle; and in this form the idea was taken up elsewhere, notably in the **Royal Circus, Edinburgh**, Scotland. Thereafter, the word was applied to any urban space that was roughly circular in shape, e.g. **Holborn Circus** and **Piccadilly Circus, London**. [see CRESCENT]

## CIST

Box-like prehistoric grave composed of rectangular slabs of stone. A cist may be above or below ground, and is often concealed beneath a cairn or barrow. [see CHAMBERED TOMB]

## CITY CHAMBERS or HALL [see MUNICIPAL BUILDINGS]

## CLACHAN

Small, scattered settlement of a type common in the Scottish Highlands until the nineteenth century. A clachan has been preserved at **Auchindrain**, *S'clyde*, Scotland. [see BLACK HOUSE, CROFT]

## CLADDING

Protective and often decorative covering of the external façade of a building, e.g. with slates, tiles, stone or weatherboard.

## CLAPBOARD [see WEATHERBOARD]

## CLAPPER-BRIDGE [see BRIDGE]

## CLASSICAL, CLASSICISM

Term derived from Latin '*classicus*' meaning 'of the highest class'. The words 'Classicism' and 'Classical' were later applied to the literary and artistic works of Greek and Roman antiquity which were considered to be of the highest order of merit. Strictly speaking, the adjective 'Classical' refers to the original products of Greece and Rome, whereas 'Neo-Classical' describes subsequent attempts at imitation. In practice, however, 'Classical' and the noun 'Classicism' embrace not only the culture of antiquity but also the revival of Classical civilization.

The Classical revival or Renaissance first reached the British Isles in the sixteenth century, mainly relayed via France and the Low Countries. In Tudor and Jacobean architecture Classical motifs such as columns and pediments were haphazardly employed for decorative effect without regard to the rules concerning the decoration of the various orders and the underlying principles governing correct proportion, e.g. the hybrid **Tower of the Five Orders** of 1613–20 in the **Old Schools Quadrangle, Oxford**, *Oxon*. The pure spirit of Classicism, as embodied by the Italian Renaissance, did not extend to Britain until the early decades of the seventeenth century, as exemplified by the buildings in London of Inigo Jones (1573–1652), e.g. the **Banqueting House, Whitehall**, and the **Queen's House, Greenwich**.

The tumult of the English Civil War (1642–9) interrupted any further development; and it was only after the Restoration of the Stuart monarchy in 1660 that Classicism was able to evolve, this time in the much freer vein of the English Baroque practised by Christopher Wren (1632–1723), e.g. at **St Paul's Cathedral, London**. A more dramatic Baroque was pursued by Nicholas Hawksmoor (1661–1736) in several London churches, e.g. **St Anne, Limehouse**; also by John Vanbrugh (1664–1726) at **Blenheim Palace**, *Oxon*, and by Thomas Archer (1668–1743) at **St John, Smith Square, London**.

The Palladian form of Classicism, more pleasing to the English taste for modesty, was taken up once again with renewed vigour at the beginning of the eighteenth century by the 3rd Earl of Burlington (1694–1753) and a group of adherents, notably William Kent (1685–1748) and Colen Campbell (d. 1729). Theirs was a relatively austere blend of Palladianism which determined the appearance of the many country houses with neat Classical porticos which were built from *c.* 1730 throughout the country.

82 *A piece of a column at Walthamstow, London, show its fluting and Ionic capital with volutes.*

approach to Classicism was adopted by the Victorians, e.g. at **St George's Hall, Liverpool**, *Mers*, of 1839–54. Classical ideas were largely eclipsed in the later nineteenth century by the Gothic Revival, but returned during the Edwardian era in the guise of a Baroque Revival. For most of the twentieth century Classicism has had to bow to various forms of Modernism, but the Classical spirit lingers on, e.g. in the architecture of a number of contemporary practitioners such as Quinlan Terry. [for examples of Classical style see ADAM STYLE, BAROQUE, BATTLE OF THE STYLES, GREEK REVIVAL, ITALIANATE, JACOBEAN, MANNERISM, PALLADIANISM, REGENCY, RENAISSANCE] [for building types and details of Classical architecture see ABACUS, ACANTHUS, ACROTERIA, AEDICULE, ANTAE, ANTHEMION, ARCH, ARCHITRAVE, ASTYLAR, ATHENAEUM, ATLANTES, ATRIUM, ATTIC, BASE, BASILICA, CAPITAL, CARYATID, CELLA, COLONNADE, COLOSSAL ORDER, COLUMN, CONSOLE, CORNICE, DECASTYLE, ECHINUS, ENTABLATURE, ENTASIS, FLUTING, FRET, FRIEZE, HEXASTYLE, HYPAETHRAL, HYPOSTYLE, METOPE, MODILLION, MONOPTERAL, MOULDING, OCTASTYLE, ORDER, PEDESTAL, PEDIMENT, PERIPTERAL, PERISTYLE, PILASTER, PLINTH, PODIUM, PORTICO, PROSCENIUM, ROTUNDA, STEREOBATE, STYLOBATE, TEMPLE, TETRASTYLE, TRIGLYPH, VILLA, VOLUTE]

**83** *Carlton House Terrace, London: note the square abacus of the Doric order supporting the balustrade.*

This vision was challenged in the second half of the eighteenth century by architects who went in search of a variety of original Greek and Roman sources rather than rely on Palladio's Renaissance version of ancient Rome. The term Neo-Classicism has been used to describe this fresh departure, spearheaded by the Greek Revivalist James 'Athenian' Stuart (1713–88) and the rival architects William Chambers (1723–96) and Robert Adam (1728–92).

By the turn of the nineteenth century the Greek Revival had emerged as the dominant Neo-Classical mode; and it continued to make an impact for several decades in the work of Robert Smirke (1781–1867), William Wilkins (1778–1839) and the idiosyncratic John Soane (1753–1837). The Regency style, as personified by John Nash (1752–1835) added a lighter, eclectic note of its own, but still operated within the framework of Classicism. A heavier, more monumental

## CLERESTORY

Upper part of the nave wall of a church containing a range of windows. Large clerestory windows were a marked feature of Perpendicular Gothic. [see **133, 383**]

## CLIFF CASTLE [see PROMONTORY FORT]

## CLOB [see COB]

## CLOCHAN [see BEEHIVE CELL]

## CLOCKTOWER

Monumental edifice housing a large clock, e.g. the **Albert Memorial Clock Tower, Belfast**, N.Ireland, and **St Stephen's Tower** at the **Houses of Parliament, London**. [see **34, 239**]

84 *The clocktower of the Houses of Parliament, London, is a prominent urban landmark.*

## CLOISTER

From Latin '*claustrum*', meaning 'enclosed place', the word 'cloister' is generally applied to the covered ambulatory around a monastery or college quadrangle. Cistercian and Benedictine cloisters were often majestic in scale, but those of the Franciscans were of more modest proportions e.g. **Moyne Friary**, *Mayo* and **Muckross Friary**, *Kerry*, Ireland. Some of the best preserved cloisters are at the ancient cathedrals, e.g. **Gloucester**, *Glos*; **Lincoln**, *Lincs*; **Norwich**, *Norfolk*; and **Salisbury**, *Wilts*. The cloister became a regular feature of collegiate architecture, e.g. at **New College** and **Magdalen College, Oxford**, *Oxon*. [see COLLEGE, FRIARY, MONASTERY, QUADRANGLE, **146, 324**]

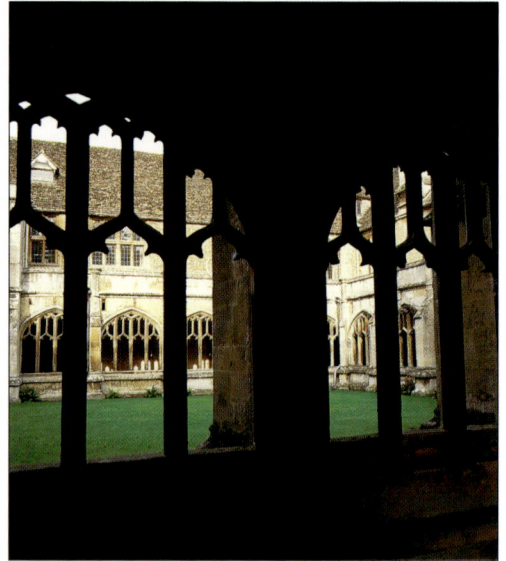

85 *The cloister at Lacock Abbey*, Wilts, *is noted for its intricate Gothic tracery.*

## CLOSE

Walled precinct surrounding a cathedral, e.g. at **Norwich**, *Norfolk*; **Salisbury**, *Wilts*.

CLUB [see ATHENAEUM, PALAZZO]

## CLUNCH
Soft, white limestone, often used for interior sculptured detail.

## CLUSTER BLOCK
Group of apartment blocks grouped around a central service tower, pioneered in the 1950s in London's East End by Denys Lasdun. [see COUNCIL HOUSING]

CLUSTERED PIER [see COLUMN]

## COADE STONE
Compound for producing artificial stone, invented in the 1720s by Richard Holt but perfected fifty years later by George and Eleanor Coade. The exact formula was lost soon after 1840 when the Coade Artificial

86 *Coade stone figure of a charity child at St Botolph's, Bishopsgate, London.*

Stone Manufactory was closed, but analysis shows that it consisted of china clay, sand and finely ground stoneware. The mixture was fired in a kiln. The weatherproof qualities of Coade Stone made it well suited for outdoor statuary, e.g. the **South Bank Lion** by **Westminster Bridge, London**, and at **Liverpool Town Hall**, *Mers.* [see TERRACOTTA]

## COB
Building material composed of clay earth, straw, lime, sand and gravel mixed with water. Cob is usually covered with limewash to protect it from the weather. It is common in south-west England, e.g. in the cottages of **Milton Abbas**, *Dorset.* Known in Cornwall as clob.

## COBBLESTONE
Rounded paving stone. Also known as sett. [see **274**]

COFFER [see CAISSON]

## COLLAR BEAM, COLLAR PURLIN
The collar beam is a horizontal transverse timber connecting the principal rafters just below the apex of a roof. The collar purlin is a timber which runs the length of a roof directly under the centre of the collar beam. [see TIMBER-TRUSSED ROOF]

## COLLEGE
From Latin '*collegium*', meaning an organized community usually with living accommodation. In the Middle Ages a college was a body of priests attached to a collegiate church; but the word came to denote a place of religious instruction and later an educational establishment in general. In England, the earliest college buildings date back to the fourteenth and fifteenth centuries in Oxford and Cambridge; and it was here that the style and plan of the medieval college evolved. This derived in almost

equal measure from the manor house with its great hall and ranges of accommodation and from the monastery with its church and cloistered quadrangle. **St Andrew's**, *Fife*, Scotland, contains colleges of the fifteenth and sixteenth centuries. From Tudor until mid-Victorian times Oxford and Cambridge set the pace for collegiate architecture in England, employing the most eminent architects of the day. Accordingly, these universities acquired a collection of college buildings ranging from medieval, Renaissance and Baroque to Greek Revival and Gothic Revival. **Trinity College, Dublin**, Ireland, set new standards in the mid-eighteenth century with its comprehensive and grandiose rebuilding in the Neo-Classical style. In the nineteenth century there was a proliferation of college building which produced some spectacular results, e.g. the **Royal Holloway College for Women** of 1886 at **Egham**, *Surrey*. [see LIBRARY, QUADRANGLE, SCHOOL, UNIVERSITY]

## COLLEGIATE CHURCH

After the great monastic foundations of the early Middle Ages there was a shift towards more modest acts of piety in the form of smaller endowments of a church staffed by a college of clergymen. The collegiate church founded by Richard, Duke of York in the 1430s at **Fotheringhay**, *Northants*, remains a noble sight even without its choir. A more typical example is at **Tattershall Castle**, *Lincs*. Scotland possesses some fine collegiate churches, e.g. at **Dunglass** and **Rosslyn**, *Lothian*. [see CHANTRY]

## COLONNADE

In Classical architecture, a row of columns supporting an entablature. The colonnade evolved in the eighteenth century as a fashionable device for linking flanking pavilions to the central block of a Palladian country house, e.g. at **Hopetoun House**, *Lothian*, Scotland; at **Russborough**, *Wicklow*, and **Castletown House**, *Kildare*, Ireland. [see 4, 301]

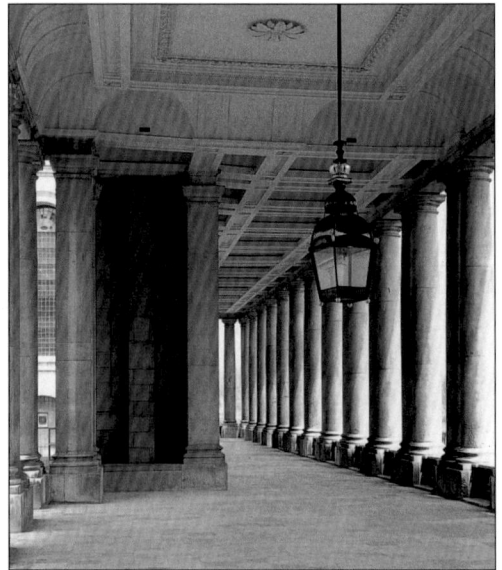

88 *This colonnade at the Royal Naval Hospital, Greenwich, London, is part of a grand composition.*

87 *The heavily fortified collegiate church at Dunglass, Lothian, Scotland. Note the stone roof.*

## COLONNETTE
A small column.

## COLOSSAL ORDER

Any Classical order, of which the columns extend in height through two or more storeys. Most grand Neo-Classical buildings employ a colossal order, e.g. the **British Museum** and the **National Gallery, London**. Also known as giant order. [see ORDER, **171, 279**]

## COLUMBARIUM

Latin for pigeon house or dovecote. [see DOVECOTE]

## COLUMN

In Classical architecture a column comprises a capital, a shaft and a base; and it serves to support an entablature. When joined to a wall, it is called an attached or engaged column. The shaft

*89 The Royal Albert Hall, Kensington, London, is in the form of a rotunda. Note the elegant frieze.*

of a column can be decorated in a number of ways, but most commonly with fluting. A blocked column has square blocks spaced at intervals on the shaft. When a group of slender columns surrounds a pier, this is known as a compound or clustered pier. [see COLONNADE, DEMI-COLUMN, FLUTING, MONUMENT, ORDER]

## COMPOSITE ORDER [see ORDER]

## COMPOUND PIER [see COLUMN]

## CONCENTRIC [see CASTLE]

## CONCERT HALL

Structure for musical performances. The **Holywell Music Room, Oxford**, *Oxon*, in continuous use since 1748, claims to be the earliest of its type in Europe; it is of more modest proportions than the palatial

concert halls of the nineteenth century, e.g. **St George's Hall, Liverpool**, *Mers*, of 1839–54; and the **Royal Albert Hall, London**, of 1868. The **Royal Festival Hall, London**, of 1951 still ranks among the best of the modern generation of concert halls. [see ASSEMBLY ROOM]

## CONCH

Half-dome of an apse or niche, in the shape of a shell. [see SCALLOP]

## CONCRETE

This material is usually associated with modern building but its use goes back more than 7500 years to ancient Egypt. Concrete is composed of sand, stones or other aggregate, and cement mixed with water, which sets in a hard mass. The word is derived from Latin *'concretus'*, meaning 'grown together'. The cement was obtained by burning limestone to produce quicklime. The technique of making concrete was perfected by the Romans, and was later used for the foundations of Norman castles and Gothic cathedrals. The development of a superior type of cement was pioneered in the eighteenth century by John Smeaton. Portland cement followed in 1824. The technology of reinforced concrete, i.e. incorporating structural elements of iron and steel, was slower to develop in Britain than in France. The fifteen-storey **Royal Liver Building, Liverpool**, *Mers*, of 1908 was Britain's first high-rise building of reinforced concrete, although it was clad with stone to disguise the fact. Pre-stressed reinforced concrete incorporating wire cables which are stretched while the concrete is still wet, opened up new possibilities, since it could be used in any variety of shapes and sizes. The massive deployment of raw concrete surfaces dominated the architecture of the 1950s and 1960s in the style known as

Brutalism. The unattractive weathering of concrete has led to its concealment behind various types of cladding, including brick. The naked use of concrete is now considered more appropriate in an overtly functional context, e.g. in bridges and tunnels. [see BRUTALISM, SHUTTERING]

## CONDUIT

Channel or pipe for the conveyance of water or other liquid. Conduits were occasionally used in medieval buildings to collect rainwater from the roof, e.g. at **Warkworth Castle**, *Northum*. Drinking water was conveyed to medieval cities such as London and Bristol through wooden conduits from the surrounding countryside. The seventeenth-century conduit house at **North Hinksey**, *Oxon*, was a reservoir for Oxford's first water mains. [see AQUEDUCT, CULVERT]

## CONSERVATORY

Structure composed of glass panels set in a framework, usually of cast iron. Large conservatories were first built in the nineteenth century to house tropical plants and trees, e.g. in 1827–30 at **Syon House, London**, by Charles Fowler. Joseph Paxton's conservatory (now vanished) of 1837 at **Chatsworth**, *Derbys*, won him much acclaim and the commission to design the vast Crystal Palace in London (also vanished) for the Great Exhibition of 1851. Still intact is the **Palm House** of 1839 in the **Botanic Gardens, Belfast**, N. Ireland, where Richard Turner's expertise with curved panels of glass was first put into service. Turner's work may also be seen in the **Palm House** of 1842–50 in the **Botanic Gardens** at **Glasnevin, Dublin**, Ireland, and in collaboration with Decimus Burton at the **Palm House** in **Kew**

**90** OPPOSITE *The Kibble Palace, Glasgow, Scotland, is essentially a large conservatory of glass and iron.*

**Gardens, London**, of 1844–48. The **Palm House** in the **Royal Botanic Gardens**, Edinburgh, Scotland, dates to 1858. Conservatories were also built as extensions to grand houses in town and country, and sometimes incorporated within a public building, e.g. the **People's Palace** of 1898 in **Glasgow**, Scotland. [see ORANGERY]

## CONSOLE
Curved ornamental bracket in Classical architecture, e.g. supporting a cornice above a doorway. Consoles are also known as ancones. [see MODILLION]

## COPING
Covering of stone or tiles on the top of a wall to prevent penetration by rainwater.

## CORBEL, CORBELLING
The technique of corbelling involves a series of oversailing courses to form a

91 *A decorative corbel supports the ribs of a Gothic vault in Southwark Cathedral, London.*

vault. A corbel is a projection which supports a beam or structure. Gothic architecture is noted for its decorative use of corbels. [see OVERSAIL, 260]

## CORBIE-STEPPED [see GABLE]

## CORINTHIAN ORDER [see ORDER]

## CORNERSTONE
Stone in the projecting angle of a building.

## CORNICE
In Classical architecture, the uppermost part of an entablature, consisting of a projecting ornamental moulding. A cornice may also adorn the top of a wall or arch. In the context of interior decoration, the cornice is an ornamental moulding around the four walls of a room just below the ceiling. [see CORONA, ENTABLATURE, 345]

## CORONA
1) Projecting element of a Classical cornice. [see ENTABLATURE]

2) Circular chapel, e.g. **Becket's Crown**, added to the apse of **Canterbury Cathedral**, *Kent*.

## COTTAGE
A simple rural residence, usually in the vernacular style reflecting the local availability of building materials. These range from the cob and thatch of Devon and the limestone of the Cotswolds to the millstone grit of the Pennines and the granite and slate of Cornwall, Cumbria and north Wales. The cottages of today are far superior to the type of homes built in the Middle Ages by the landless class of 'cottars' or 'cottiers', named after their primitive and flimsy 'cots'. These makeshift dwellings were improvised from wooden branches, sods of turf, wat-

92 *Hardy's Cottage, Higher Bockhampton, Dorset, has a picturesque rustic appearance that is typical of the genre.*

tle and daub. Most of the cottages of rural England today, including the familiar half-timbered variety, are no older than the sixteenth century when a great rebuilding occurred. Since then, the construction of various types of cottage has continued without interruption. In the eighteenth century many landlords began to rehouse their tenants in neat rows of cottages in planned villages. Workers' cottages were built by industrial magnates in the nineteenth century. Some of these imitated the style of the Tudor period,

e.g. at **Port Sunlight**, *Mers*. The word 'cottage' is nowadays applied indiscriminately to any small house in town or country, but it still evokes the quintessential image of a snug dwelling in a rural setting with a bright, informal flower garden. [see BLACK HOUSE, COTTAGE ORNÉ, CROFT, LONGHOUSE, PLANNED VILLAGE]

## COTTAGE ORNÉ

The style of the thatched cottage was imitated in the late eighteenth and early nineteenth centuries as a picturesque idiom of studied rustic charm for structures such as the lodge of a country estate or the houses of a planned village. The artful qualities of the cottage orné were fully explored by John Nash in 1810 at **Blaise Hamlet**, *Avon*. The famous **Swiss Cottage** at **Osborne House, Isle of Wight**, presented to Queen Victoria by the people of Switzerland, inspired several similar variants of the cottage orné. [see PLANNED VILLAGE]

## COUNCIL HOUSING

The provision of affordable housing by municipal authorities was pioneered in the nineteenth century in industrial cities such as **Birmingham**, *W Mids*. It was not until 1890 that the London County Council was enabled to build public hous-

**93** *The Boundary Street Estate, London, was a pioneer of council housing. Note the banded decoration.*

ing. The first LCC schemes reflected the ideals of the Arts and Crafts movement, e.g. at the **Boundary Street Estate** of 1894–1900 in **Shoreditch**. From 1900 the LCC built many blocks of flats in the inner city as well as vast dormitory suburbs beyond its own boundaries, e.g. at **Borehamwood**, *Herts*, and **Becontree**, *Essex*. Extensive destruction in many cities during the Second World War (1939–45) opened the way for massive council housing projects in the 1950s and 1960s. The old cityscapes of terraced houses were generally replaced by tower blocks and vast complexes which have failed to live up to the expectations of the planners. During the 1980s the task of building public housing for rent passed to myriad housing associations. [see CLUSTER BLOCK, GARDEN CITY, NEW TOWN, PEABODY BUILDINGS, TENEMENT]

## COUNTERSCARP

Outer slope of a ditch surrounding a castle or fortification. [see EARTHWORK, SCARP]

## COUNTRY HOUSE

The idea of an undefended noble residence set in its own parkland or garden at the heart of a rural estate evolved at the end of the Middle Ages when the more settled conditions in England made it safe for the landed gentry to move from their castles and fortified manor houses. This trend gradually gathered force in the sixteenth and seventeenth centuries, though sporadic unrest in Scotland and Ireland ensured that medieval strongholds such as the tower house continued to be built at this time. Elizabethan bravado and inventiveness left their mark on a series of remarkable country houses, e.g. **Longleat**, *Wilts*; **Hardwick Hall**, *Derbys*; and **Burghley House**, *Lincs*. The exuberance of the early Stuart period, e.g. at **Blickling Hall**, *Norfolk*, and **Wilton**

94 *Trelissick House,* Cornwall: *a country house with a portico in the style of the Greek Revival.*

House, *Wilts*, was brought to a sudden halt by the Civil War of the 1640s; and many medieval castles were hastily reoccupied for the duration of the fighting. Building activity resumed in spectacular fashion after the Restoration of 1660, e.g. at **Chatsworth House**, *Derbys*.

The eighteenth century witnessed a veritable boom in the building of country houses throughout the British Isles, as radical estate improvements boosted the revenues of the great landowners. This coincided with a widespread enthusiasm for the Classical style in architecture. The golden age of the country house is thus closely associated with the image of a stately mansion decked out with all the

**95** *Wrest Park House*, Beds: *a country house with the flair of a French château.*

trappings of portico, pediment and colonnade, often combined with statues and fountains to create a most noble impression. Only the wealthiest of patrons could indulge in the Baroque magnificence of **Blenheim Palace**, *Oxon*, or **Castle Howard**, *N Yorks*; and the Palladian style was found to be more versatile for a wide range of country houses, from the stately **Holkham Hall**, *Norfolk*, to the more modest **Constable Burton Hall**, *N Yorks*. Alternatives to the omnipresent Palladian style were sought in a variety of exotic conversions by Robert Adam, e.g. at **Syon House** and **Osterley Park House, London**. Rococo made a striking appearance at **Claydon**

**House**, *Bucks*; and the austere simplicity of the Greek Revival was taken up at the beginning of the nineteenth century for a number of country houses, e.g. **Belsay Hall**, *Northum*. The Gothic Revival had begun to emerge during the second half of the eighteenth century, e.g. at **Arbury Hall**, *Warw*; and at **Slane Castle**, *Meath*, Ireland. These early essays were regarded as rather frivolous by the arbiters of taste, but in the course of the nineteenth century the Gothic Revival became a deadly serious affair as the builders of country houses increasingly sought inspiration in the castle architecture of the Middle Ages, e.g. at **Gosford Castle**, *Armagh*, N. Ireland; **Penrhyn Castle**, *Gwynedd*, Wales; and **Dunrobin Castle**, *Highland*, Scotland. This Baronial style endured into the Edwardian era and even beyond, although the First World War (1914–18) generally marked the end of country-house building in the grand manner. Twentieth-century country houses are on a more modest scale, both as a result of reduced ambitions on the part of their owners and also as a response to the difficulties of recruiting the numbers of low-paid staff needed to run the larger establishments. [see: ADAM STYLE, BARONIAL, BAROQUE, DOWER HOUSE, E-PLAN, ELIZABETHAN, FOLLY, GOTHIC REVIVAL, GREEK REVIVAL, JACOBEAN, MANOR HOUSE, PALACE, PALLADIANISM, PIANO NOBILE, STABLE, STATELY HOME, STUART, VILLA]

## COURSE

Horizontal layer of a building material such as stone or brick. [see OPUS LISTATUM, STRING COURSE]

## COURT CAIRN [see CHAMBERED TOMB]

## COURT or COURTYARD

Area enclosed by buildings and usually entered through an arch or gateway. In a medieval castle it may be called a bailey or ward. [see BAILEY, QUADRANGLE]

## COURTYARD HOUSE

Type of Iron Age dwelling in which the rooms are entered via a central area or courtyard, e.g. at **Chysauster**, *Cornwall.*

## COVE

U-shaped setting of standing stones, usually in association with a prehistoric stone circle, e.g. at **Stonehenge**, *Wilts.*

## COVERED MARKET

Since the Middle Ages many guildhalls and market houses provided a covered space under an arcade or colonnade for local traders. With the dramatic expansion of towns and cities in the nineteenth century larger structures were required, e.g. the **Covent Garden Market, London**, of 1830 for flowers, fruit and vegetables. The new building technology of iron and glass was widely adopted, e.g. for the meat market at **Smithfield, London**, which opened in 1868. **Leadenhall**

96 *The sheltered courtyard of Skipton Castle, N Yorks.* Note the prominent mullions.

97 *Leadenhall Market in the City of London, a small masterpiece of Victorian design using iron and glass.*

**Market** of 1881 still supplies the City of London with fresh provisions. There are many fine covered markets elsewhere, e.g. at **Oxford**, *Oxon*, and **Barnstaple**, *Devon*, where the **Pannier Market** was built in 1854. [see ARCADE, MARKET HALL, SHOP]

## COVING
Concave moulding at the angle of a wall and a ceiling.

## COWL
Cover for a chimneystack or other ventilation outlet, e.g. on an oast house. The name was inspired by the form of a monk's cowl or hood.

## CRADLE-ROOF [see WAGON ROOF]

## CRANNÓG
Type of lake-dwelling, particularly widespread during the Iron Age. The most durable crannógs were made by pile-driving tree trunks into the bed of a lake to form a solid foundation. The term is derived from the Irish '*crannóg*' meaning 'wood' or 'timber'. An artificial island could then be built up by the addition of rubble, brushwood, clay and stones. Finally, a light dwelling was constructed on top. Since the islands remain long after the houses have perished, crannóg sites can be identified. Many have been found in Ireland. The draining of the marshes led to the discovery of a cluster of crannógs just outside **Glastonbury**, *Somerset*; but these are now no more than circular bumps in a grassy field. A crannóg still surrounded by water and with a stone revetment is at **Fair Head**, *Antrim*, N.Ireland.

## CRENELLATION
Alternative term for a battlement, derived from French '*crenelle*', meaning the opening between the solid portions or 'merlons'. In the Middle Ages a licence to crenellate had to be obtained from the Crown before a castle could be built. [see BATTLEMENT, CASTLE]

## CRESCENT
The concave shaping of a street of houses was an urbanistic invention of John Wood the Younger. His **Royal Crescent** of 1765–75 at **Bath**, *Avon*, was a palatial rendering of terrace architecture, and it remains the most majestic of crescents. Also of note is John Carr's **Crescent** of 1784 at **Buxton**, *Derbys*. The **Royal York Crescent, Bristol**, *Avon*, of 1791–1820 is reckoned to be the longest in Europe. [see CIRCUS, TERRACE]

## CREST, CRESTING
Ornamental finish, resembling a miniature battlement, to crown the parapet of a wall or roof ridge. [see BRATTISHING]

**98** *Roof cresting on the Temple Gardens Building, Middle Temple, London. Note gabled dormer windows.*
**99** OPPOSITE *The Royal Crescent, Bath, Avon. Note the iron railings in front of the area.*

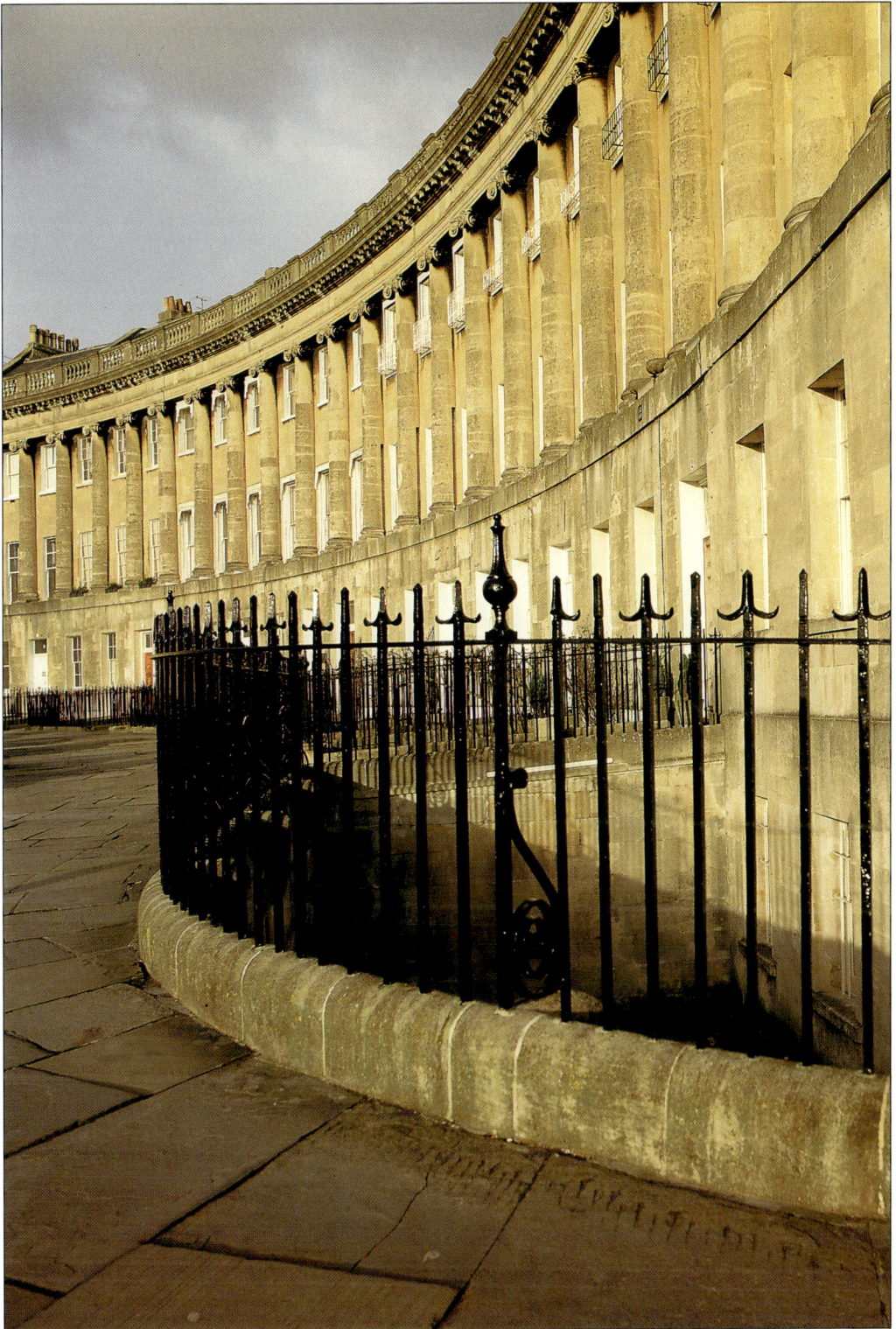

## CRINKLE-CRANKLE
Garden wall following a curved course.

## CROCKET
Leaf-like projection carved in stone or wood which embellishes Gothic spires, pinnacles and gables. [see CAPITAL, **158**]

## CROFT
Scottish smallholding, especially in the Highlands and Western Isles. The word also denotes the simple house which provides the living accommodation of the croft. [see BLACK HOUSE, CLACHAN, LONGHOUSE]

## CROMLECH [see DOLMEN]

## CROSS PILLAR, CROSS SLAB
The earliest carved crosses, the predecessors of the high crosses of Celtic Ireland, were tooled on standing stones known as pillar stones, e.g. at **Kilnasaggart**, *Armagh*, N. Ireland, dating back to *c.* AD 700. At **Fahan Mura**, *Donegal*, Ireland, the eighth-century cross is an intricate pattern of intersecting lines on each side of an upright stone slab. The art of the cross slab was elaborated in a unique manner by the enigmatic productions of the Picts in Scotland. These feature on one side an elaborate cross, and on the other a bizarre array of pagan symbols. The Pictish cross slab at **Aberlemno**, *Tayside*, Scotland, displays on its reverse face an impressive battle scene. The **Meigle Museum**, near **Forfar**, *Tayside*, Scotland, houses a large collection of Pictish symbol stones and cross slabs. [see HIGH CROSS]

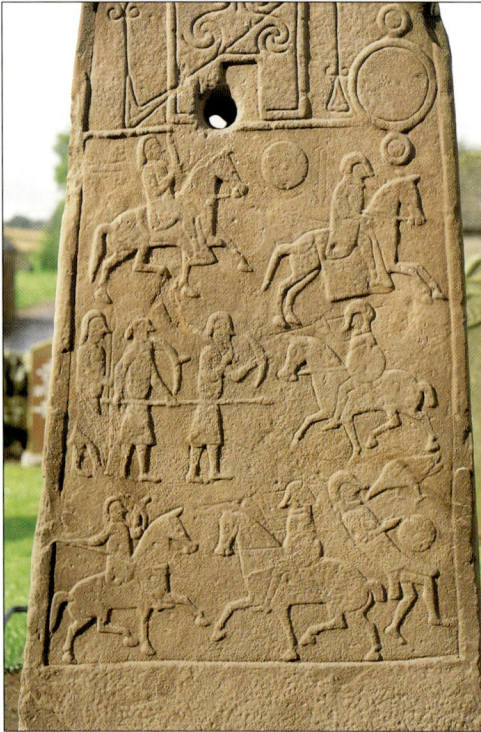

**100** *Battle scene on the reverse face of the Pictish cross-slab at Aberlemno,* Tayside, *Scotland.*

## CROSSING
Intersection of the transepts with the nave and chancel of a church. The crossing may be surmounted by a tower in a Norman or Gothic church, or by a dome in a Baroque church. [see CRUCIFORM, TRANSEPT, **64**]

## CROSS-VAULTING [see GROIN VAULT]

## CROWN POST
Vertical timber standing at the centre of a tie beam and supporting a collar purlin. [see TIMBER-TRUSSED ROOF]

## CROWN SPIRE [see SPIRE]

## CROW-STEPPED [see GABLE]

## CRUCIFORM
Having the shape of a cross. The word is applied to the groundplan of a church or cathedral having transepts which cross the main axis of the building. [see CROSSING, GREEK CROSS, LATIN CROSS, **64**]

# CRUCK

Half-timbered structure supported by pairs of inclined timbers known as crucks or blades which generally meet at the ridge of the roof. When exposed to view and rising directly from the sill, the crucks constitute a bold feature of the gable end. Some impressive crucks may be seen in the old houses at **Weobley**, *Heref & Worcs*. [see HALF-TIMBERING]

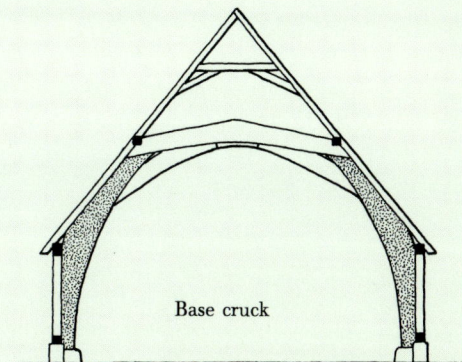

Base cruck

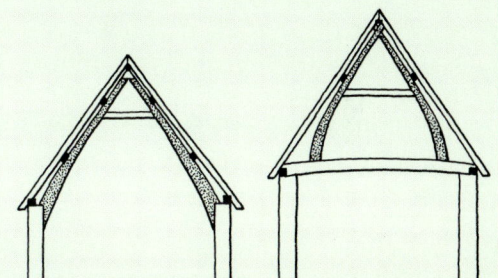

Raised cruck          Upper cruck

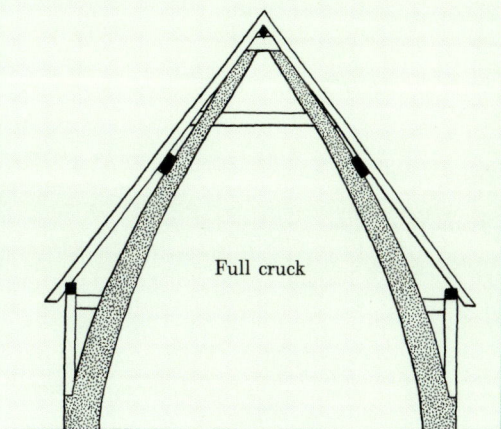

Full cruck

**101** *A prominent cruck on display in this house in the village of Lacock,* Wilts.

# CRYPT

A vaulted chamber or undercroft beneath a church or cathedral. Inevitably, the crypt is the oldest part of the building fabric. Magnificent early Saxon crypts survive at **Ripon Cathedral**, *N Yorks*, and at **Hexham Abbey**, *Northum*. Fine examples from the Norman period are at **St Mary, Lastingham**, *N Yorks*; **Rochester Cathedral** and **Canterbury Cathedral**,

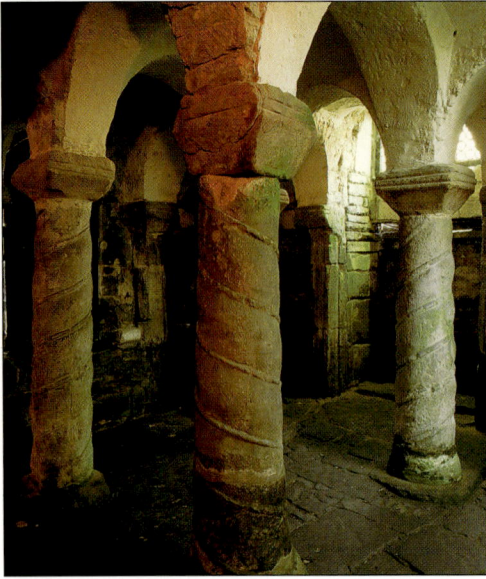

102 *Saxon crypt of St Wystan, Repton, Derbys. Note the spiral on the shafts and the primitive capitals.*

*Kent*. Normally, a crypt does not extend much beyond the chancel of the church above, but that at **Christ Church Cathedral, Dublin**, Ireland, runs the full length of the nave. [see CATACOMB, SAXON, UNDERCROFT]

## CUBE

The idea of constructing a room in the form of a perfect cube, i.e. with the same dimensions in height, width and depth, was a feature of Palladian architecture. It was pioneered in England by Inigo Jones at the **Queen's House, Greenwich, London**, from 1616; and at the **Banqueting House, Whitehall, London**, from 1619 he designed the entire building around a double cube. At **Wilton House**, *Wilts*, in *c.* 1650 Jones incorporated at the heart of the structure both a single cube room (30 x 30 x 30 ft) and a double cube room (60 x 30 x 30 ft). This passion for the cube was taken even further in the eighteenth century with the great triple cube room (72 x 24 x 24 ft) at **Corsham Court**, *Wilts*. [see PALLADIANISM]

## CULVERT

Drain or channel for the passage of water, which may be built of brick or stone. [see AQUEDUCT, CONDUIT]

## CUP AND RING MARK

Type of prehistoric rock decoration consisting of a carved circular depression surrounded by one or more rings. These designs occur at several locations, e.g. at **Roughting Linn**, *Northum*, and may date back to the New Stone Age. [see MEGALITHIC, PREHISTORIC]

## CUPOLA

A small dome. [see DOME, 26]

## CURTAIL STEP

Lowest step of a staircase, of which the outer edge protrudes in a scroll-like shape. [see STAIR, STAIRCASE]

## CURTAIN WALL

1) In medieval architecture, an outer wall surrounding a castle, and linking towers and bastions. [see CASTLE]

2) In modern building technology, a non-loadbearing wall fixed to the framework of a structure. It can be made of glass or aluminium. A famous early example was the factory/warehouse of the Boots Pure Drug Company at **Beeston**, *Notts*, of 1932.

## CURTILAGE

The area immediately adjacent to a house, usually enclosed by a wall or fence.

## CURVILINEAR TRACERY [see TRACERY]

## CUSHION CAPITAL [see CAPITAL]

## CUSP

Point formed in Gothic tracery by the

meeting of two curved lines, e.g. the segments of foils. [see FOIL, TRACERY]

## CUTWATER

Pointed profile given to a bridge pier which reduces the impact of the current on the structure. Also known as a starling.

## CYCLOPEAN

Denotes masonry consisting of huge, irregular blocks. The term derives from the pre-Classical architecture of Mycenae, which the ancient Greeks attributed to the superhuman powers of the mythical

Cyclopes. The term also describes a rough finish to masonry. [see RUSTICATION]

## CYMA RECTA

Cornice moulding in the form of an ogee, in which the concave part is uppermost. [see ENTABLATURE]

## CYMA REVERSA

Cornice moulding in the form of an ogee, in which the convex part is uppermost. [see ENTABLATURE]

## CYMATIUM

The uppermost element of the cornice in a Classical entablature.

**103** *Curtain wall: the Bishop's Palace, Wells,* Somerset.

# D

## DAB
To dress stone by picking the surface to give it a rough, dappled finish.

## DADO
1) In Classical architecture, that part of a pedestal between cornice and base. Also known as die. [see PEDESTAL]

2) In the context of interior decoration, the lower part of a wall up to the chair rail.

## DAIS
Raised platform at one end of a medieval hall, where the high table of the master of the house was located. The dais is still a common feature in the dining halls of many colleges.

## DART [see EGG AND DART]

## DAUB [see WATTLE AND DAUB]

## DECADENT
The word describes a moment in architectural evolution when a style descends from a height of purity or artistic merit, and is interpreted in a less accomplished manner.

## DECASTYLE
A portico with ten columns on its front elevation.

## DECORATED GOTHIC [see GOTHIC]

## DEER HOUSE
Shelter built for the use of deer, e.g. in the deer park of **Auckland Castle**, *Durham*, built in 1760 by the Bishop of Durham.

## DEMI-COLUMN
A type of attached or engaged column having a cross-section of 180 degrees and recessed into a wall. [see COLUMN]

## DEMILUNE
Half-moon-shaped outer defence to protect the bastion of a fort.

## DENTIL
Element in a Classical cornice, consisting of a small square block ranged in a series. The term is derived from Latin *'denticulus'*, meaning 'little tooth'. [see ENTABLATURE]

## DEPARTMENT STORE
Large-scale type of emporium pioneered towards the end of the nineteenth century, offering through its various departments a comprehensive range of goods otherwise obtainable only through a number of individual retailers. London generally set the style for the palatial architecture of the department store, e.g. the fantastic terracotta façade of **Harrods, Knightsbridge**, of 1901–5. **Selfridges** in

104 *The department store of Selfridges, London, displays a colossal order rising from first-storey level.*

**Oxford Street**, completed in 1928, stands out as one of the most impressive Neo-Classical buildings of the early twentieth century. **Liberty & Co** in **Regent Street** of the 1920s combines Baroque elements with mock Tudor. Department stores were built in all major towns and cities, e.g. **Jenners** of **Edinburgh,** Scotland, as early as 1895. However, London remained in the vanguard with the sheer number and variety of its department stores, from the Edwardian magnificence of **William Whiteley** in **Bayswater** of 1911 to the sleek Modernism of **Peter Jones** of **Sloane Square** of 1936, which still looks up-to-date behind its glass façade. [see ARCADE, SHOP]

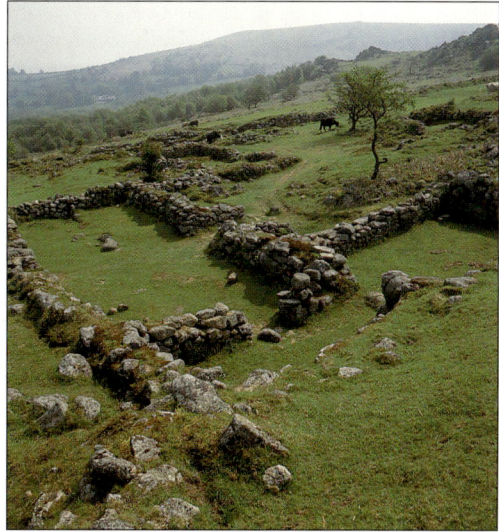

105 *Only the house foundations remain of the deserted village of Hound Tor on Dartmoor,* Devon.

## DEPRESSED ARCH

Flattened arch of late medieval and Tudor times. [see ARCH]

## DESERTED VILLAGE

The abandonment of rural settlements has been a recurrent theme in the British Isles since the New Stone Age. A violent storm buried the Neolithic village of **Skara Brae** on **Orkney**, Scotland, in *c.* 2450 BC beneath a mound of sand. Bronze Age **Grimspound** on **Dartmoor**, *Devon*, fell victim in the Iron Age to a worsening of the climate which ruined the farming potential of this upland site. In England the sites of some 3000 deserted medieval villages have been identified. The Black Death of 1348–9 was a significant factor, but the expansion of sheepfarming between 1450 and 1550 had a telling impact on rural life. Where previously many people had scratched a living from the soil, henceforth there was work for just a handful of shepherds. The sites of deserted villages are often visible only from the air as bumps in the ground indicating house walls and field boundaries. Of particular interest are **Wharram Percy**, *N Yorks*, and **Gainsthorpe**, *Humbs.* **Hound Tor** on Dartmoor, *Devon*, was abandoned during another worsening of the climate in the fourteenth century. In the eighteenth and nineteenth centuries many industrial villages were built, and some in remote locations were subsequently abandoned, e.g. the deserted quarry village of **Porth-y-Nant**, *Gwynedd*, Wales, which has recently been reoccupied by the Welsh National Language Centre. The Highland Clearances in Scotland of the late eighteenth and early nineteenth centuries resulted in the permanent abandonment of hundreds of rural settlements, of which little now remains to be seen. [see CLACHAN]

## DIAMOND WORK

Style of masonry composed of stones cut individually to form pointed or diamond shapes. Such stones may be used to embellish an entire façade, e.g. the new lodgings of the 1580s at **Crichton Castle,** *Lothian*, Scotland, which were inspired by

106 *A striking example of diamond work adorns the courtyard façade of Crichton Castle*, Lothian, *Scotland.*

the famous Palazzo dei Diamanti at Ferrara, Italy. [see RUSTICATION]

## DIAPER WORK

Surface decoration consisting of a repetition of square or diamond shapes. In Gothic architecture this is often composed of a floral motif. Brick diapering consists of diagonal patterns created by darker bricks. The word 'diaper' derives from the characteristic patterns of Belgian cloth from Ypres, i.e. 'd'Ypres' in French. [see BRICKWORK]

## DIAPHRAGM ARCH

Transverse arch supporting a stone gable in the nave of a church or used as a partition in a wooden roof to hinder the spread of fire.

## DIE [see DADO, PEDESTAL]

*107 Distance slab from the Antonine Wall in Scotland.*

## DISTANCE SLAB

Roman commemorative stone tablet marking the completion of a stretch of defensive wall, e.g. those from the **Antonine Wall**, Scotland, now in the **Hunterian Museum, Glasgow**. [see ROMAN, WALL]

## DOG-LEG STAIR

Stair consisting of parallel flights of steps joined at right angles by a landing. [see STAIR, STAIRCASE]

## DOGTOOTH

Gothic ornament, especially of the Early English period, consisting of a series of small pyramid-like shapes of which the sides are in the form of a leaf.

## DOLMEN

Also known as a cromlech, portal tomb or quoit, this prehistoric structure consists of a large capstone resting on two or more upright stones. It is thought that some dolmens may once have been covered by a cairn or barrow, but the dramatic style of many dolmens gives reason to believe that they were intended to be seen, e.g. **Lanyon Quoit** and **Trethevy Quoit**, *Cornwall*; and in Ireland, **Poulnabrone Dolmen**, *Clare*; **Kilclooney Dolmen**, *Donegal*; **Legananny Dolmen**, *Down*.

108 *Kilclooney Dolmen*, Donegal, *Ireland: there is a graceful quality to this megalithic structure.*

Dolmens date back to the New Stone Age and were used for burials and associated rituals. [see BARROW, CHAMBERED TOMB, 222]

## DOME

Half-spherical structure crowning a building of some importance. This architectural feature was fully evolved in Byzantium and eventually reached the British Isles via the Italian Baroque. The word is derived from Italian '*duomo*', meaning 'cathedral'. The dome generally appears in an ecclesiastical context, e.g. **St Paul's Cathedral** and the **Brompton Oratory, London**; but it has also found an effective role in other buildings such as libraries, e.g. the **Radcliffe Camera, Oxford**, *Oxon*, and the **Round Reading Room** of the **British Museum**, London. The dome features prominently in Edwardian Baroque buildings such as **Cardiff City Hall**, *S Glam*, Wales, and **Belfast City Hall**, N. Ireland [see CUPOLA, 33, 236, 239]

## DONJON

The tower or keep of a medieval castle. Not to be confused with 'dungeon', although this is derived from the same French word. [see DUNGEON, KEEP]

## DOOR, DOORWAY

The entrance to a building and its surround have long attracted special architectural treatment. The Normans transformed the doorway of even a small church into an exuberant work of art laden with symbolism, e.g. at **St Nicholas, Barfreston**, *Kent*, and **St Mary & St David, Kilpeck**, *Heref & Worcs*. With the transition to the pointed arch of Gothic the doorways on the west front of cathedrals were given dramatic expression by majestic arches which dominated the entire façade, e.g. at **Lincoln**, *Lincs*, and **Peterborough**, *Cambs*. During the Tudor period the doorway reflected the move to a flatter and less spectacular form of arch, which came to be enclosed within a

| | | |
|---|---|---|
| A architrave | E top panel | I lock rail |
| B top rail | F frieze rail | J bottom panel |
| C shutting stile | G muntin | K bottom rail |
| D hanging stile | H middle panel | |

109 *An elegant Georgian door in Lansdown Crescent, Bath,* Avon. *Note the fanlight and the smooth rustication.*

110 *The west door of St Germans,* Cornwall, *is typically Norman. Note the chevron design carved on the archivolts.*

square surround. With the introduction of Classical ideas in the seventeenth century, the arched doorway gave way to the horizontal lintel.

During the Georgian era the door itself was subjected to a Classical treatment whereby the vertical stiles and muntins joined to the horizontal rails followed established formulae of proportion. Yet within the overall context of the doorway there was a great variety of individual features, e.g. hoods, fanlights, porticos etc. which made for artistic diversity. In the nineteenth century doors were increasingly embellished, often with striking results, e.g. at the **Old Swan House** on the **Chelsea Embankment, London**. Commercial and public buildings enhanced the doorway as a bold architectural feature, e.g. at the **Natural History Museum, London,** of 1872. The **City Hall, Swansea,** *W Glam*, Wales, of 1930 sports an imposing doorway in the Classical tradition. Thereafter, the doorway was generally given a more modest appearance devoid of any aspirations to grandeur. [see DOOR FURNITURE, FANLIGHT, HOOD, PEDIMENT, PORCH, PORTICO, SOPRAPORTA, TYMPANUM, WICKET, **244, 257**]

## DOOR FURNITURE

Generic term denoting the various fixtures and fittings attached to a door, e.g. knobs, knockers, fingerplates, letterboxes and handles. In the Middle Ages vast and intricate patterns were created by iron hinges which spread like branches over the surface of a door, e.g. the thirteenth-century hall door at **Merton College, Oxford**, *Oxon*. At **Durham Cathedral**, *Durham*, there is a powerful twelfth-century door knocker in the form of a grotesque head with a ring in its mouth. Although door furniture became increasingly standardized in the eighteenth century, the Georgians did permit themselves some flourishes; and interior designers such as Robert Adam devised fanciful shapes for door handles and even the surrounds of keyholes.

111 *Wonderful patterns are created by the iron hinges of this door in St David's Cathedral,* Dyfed, *Wales.*

## DORIC ORDER [see ORDER]

## DORMER WINDOW

Window projecting from a sloping roof to form a small structure beneath a tiny roof of its own. The word is derived from French '*dormir*', meaning 'to sleep', since the attic storey was originally used as sleeping quarters for the servants. There is a spectacular array of decorative dormers at **St Pancras Station, London**, and the **University Museum, Oxford**, *Oxon*. The dormer window is also known as a lucarne. [see WINDOW, **98, 112, 165**]

## DORTER

Monastic dormitory. [see MONASTERY]

## DOVECOTE

Pigeons once provided a valuable supply of fresh meat; and special structures with nesting boxes were built to accommodate the birds. In its common circular form, the medieval dovecote contained a multitude of roosts beneath a conical roof, e.g. at **Minster Lovell**, *Oxon*. The dovecote at **Willington**, *Beds*, contains 1500 nesting boxes in a prominent gabled structure. A dovecote could also be accommodated in the loft or gable end of a barn, e.g. at **Great Coxwell**, *Oxon*. Dovecotes were much resented by the peasantry in the Middle

112 *Dovecote at Erddig,* Clwyd, *Wales. The roof lantern and dormer windows serve as entrances for the doves.*

113 *Piccadilly Drawing Room, Apsley House, London, by Robert Adam. Note the apse and marble chimney-piece.*

Ages, since the lord's pigeons fed themselves free of charge on the corn of the tenants. [see 30]

## DOWER HOUSE

A smaller but nonetheless spacious house built on a country estate to accommodate the widow of the landowner. The big house could thus be occupied by the family of the next generation.

## DRAWBRIDGE

Retractable wooden bridge across the moat of a medieval castle. The drawbridge would be raised by a system of chains and windlasses in an upper chamber in the gatehouse.

## DRAWING-ROOM

One of the main rooms of a mansion or country house. The term derives from 'withdrawing room', i.e. one to which the ladies would withdraw after dinner.

## DRESSINGS

Finely worked stones deployed prominently and decoratively as door and window surrounds or as quoins at the angles of a building. Stone dressings provide a pleasing contrast against brickwork, especially in the domestic architecture of Chistopher Wren

114 *Bold stone dressings at Lambeth Palace, London.*

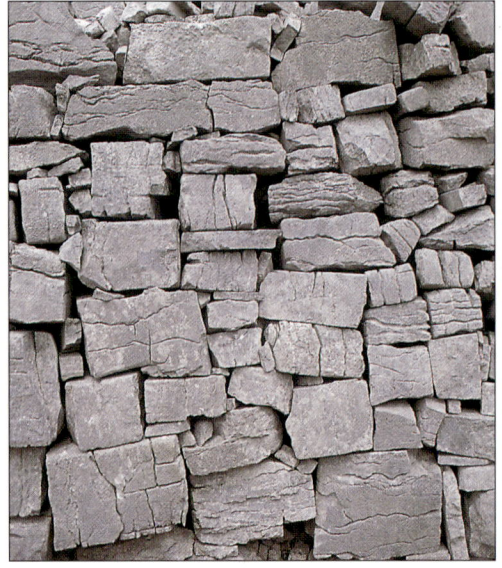

115 *Drystone at Dun Aengus, Aran Islands, Ireland.*

and his contemporaries from the late seventeenth century. [see FLINT, **178**]

## DRIP

Element projecting from a cornice, designed for rainwater to run off without wetting the face of a wall. [see GARGOYLE]

## DRIPSTONE [see HOOD-MOULD]

## DRUM

Cylindrical structure supporting a dome.

## DRUM TOWER

Cylindrical tower, usually of a castle.

## DRYSTONE

Masonry technique which does not employ mortar to bond the stones but relies on the skilful positioning of the stones to achieve stability. The architecture of prehistory – from chambered tombs to brochs and cashels – is noted for its durable drystone work. The most common application for drystone today is in field boundaries which constitute a distinctive regional feature in upland areas, e.g. in Yorkshire, Cumbria, Wales, Cornwall, the Cotswolds and the west of Ireland. [see **58, 70, 81, 255**]

## DUN

Circular fortified enclosure associated with Iron Age settlements in Scotland and Ireland. The semicircular **Dun Aengus** on **Inishmore**, Aran Islands, Ireland, is the most spectacular example of this class of monument. [see CASHEL, RATH, **75**]

## DUNGEON

The French word '*donjon*', meaning 'keep', has been anglicized to describe just one of the several functions of a castle keep, i.e. as a place for the incarceration of prisoners. The word 'dungeon' in English has thus come to denote the subterranean cells of a medieval castle which were used for the confinement and torture of captives. [see OUBLIETTE]

## DUTCH GABLE [see GABLE]

## DYKE [see EARTHWORK]

# E

## E-PLAN

During the Tudor period the typical country house evolved as an open layout comprising a principal range with two parallel wings extending at right angles. The centrally located entrance was often enhanced by a projecting porch, so that the groundplan resembled the letter 'E'. It has been suggested that the E-plan was a flattering tribute to Elizabeth I, but it was probably a happy coincidence that the initial letter of the monarch's name was formed in this grand manner; indeed, the E-plan actually predates Elizabeth's accession. **Barrington Court**, *Somerset*, is a classic example of the E-plan; and **Montacute**, *Somerset*, resembles two E-plans placed back to back. A common variation on the theme was the H-plan, which was formed when the wings of the house extended symmetrically in both directions. [see ELIZABETHAN]

## EARLY ENGLISH GOTHIC [see GOTHIC]

## EARTH HOUSE [see FOGOU]

## EARTHWORK

Structure created by the excavation and piling-up of earth, most commonly for defensive purposes. The most spectacular earthworks are the great hillforts of the Iron Age. However, the creation of

**116** *The E-plan of Barrington Court,* Somerset, *is apparent from this elevation. Note the finials on the gables.*

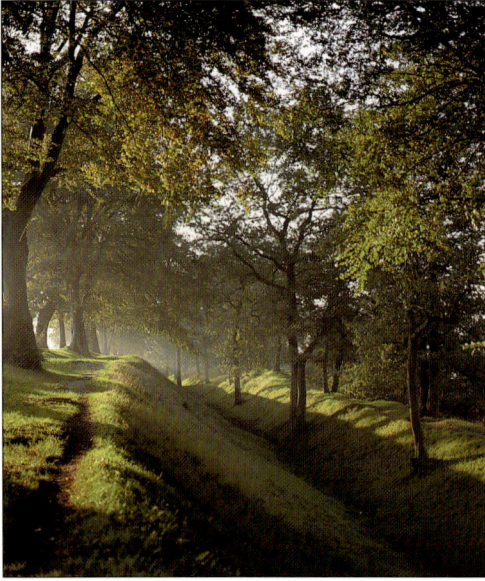

117 *The earthwork of the Antonine Wall, Scotland, is a simple ditch-and-rampart structure.*

mighty earthworks extends far back into prehistory with the Neolithic henges at **Avebury** and **Stonehenge**, *Wilts*. The Roman **Antonine Wall** in central Scotland is an earthwork consisting of a ditch or fosse and rampart. Great linear earthworks, known as dykes, were built in the post-Roman era to mark frontiers, e.g. **Wansdyke**, *Wilts*, and **Offa's Dyke** along the border of England and Wales. [see BURH, CAUSEWAYED CAMP, FOSSE, HENGE, HILLFORT, RATH]

**EASTER SEPULCHRE** [see SEPULCHRE]

**EAVES**
Part of a pitched roof projecting beyond the gable end. [see ROOF]

**ECHINUS**
Element of a Classical capital, consisting of a round moulding, e.g. beneath the abacus in Greek Doric. [see CAPITAL, ORDER]

**EDGE ROLL** [see BOWTELL]

**EDWARDIAN**

In the context of medieval architecture, the term refers to the castles built during the reign of Edward I (1272–1307). But the word is more readily associated with the opulent and bombastic style of architecture which flourished during the reign of Edward VII (1901–10). Many of the grander buildings of this era belong to the revival of a monumental Baroque, as exemplified by a host of commercial and public buildings, e.g. the **City Hall, Belfast**, N. Ireland; the **Port of London Authority** and the **Central Criminal Court** at the **Old Bailey, London**. In domestic architecture, the Edwardian age drew its inspiration from the vernacular buildings of the past with their pitched roofs, fanciful gables and prominent chimney stacks, but it added new elements, such as verandas, and it experimented with novel materials for external display, such as terracotta and glazed tiles, e.g. at **Debenham House, London**, of 1905–7 by Halsey Ricardo, which is covered with blue, green and white glazed tiles.

118 *The colourful tiled approach to Debenham House, London, gives an idea of the splendours within.*

**119** *The palatial treatment of the interior at Oldway, Paignton, Devon, represents the summit of Edwardian opulence.*

Mansion blocks sported a bewildering blend of Baronial and Baroque features to impress the onlooker. The exuberance of the Edwardian era expressed itself in a multitude of buildings devoted to leisure and entertainment, e.g. theatres, opera houses, grand hotels, and the seaside architecture of piers and pleasure pavilions. Although Edward VII died in 1910, the style identified with his name lived on until 1914 when the outbreak of the First World War (1914–18) brought most building activity to an abrupt halt. [see APARTMENT HOUSE, DEPARTMENT STORE, HOTEL, MONUMENT, MUNICIPAL BUILDINGS, SEASIDE PIER, THEATRE]

**120** *The Port of London Authority exudes Edwardian self-confidence.*

**EFFIGY** [see TOMB SCULPTURE]

## EGG AND DART
Moulding composed of alternating shapes resembling an ovoid and a dart or arrowhead. [see MOULDING]

## EGYPTIAN
The influence of ancient Egyptian architecture in the British Isles is limited, but it has left its mark in a number of places. The columns of Egyptian temples have occasionally been imitated in a light-hearted manner to produce an exotic effect, e.g. the **Egyptian House, Penzance**, *Cornwall*, of 1835. A more surprising Egyptian creation was **Temple Mill, Leeds**, *W Yorks*, of 1840 which was based on the Temple of Karnak; its original chimney was in the style of an Egyptian obelisk, but it cracked in 1852 and was replaced by a more conventional affair. Egyptian motifs made a frequent appearance in the tombs of Victorian cemeteries; and sphinxes guarded the terraces of the **Crystal Palace** at its new location in south London after the Great Exhibition of 1851. The garden at **Biddulph Grange**, *Staffs*, contains an **Egyptian Court**. In recent years, the squat columns, colourful decoration and massive entablature of ancient Egyptian architecture have been rediscovered by the Post-Modernists, e.g. John Outram's design for the **Pumping Station** on the **Isle of Dogs, London**. [see OBELISK, PYLON, PYRAMID]

## EGYPTIAN HALL
This has no direct link with Egypt, but denotes a Palladian type of hall with an internal peristyle, e.g. Lord Burlington's

**Assembly Rooms** at **York**, *N Yorks*. [see PERISTYLE]

## ELEANOR CROSS
When Edward I's queen, Eleanor of Castile, died in 1290 at Harby, *Lincs*, the king ordered that her body be embalmed and brought back to London for burial in Westminster Abbey. As a token of his grief he had monuments erected at each resting place of the funeral cortège. These were Gothic structures, similar to market crosses, with canopied niches for statues. The best preserved of the original Eleanor crosses are at **Geddington** and **Hardingstone**, *Northants*. **Waltham Cross**, *Essex*, is much restored; and the famous **Charing Cross, London**, is a replica made in 1863. [see HIGH CROSS, MARKET CROSS]

122 *The Eleanor Cross at Geddington*, Northants, *is a richly carved monument similar to a Gothic high cross.*

## ELEVATION [see FAÇADE, 116, 265]

## ELIZABETHAN

The word refers to the architecture of
the reign of Elizabeth I (1558–1603).
The characteristics of Elizabethan style
are best exemplified by the great country
houses of the period, e.g. **Longleat**, *Wilts*;
**Kirby Hall**, *Northants*; **Burghley House**,
*Lincs*; **Wollaton Hall**, *Notts*; and
**Hardwick Hall**, *Derbys*. These combine
Renaissance features, such as symmetrical
fenestration, with all manner of fantastic
decorative flourishes, notably turrets with
cupolas, pinnacles and fanciful chimneystacks, to create a highly original con-
coction that has been aptly described as

**123** *Trerice*, Cornwall, *is a charming example of Elizabethan domesticity. Note the decorative gables.*

**124** *Burghley House*, Cambs, *a veritable 'prodigy house'. Note the parade of architectural showmanship.*

125 *Little Moreton Hall*, Cheshire, *shows the grand effects that can be achieved with half-timbering.*

the 'prodigy house'. Inside, the long galleries, ornate plaster ceilings and rooms lit by huge windows containing a riot of carved wood-work express all the enthusiasm and invention of the Elizabethan era.

Although Elizabeth built very little herself, many houses were built in her honour by wealthy courtiers who were anxious to offer the queen lavish hospitality in the course of her frequent royal progresses around the country. The period also witnessed significant building activity by the rural squires and yeomen, e.g. at **Little Moreton Hall**, *Cheshire*. By contrast, there was a dearth of ecclesiastical construction: the process of secularization of the social economy was already well under way. [see E-PLAN, RENAISSANCE, TUDOR, **39**]

126 *An enfilade is formed by these two elegant Palladian doorways at Chiswick House, London.*

**EMBRASURE** [see BATTLEMENT]

**ENCAUSTIC TILES** [see TILES]

**ENCEINTE**

In medieval military architecture, the curtain wall and its towers which enclose a castle. Also the enclosure itself.

**ENFILADE**

Series of doors aligned on a straight axis which permit an unencumbered line of sight. Such an internal vista was of particular appeal in Baroque palaces and also occurs in Palladian houses, e.g. **Chiswick House, London**. The word is derived from French '*enfilade*', meaning a succession of rooms.

**ENGAGED COLUMN** [see COLUMN]

127 *The engine house at East Pool,* Cornwall, *now in the care of the National Trust.*

## ENGINE HOUSE
Industrial structure built to contain the engines required for the pumping of mines. A marked feature of the Cornish landscape are the tall chimneys of redundant engine houses, e.g. at **Botallack** and **Towanroath** on the north coast, and inland at **East Pool**.

## ENTABLATURE
In Classical architecture, the upper horizontal part of a building supported by a colonnade and consisting of an architrave, frieze and cornice. [see ORDER]

## ENTASIS
Technique borrowed from Classical Greek architecture which gave a slight convex swelling to a column in order to counter-act the optical illusion of concavity which would have resulted from perfectly straight-sided shafts. The point of maxi-mum entasis is at roughly one third of the height of the column. Entasis is also a feature of the round towers of early Christian Ireland. [see **273, 309**]

## ENTRESOL [see MEZZANINE]

## ESCARP [see SCARP]

## ESCUTCHEON
Heraldic shield with armorial bearings which occurs in Gothic and Baronial architecture on bosses, spandrels and chimneypieces. Escutcheons may be carved of stone or wood, but they may also be moulded in lead on a rainwater head or represented in stained glass. The Garter Stalls in **St George's Chapel, Windsor Castle**, *Berks*, display a rich collection of painted escutcheons. [see ACHIEVEMENT, HATCHMENT, **152**]

128 *Colourful escutcheons adorn the side panels of this medieval tomb at Minster Lovell,* Oxon.

## ETRUSCAN
Strictly speaking, this refers to the architecture of the ancient civilization of central Italy which preceded the Roman era. The name entered the design vocabulary in the eighteenth century when Robert Adam applied it to one of his imaginative

**129** *The Exchange, Bristol,* Avon: *a Palladian design.*

styles derived from the decoration of Etruscan vases. Adam's Etruscan decors incorporated trellis-work, ancient urns and bas reliefs, e.g. the **Etruscan Dressing Room** at **Osterley Park House, London.** [see ADAM STYLE]

## EXCHANGE

Building designed for the conduct of commercial transactions. London's original Royal Exchange, built largely at the expense of the merchant Thomas Gresham, was opened in 1567. Inspired by the Bourse at Antwerp, Gresham's building was destroyed in the Great Fire of 1666. Its successor also fell victim to a fire which paved the way for the present Neo-Classical **Royal Exchange**, built in

1844. **Bristol**, *Avon*, had built its own **Exchange** in 1743 according to a Palladian design by John Wood the Elder. The **Corn Exchange in Leeds**, *W Yorks*, of 1863 is an imposing Baroque rotunda. **London**'s present **Stock Exchange** is an undistinguished office block of the 1970s.

## EXTRADOS [see ARCH]

## EYE-CATCHER

Any structure placed in a park, garden or landscape solely or principally to provide a visual attraction, e.g. to terminate a vista. This could be anything from a sham Gothic ruin to a lofty obelisk or Classical monument, e.g. at **Castletown House**, *Kildare*, Ireland. [see FOLLY, OBELISK, TEMPLE]

# F

## FAÇADE

Face, front or elevation of a building which is given some form of architectural expression. [see FRONTISPIECE]

## FACTORY

The Industrial Revolution, which began in the closing decades of the eighteenth century, introduced the concept of mechanized mass production and along with it a new type of building to accommodate the machines and their workers. The first factories were the textile mills of Lancashire, which were rapidly followed elsewhere. Early factory buildings were inspired by the prevalent Classical style of architecture with its insistence on regularity and proportion; unnecessary embellishment was avoided, e.g. at **New Lanark**, *S'clyde*, Scotland, where reticence and sobriety reflect the moral purpose of the owner's work ethic. Later, Victorian enthusiasm for industry brought forth a very different style of factory.

**130** *Manningham Mill, Bradford,* W Yorks: *a noble vision of the factory. The campanile is in fact a chimney.*

131 *Abbey Mill, Bradford-on-Avon*, Wilts: *a fine Classical structure for textile manufacture.*

**Manningham Mill, Bradford**, *W Yorks*, of 1873 is a vast palazzo crowned by a lofty chimney masquerading as a campanile. **Bliss Mill, Chipping Norton**, *Oxon*, could almost be taken for a Baroque mansion, were it not for the huge chimney protruding from the cupola. Even more outlandish was the exotic **Templeton's Carpet Factory** of 1890 in **Glasgow**, Scotland, which is a fairytale vision of polychrome brickwork in the Venetian Gothic manner. In the 1920s and 1930s factory design was revolutionized by the sleek lines of Art Deco e.g. the **Hoover Factory, London**. Modern factories prefer a style such as High Tech which expresses engineering and technology rather than architecture. [see WAREHOUSE, **16, 368**]

**FACTORY VILLAGE** [see PLANNED VILLAGE]

## FANLIGHT

Fixed window above a front door, essentially semicircular in shape and with radiating glazing bars which suggest the segments of an open fan. The device was extremely popular in Georgian and Regency houses, especially in **Bath**, *Avon*; **Dublin**, Ireland; and **Edinburgh**, Scotland. The word has come to denote any shape of window above a door. [see **109, 332**]

132 *A fanlight over a Georgian door in Dublin, Ireland. Note the Ionic capitals and unfluted shafts.*

## FAN VAULT

Late development of Perpendicular Gothic in which the vaulting appears to spring in a fan-like profusion of radiating ribs. Fan vaulting made an early

133 *The fan-vaulted nave of Sherborne Abbey, Dorset. Note the vast expanse of the clerestory windows which illuminate the stonework with a flood of light.*

appearance during the first half of the fifteenth century in the cloister of **Gloucester Cathedral**, *Glos*, and then to spectacular effect at **Sherborne Abbey**, *Dorset*, of *c*. 1475–1500; **King's College Chapel, Cambridge**, *Cambs*, of 1446–1515; the choir of **Peterborough Cathedral**, *Cambs*, *c*. 1496–1508; and the

**Henry VII Chapel** in **Westminster Abbey, London,** of 1503–19. [see GOTHIC, PENDANT, VAULT, **161**, **231**]

## FASCIA

Unadorned horizontal band on an architrave or cornice which provides a plain interspace between decorative mouldings. [see ENTABLATURE]

## FENESTRATION

The disposition of windows in a façade.

117

**134** *Festoons, designed by Robert Adam, adorn the façade of 20 Portman Square, London.*

# FESTOON

Decorative motif consisting of a garland of fruit and/or flowers draped between two supports and tied with swirling ribbons. It may be carved in wood or stone or moulded in plaster. It was a favourite device of Baroque and Neo-Classical architecture and interior design. [see SWAG]

# FILLET

Narrow, flat band between mouldings or the flutes of a column. It is also the top element of a Classical cornice, sometimes known as a listel. [see ENTABLATURE, FLUTING]

# FINIAL

Crowning ornament or termination of a gable, canopy, spire or newel post. A variety of finials adorn bench ends of church pews. [see PINEAPPLE, POPPYHEAD, **26, 116, 269**]

# FIREPLACE [see CHIMNEYPIECE]

118

# FIRE-DOGS

A wrought-iron structure, also known as andirons, designed to serve as a brazier and generally to be found in large open fireplaces. [see CHIMNEY]

# FLAG, FLAGSTONE

Flagstones are extracted from stratified rock formations, sometimes with the help of natural frosting which causes the water in the joints to freeze and expand, thereby separating the individual strata. When used for roofing, flagstones are referred to as stone slates; flatstone and thackstone are alternative names. Flagstone roofs may be of limestone or sandstone. Limestone roofs are much in evidence in the buildings of the Cotswolds, e.g. at **Stanway**, *Glos*, and also in Wiltshire, e.g. the **Barton Farm Tithe Barn** at **Bradford-on-Avon** and **Great Chalfield Manor**. Sandstone flags are generally thicker and heavier than their

**135** *The roof of the great tithe barn at Bradford-on-Avon, Wilts, is made of limestone flags.*

limestone counterparts, and are sometimes described for that reason as slabs; e.g. at **Stokesay Castle**, *Shrops*. The term flagstone also designates the paving slabs of a courtyard.

## FLANK

In medieval military architecture, the side of a bastion. [see BASTION]

## FLATSTONE [see FLAGSTONE]

## FLÈCHE

From the French, meaning 'arrow' or 'spire', and used in English to denote a particularly slender type of spire made of wood or metal. It could be mounted on the roof ridge of a church or cathedral since it did not require buttressing. Also known as spirelet. [see SPIRE]

*136 Flushwork on the gatehouse of St Osyth Priory, Essex. Note St George and the dragon in the spandrels.*

## FLEURON

From the French meaning 'small flower', a carved ornament representing a leaf or flower. [see FOLIATED]

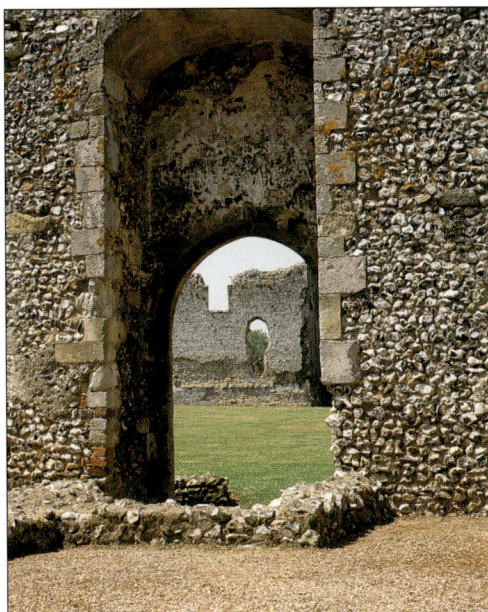

*137 Walls of knapped flint at Bishop's Waltham Palace, Hants. Note how the flint nodules have been split.*

## FLINT

Hard material composed of silica found in irregular nodules which are relatively easy to split. In prehistoric times flint was used for fashioning a variety of tools, and it was even extracted from subterranean deposits, as evidenced by the Neolithic flint mines near **Thetford**, *Norfolk*, known as **Grime's Graves**. As a building material flint can be used for robust walls composed of entire nodules set in mortar. During the Middle Ages the practice evolved of knapping, i.e. splitting, the nodules and mounting them so as to present a flattish dark face. When used in conjunction with dressings of white stone, knapped flints provide an attractive contrast in tone and texture; the technique, known as flushwork, is a particular feature of East Anglia and southern England, e.g. the gatehouse of **St Osyth Priory**, *Essex*, and at **Holy Trinity, Long Melford**, *Suffolk*. In the Chilterns, flint is used in conjunction with red brick to create a pleasing decorative effect. [see CHEQUER-WORK, CHERT]

## FLORIATED [see FOLIATED]

## FLOWING TRACERY [see TRACERY]

## FLUSHWORK [see FLINT]

## FLUTING

In Classical architecture, the vertical concave grooves carved into a column to give it a profile. The grooves may meet in a sharp edge, known as an arris, or be separated by a flat interspace or fillet. [see ORDER, 82]

## FLYING BUTTRESS [see BUTTRESS, SPIRE]

## FLYING STAIR

A staircase supported on the cantilever principle, i.e. without visible internal support, apart from the walls of the stairwell, so that it appears to be suspended in space. A flying stair, of which the inner ends of the steps form a circular or elliptical shape, is known as a geometric stair, e.g. the **Tulip Staircase** in the **Queen's House, Greenwich**, London. [see STAIR, STAIRCASE]

## FOGOU

Type of subterranean chamber and passage which is found in association with ringforts and other Iron Age settlements. It has been variously interpreted as a bolt-hole or storage cellar. The word is Cornish, meaning cave; and some of the best preserved fogous are those at **Trelowarren** and **Carn Euny**, *Cornwall.* Elsewhere, the fogou is known as an earth house, souterrain or, in Scots dialect, a weem. Scottish examples include **Ardestie** and **Carlungie**, *Tayside*; **Grain** and **Rennibister,** Orkney.

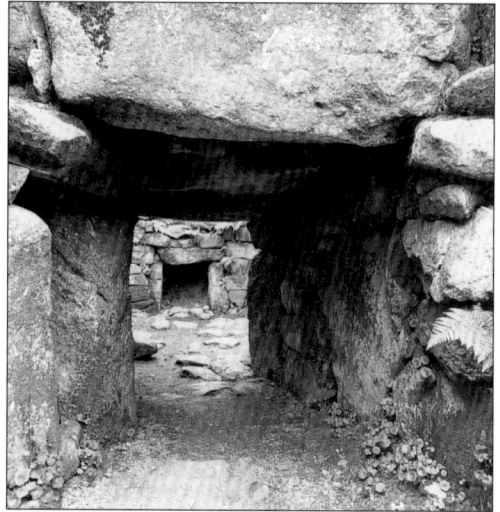

**138** *The fogou at Carn Euny, Cornwall. The heavy granite lintel rests on two equally solid orthostats.*

## FOIL

From French *'feuille'*, meaning leaf, this form of Gothic tracery consists of circles in a cluster, separated by cusps. The number of circles determines the shape and name of the pattern, i.e. trefoil (3), quatrefoil (4), cinquefoil (5) etc. [see TRACERY]

## FOLIATED

Describes a leaf-like ornament, also known as floriated. [see FLEURON]

## FOLLY

An eccentric structure having a limited practical purpose, built mainly to indulge the whim of its creator. The word is derived from old French *'folie'*, originally meaning a delight. The word is thought to have acquired its pejorative sense in *c.* 1228 when Hubert de Burgh was obliged by royal command to demolish his *'folie'* or favourite abode, a castle in the Welsh borders, even before he had moved in. However, the deliberate building of follies did not become widespread until the eighteenth century when it became fashionable for the gen-

**139** *The Gothic Temple at Stowe,* Bucks, *is an elaborate folly designed essentially for scenic effect.*

try to enliven their parks with picturesque structures, ranging from Gothic ruins to Classical temples and Chinese pagodas, as may be seen in the great landscape gardens e.g. **Stourhead**, *Wilts*, and **Stowe**, *Bucks*. [see BANQUETING HOUSE, CHINOISERIE, EYE-CATCHER, GROTTO, LODGE, PAVILION, PINEAPPLE, ROTUNDA, TEMPLE, TOWER]

## FONT

The vessel containing the holy water for the ceremony of baptism is by tradition an impressive piece of stone sculpture occupying a prominent position at the west end of the church near the main entrance. The origins of the font go back to the very beginning of church architecture. The enduring symbolism and significance of the font is reflected in the preservation of many ancient examples, e.g. at **St Morwenna, Morwenstow**, *Cornwall*, where a Saxon font is still in use. Cornwall possesses many remarkable Norman fonts from the twelfth century e.g. at **Bodmin Priory** and at **St Nonna, Altarnun**. Vigorous sculpture framed by interlace carving flows dramatically around the Norman fonts at **St Mary Magdalene, Eardisley** and **St Michael, Castle Frome**, *Heref & Worcs*. In the thirteenth century figurative carving gave way to an abstract decoration of the font imitating the evolution of Gothic window tracery. The fourteenth-century font at

140 *Font in All Saints, Margaret Street*, London.

North Hinksey, *Oxon*, displays faithful reproductions of Decorated tracery. Perpendicular style fonts, usually octagonal, are particularly in evidence in East Anglia, and there is a partial return to figurative sculpture e.g. at **All Saints, Walsoken,** *Norfolk*. Heraldic devices also feature, e.g. at **St Mary, Ufford,** *Suffolk*, where the font sports a towering wooden canopy of intricately carved tiers which dwarfs the font itself. The fashion for elaborate font canopies continued in the post-Reformation era. **All Hallows by the Tower, London**, has one carved by Grinling Gibbons which portrays two cherubs flanking a pile of flowers under the watchful eye of a dove. The font of **St Clement, Eastcheap,** London, shows the emergence of Classical design. The Gothic Revival of the nineteenth century brought with it some spirited productions, e.g. at **St Mary Abbots, Kensington,** London; and there are some exotic Byzantine fonts of coloured marble, e.g. at **St Mary, Ottery St Mary,** *Devon*. Some twentieth century fonts have followed the trends of modern sculpture using materials such as steel and hollowed-out boulders.

**141** *The Norman font in Bodmin Priory,* Cornwall.

**FORMWORK** [see SHUTTERING]

## FORT, FORTRESS

The difference between a fort and a castle is not always clear-cut, since both are essentially fortified buildings. However, a fort is generally a stronghold built for a garrison rather than as a residence for a nobleman. The military camps of the Romans are known as forts. Some of the best preserved are those along Hadrian's Wall, e.g. **Corbridge, Chesterholm, Housesteads** and **Birdoswald,** *Northum*. The term fortress may be used to distinguish the larger camps of the legions from the smaller forts of the auxiliaries.

During the Middle Ages baronial castles maintained control of the land. In

**142** *Fort George, near Inverness,* Highland, *Scotland, was built in the aftermath of the Jacobite uprising.*

143 *St Mawes*, Cornwall: *a coastal fort built by Henry VIII against the threat of invasion from Europe.*

the sixteenth century, the threat of invasion from continental Europe prompted Henry VIII to construct a chain of artillery forts along the English Channel coast from **Pendennis** and **St Mawes**, *Cornwall*, via **Portland**, *Dorset*, to **Walmer** and **Deal**, *Kent*. Although these are designated as castles, they are fundamentally different to their medieval namesakes in their exclusively military purpose. Apart from the royal coat of arms above their entrances there is nothing royal or even baronial about them; instead of a great hall and noble apartments, there are guardrooms and barrack-style sleeping quarters. These forts were built according to the latest theories of artillery defence, but they were soon superseded in the seventeenth century by a new generation in which angular outworks, known as ravelins, replaced the circular towers, e.g. **Tilbury Fort**, *Essex*, and **Charles Fort, Kinsale**, *Cork*, Ireland. Scotland retains some fine Hanoverian forts, most notably **Fort George**, near **Inverness**, *Highland*. **Fort Brockhurst** at **Gosport**, *Hants*, of 1858–62 was one of the last major forts to be built in Britain, but the changing pattern of warfare soon rendered it obsolete. [see BARRACK, CASTLE, CASTRUM, DEMILUNE, HILLFORT, MARTELLO TOWER, RATH, RAVELIN, ROMAN]

## FOSSE
Defensive ditch or moat, either part of an earthwork or in front of a fortified wall. [see EARTHWORK]

## FOUNTAIN
Ornamental structure, often decorated with sculpture, with water falling through one or more outlets into a basin. The idea of the fountain as a central feature of a formal square or garden was taken from the repertoire of the Italian Renaissance, and is seen to grandest effect at stately homes and palaces, e.g. **Hampton Court**, London; **Castle Howard**, *N Yorks*, and **Blenheim Palace**, *Oxon*. Fountains are also prominent in the urban context, e.g. at **London's Trafalgar Square**, where the fountains by Edwin Lutyens were installed in 1939.

## FOUR-CENTRED ARCH [see ARCH]

## FOYER
French word meaning 'hearth' or 'home', but in English it has come to denote the entrance hall of a cinema or theatre.

## FRAMED BUILDING
System of construction whereby the building is supported not by load-bearing walls but by a framework, whether

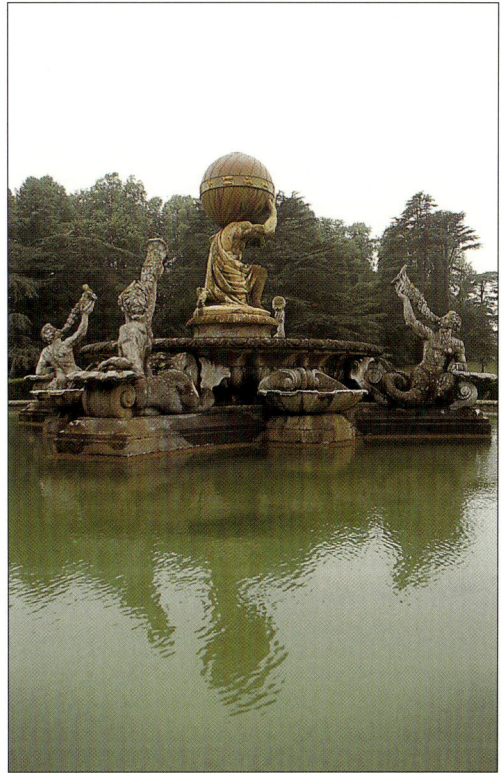

144 *The Atlas Fountain at Castle Howard*, N Yorks, *is the centrepiece of a formal garden adjoining the house.*

of wood, iron, steel or reinforced concrete. [see CRUCK, HALF-TIMBERING, STEEL-FRAME]

## FRATER
Dining-hall or refectory of a monastery. [see MONASTERY]

## FREESTONE
Denotes any building stone, but usually best-quality limestone or sandstone, which can be cut in any direction. Freestone is employed for the ornate dressings of a building, requiring a finer finish.

## FRENCH WINDOW
A pair of casement windows, extending down to the floor, which also serve as doors. The device was put to prominent

**145** *Kilconnell Friary*, Galway, *Ireland, shows the compact grouping of buildings typical of Franciscan houses.*

use at Versailles in the 1680s, hence the association with France.

## FRESCO

Strictly speaking this refers to the Italian technique of painting directly on to fresh plaster, but the term is often loosely applied to denote wall paintings in general. [see MURAL]

## FRET

Classical ornament composed of continuous interlocking vertical and horizontal lines. One of the most popular forms of fret is the Greek Key design, often found on a frieze.

## FRIARY

Monastery established by one of the mendicant orders of friars, e.g. Dominicans, Carmelites and Franciscans. By contrast to most other monastic orders which sought to establish closed communities away from human society, the friars endeavoured to bring their ministry to the people. Consequently many friaries were set up in towns and cities, but have long since disappeared in the course of urban redevelopment. Notable Dominican buildings survive at **Canterbury**, *Kent*; **Gloucester**, *Glos*, and **Norwich**, *Norfolk*. The **Canterbury Greyfriars** was the earliest Franciscan friary in Britain, founded in 1224. Elsewhere, the existence of vanished friaries is recorded in names, e.g. **Blackfriars** and **Carmelite Square**,

146 *The cloister of Quin Friary,* Clare, *Ireland, creates an intimate and sheltered environment.*

London. Some of the best-preserved Franciscan friaries in Europe are in the west of Ireland, e.g. **Moyne** and **Rosserk**, *Mayo*: these display a modest architectural treatment in line with the social commitment of the order. [see CLOISTER, MONASTERY]

## FRIEZE

A broad band, either plain or decorated with a pattern, e.g. fretwork, running along the upper part of a wall immediately below the cornice. In Classical architecture the frieze occurs on an entablature between the architrave and cornice. [see ENTABLATURE, **21, 89, 170**]

## FRONT [see FAÇADE, FRONTISPIECE]

## FRONTISPIECE

Principal façade of a building which is given special architectural treatment.

## FUNCTIONALISM

One of the principal ingredients of Modernism, this design philosophy of the 1920s and 30s placed the functional aspect of a building as the paramount factor in architecture. Accordingly, any aesthetic consideration had to derive from the expression of a functional purpose, in line with the dictum that 'form follows function'. In practice however, it proved extremely difficult to apply the pure principle of Functionalism. [see MODERNISM]

# G

## GADROONED

Decorated with a series of convex curves in relief, like fluting in reverse.

## GABLE

Triangular upper portion of a wall whose shape is determined by the pitch of the sloping roof. The form of the gable can be treated in a number of ways. A crow-stepped gable consists of a number of square steps rising to a flat apex; this is known in Scotland as a corbie-stepped gable. A Dutch gable has curved sides and is crowned by a pediment. A shaped gable has a multi-curved profile. [see GAMBREL, 30, 116, 123, 267]

Crow-stepped gable

Dutch gable

Shaped gables

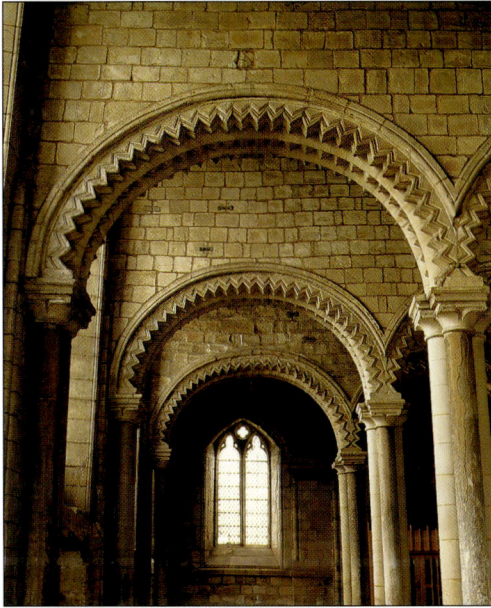

147 *The Galilee at Durham Cathedral is an aisled Norman structure with chevrons on its arcades.*

148 *The George Inn, Southwark, London. Such court-yard galleries were once a typical feature of hostelries.*

## GALILEE

Porch-like structure, sometimes known as narthex, at the western end of a large church which may serve as a separate chapel, e.g. at **Durham Cathedral**, *Durham*, and **Ely Cathedral**, *Cambs*. The **Galilee Porch** at **Lincoln Cathedral**, *Lincs*, is a westerly extension of the south transept.

## GALLERIA

Italian word meaning 'a shopping arcade'. The name has been taken up by some modern commercial developments, e.g. the **Hays Galleria** near **London Bridge**. [see ARCADE]

## GALLERY

In churches of the Middle Ages the triforium is sometimes loosely described as a gallery, but in strict parlance the gallery is an open upper storey overlooking the nave. It evolved as a feature of post-Reformation churches from the seventeenth century,

sometimes just at the west end of the nave but often extending also over the aisles. In secular architecture a minstrels' gallery was frequently built over the screens passage of a medieval hall. Open galleries were a feature of courtyard inns and of the early theatres. An innovation of the Elizabethan age was the provision of a long gallery, which was actually a room on an upper storey of a country house for the purpose of recreation, entertainment and the hanging of pictures, e.g. at **Montacute**, *Somerset*; and at **Lanhydrock**, *Cornwall*, of Jacobean date. [see ART GALLERY, AUDITORY CHURCH, TRIBUNE, TRIFORIUM]

## GALLERY GRAVE [see CHAMBERED TOMB]

## GALLETING

Technique of inserting small pieces of chipped flint, pebble or other stone into masonry joints before the mortar has set hard. This gives additional strength to the

149 *Hampstead Garden Suburb, London, has retained the pastoral values intended by its founders.*

mortar, but the purpose is also decorative.

## GAMBREL

Type of pitched roof with an additional, small gable at the ridge. [see ROOF]

## GAOL [see PRISON]

## GARDEN BUILDINGS

[see AVIARY, BELVEDERE, CONSERVATORY, CRINKLE-CRANKLE, EYE-CATCHER, FOLLY, FOUNTAIN, GAZEBO, GROTTO, HA-HA, ORANGERY, PAGODA, PAVILION, PERGOLA, SCULPTURE, SUMMERHOUSE, TEMPLE, TERRACE]

## GARDEN CITY, GARDEN SUBURB

The idea of imitating a rural settlement in the context of the city was first expressed in the form of the garden suburb, e.g. **Bedford Park, London**, of 1875. This set the tone for future developments with tree-lined streets, homely dwellings and large gardens. **Hampstead Garden Suburb, London**, of 1906 took up the idea on a larger scale, but the concept was given wider relevance by Ebenezer Howard (1850–1928) who formulated the practical aims of the garden city as an independent community which were realized at **Letchworth**, *Herts*, from 1903 and at nearby **Welwyn**, *Herts*, from 1920. Howard's ideas lay behind many of the provisions of the New Towns Act of 1944. [see NEW TOWN, PLANNED VILLAGE]

## GARDEROBE

The French word for a small chamber for the storage of clothes became a euphemism for the medieval toilet or privy. In castles the garderobe was sometimes projected externally on a corbel, e.g. at **Bothwell Castle,** *S'clyde,* Scotland.

## GARGOYLE

Carved stone waterspout projecting from the gutter of a medieval building. Gargoyles were also used for decorative effect; and they served as symbolic guardians against evil spirits. Oxford colleges abound in gargoyles and non-functional carvings known as grotesques.

**150** *A gargoyle maintains a symbolic vigil on the tower of St Peter-in-the-East, Oxford, Oxon.*

## GARRET

Attic room of small dimensions.

## GARTH

Yard or garden, especially of a monastery, where the term may denote the open area surrounded by cloisters, i.e. the cloister garth. [see MONASTERY, PARADISE]

## GATE

1) Originally the entrance to a castle or walled city, generally of stout planks of wood and often reinforced by a portcullis of iron. In the post-medieval era ornamental iron gates appeared at stately homes, e.g. **Chirk Castle,** *Clwyd,* Wales, and **Hampton Court, London,** as well as at colleges such as **Trinity, Oxford,** *Oxon* and **Clare, Cambridge,** *Cambs*; also at parks and gardens, e.g at **Kew Gardens, London.** [see GATEHOUSE, PORTCULLIS, WATERGATE, 220, 258]

**151** *The wrought-iron gates at Chirk Castle,* Clwyd, *Wales: a triumph of eighteenth-century craftsmanship.*

2) The suffix '-gate' often appears in the street names of eastern England, such as **Colliergate, York,** *N Yorks,* and **Michaelgate, Lincoln,** *Lincs.* In this context the meaning is simply 'street', from the Scandinavian *'gatan'.*

## GATEHOUSE

A structure containing a gate, e.g. at **Beeston Castle,** *Cheshire,* and the **Nevill Gatehouse** at **Raby Castle,** *Durham.* The

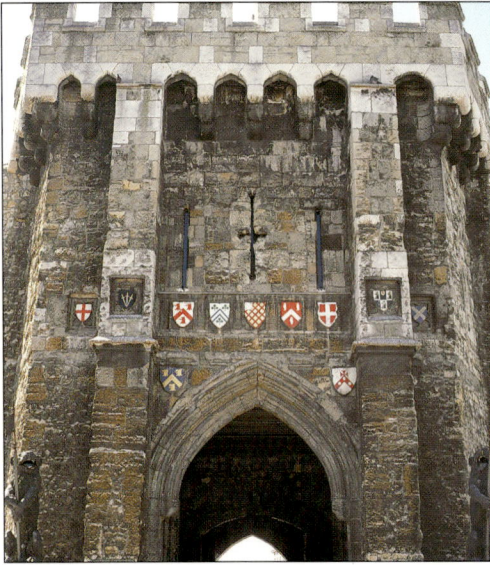

152 *The Bargate, Southampton*, Hants, *is a medieval gatehouse. Note the escutcheons and machicolation.*

entrances to the walled cities of the Middle Ages were usually equipped with imposing gatehouses, e.g. **Micklegate Bar** and **Monk Bar** in **York**, *N Yorks*, and the **Bargate, Southampton**, *Hants*. Medieval monasteries also had gatehouses of consequence, e.g. **Cleeve Abbey**, *Somerset*; **Thornton Abbey**, *Humbs*; **Forde Abbey**, *Dorset*; **St Osyth Priory**, *Essex*. The medieval gatehouse was retained in many Tudor buildings, e.g. **St James's Palace, London**; **Layer Marney**, *Essex*; and in the Jacobean era, e.g. **Lanhydrock**, *Cornwall*, and **Stanway**, *Glos*. The gatehouse remained a standard feature of Oxford and Cambridge colleges well into the nineteenth century. [see BARBICAN, LODGE, **136**, **215**, **261**]

## GAZEBO

Summerhouse in a landscape garden sited for the enjoyment of a view. [see BELVEDERE, SUMMERHOUSE]

## GEOMETRIC STAIR [see FLYING STAIR]

## GEORGIAN

The consecutive reigns of George I to George IV (1714–1830) correspond very closely to the fashion for Classical archi-

153 *Stately but sober exterior of a Georgian town house in Bedford Square, London.*

## GEOMETRICAL TRACERY [see TRACERY]

## GIANT ORDER [see COLOSSAL ORDER]

## GIBBS SURROUND

Stone dressing around a door or window consisting of square blocks set at intervals and crowned by a multiple keystone. Named after James Gibbs (1682–1754) who made frequent use of the device. It also features on many buildings in the Baroque Revival style of the Edwardian period, e.g. **County Hall, London**. It remains popular with contemporary Neo-Classicists. [see **214**]

tecture. As a stylistic label the word 'Georgian' thus conveys the chief attributes of Classicism, namely order, proportion, restraint, purity and elegance. Uniformity was preferred to originality by a society which believed it had discovered universal rules of taste in the works of the ancient Greeks and Romans. In spite of its experiments with Gothick, Rococo and Chinoiserie, the Georgian style is noted for its homogeneity, by contrast to the ensuing eclecticism of the Victorian age. The Georgian era witnessed a prolific building of country houses as well as a boom in Classical urbanism which transformed every major town and city. [see ADAM STYLE, BAROQUE, CIRCUS, CLASSICISM, COUNTRY HOUSE, CRESCENT, GREEK REVIVAL, ITALIANATE, PALLADIANISM, PLANNED VILLAGE, REGENCY, TERRACE, 242]

**154** *The staircase at 44 Berkeley Square, London. Georgian interiors were often quite lavish in contrast to their restrained exteriors.*

Gibbs surround

## GLACIS
In military architecture, a sloping bank in front of a fortification.

## GLASGOW STYLE
Late nineteenth-century style related to Art Nouveau evolved by the Glasgow architect and designer Charles Rennie Mackintosh (1868–1928) whose interiors are noted for their Japanese-like simplicity of line and telling use of an isolated floral motif. Every detail of a room was conceived as part of an overall vision which was more concerned with aesthetics than with tradi-

133

**155** *The Mackintosh style at Hill House, Helensburgh.*

tional ideas of comfort. Notable examples survive at **Hill House, Helensburgh**, *S'clyde*, and in the **Hunterian Art Gallery, Glasgow**, Scotland. The rallying point for the movement was Mackintosh's **Glasgow School of Art** of 1896, which was more highly acclaimed in Europe than in Britain at the time. [see **318, 319**]

## GLASS

The use of glass in windows was introduced to Britain by the Romans. Although it later featured extensively in medieval churches and cathedrals, it did not enter widespread domestic use except in the grandest dwellings until the sixteenth century. The Elizabethan prodigy houses performed spectacular feats with glass, e.g. at **Hardwick Hall**, *Derbys*, which – according to the rhyming couplet – was 'more glass than wall'. However, such huge windows were composed of many relatively small panes of glass. This was also true of the Georgian era when crown glass was produced by a centrifugal process which involved spin-

**156** *A glass-fronted office building in central London.*

ning the molten glass into flat, circular plates which were then cut into smallish squares or rectangles. It was not until the early nineteenth century that the manufacture of sheet glass was mastered. This permitted ever larger and stronger panes, which in turn triggered off a revolution in building design. In combination with cast iron, glass became a construction material for walls and roofs in conservatories, art galleries, covered markets and railway stations. The Crystal Palace in London of 1851 marked the grandest achievement of this kind. Also of note are the **Royal Scottish Museum, Edinburgh**, and **Gardner's Warehouse, Glasgow**, Scotland. Entire facades are now made of glass, e.g. the **Wills, Faber & Dumas Office, Ipswich**, *Suffolk.* [see CONSERVATORY, COVERED MARKET, STAINED GLASS, WINDOW, 243, 245]

## GLAZING BARS
Wooden bars arranged vertically and horizontally to retain window panes. [see CAME, WINDOW]

# GOTHIC

The term was first applied by Renaissance observers to the architecture of the Middle Ages in a pejorative sense to suggest that the style was the true inheritance of the barbarian Goths who had sacked Rome in AD 410. The Tudor chronicler John Stow described Westminster Abbey 'whose Arches turn not upon Semi-Circles, according to the Roman Manner of Architecture practised in our Days, but meet in acute Angles, in Imitation of the Gothic Way of Building'. Thus Gothic is now associated specifically with the pointed arch; and

the round-arched style of the Normans is excluded from the term. It was the scholar Thomas Rickman who in 1817 devised the categories of Early English, Decorated and Perpendicular which are still in use. Although their details are fairly distinct, the chronologies of the three phases overlapped in reality.

Early English (c. 1150 to c. 1275) is characterized by the austere simplicity of unadorned vaults, narrow lancet windows and thin ribs of masonry as if to underline its antithesis to the massive squatness of Norman building. Early English was preceded by a phase known as the Transitional, in which round arches and pointed arches occur within one building, e.g. the crypt of **St John's, Clerkenwell, London**. Early English at its purest and

**157** *The Decorated Gothic nave vault of Exeter Cathedral,* Devon. *Note the bosses at the rib intersections.*

158 *The chapter-house of Southwell Minster, Notts: fanciful detail formed part of the Gothic repertoire. Note the crockets.*

160 *Early English Gothic in the retro-choir of Southwark Cathedral, London.*

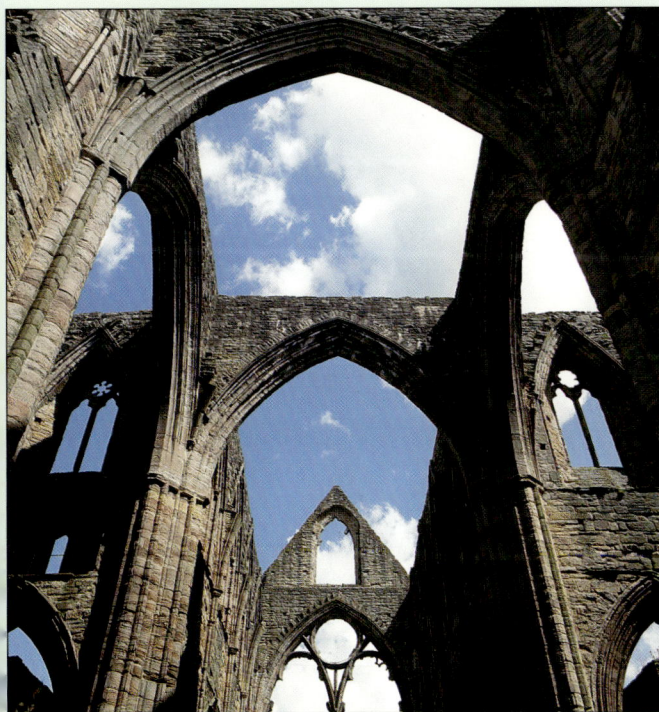

159 *The roofless shell of Tintern Abbey, Gwent, Wales, reveals the structural power of Gothic architecture.*

most spectacular may be seen at **Salisbury Cathedral**, *Wilts*, and the retro-choir of **Southwark Cathedral, London**.

Decorated (*c.* 1275 to *c.* 1375) represents a flowering into a more sophisticated and ornate style. Windows became more elaborate as the tracery adopted fanciful and complex forms. The number of ribs in a vault proliferated far beyond what was needed to support it, and their intersections were marked by colourful carved bosses e.g at **Exeter Cathedral**, *Devon*, **York Minster**, *N Yorks*, and **St Mary Redcliffe, Bristol**, *Avon*. Perpendicular (*c.* 1375 to *c.* 1510) resulted from the growing technological ingenuity of the masons who were able increasingly to dispense with solid walls for the

## GOTHIC continued

sake of vast expanses of glass, e.g. the east window of **Gloucester Cathedral**, *Glos.* The hallmark of the style was the multitude of vertical divisions, hence the name Perpendicular; but the overall effect of the style also created an impression of squareness and horizontality as arches became flattened. Many of England's most stately parish churches date from this period. The fan vault marks the grand finale of Perpendicular

Gothic. [see AMBULATORY, ANGEL ROOF, APSE, ARCH, CATHEDRAL, CHANCEL, CHANTRY CHAPEL, CHAPTER HOUSE, CHOIR, CHURCH, CLERESTORY, CLOISTER, COLLEGIATE CHURCH, CROCKET, CROSSING, CRYPT, DOGTOOTH, FAN VAULT, FLÈCHE, FLYING BUTTRESS, GALILEE, GARGOYLE, LADY CHAPEL, LIERNE, MINSTER, MONASTERY, OGEE, ORIEL, PULPITUM, RETRO-CHOIR, ROSE WINDOW, SCISSOR ARCH, SPANDREL, SPIRE, STAINED GLASS, STEEPLE, STIFF-LEAF, TRACERY, TRANSEPT, TRIFORIUM, VAULT, WOOL CHURCH]

**161** *The fan vault of the Henry VII Chapel, Westminster Abbey, London. Note the pendants.*

## GOTHIC REVIVAL

With the advent of Renaissance style in the sixteenth and seventeenth centuries the native Gothic of the Middle Ages was almost totally eclipsed. The pointed arch was virtually extinct save in a few buildings, e.g. Christopher Wren's **St Mary Aldermary** of 1682 in the **City of London**, which belongs to what has been described as the 'Gothic Survival'.

The early eighteenth century marked the nadir for Gothic, although the style

*162 Royal Courts of Justice, London: one of the most impressive products of the Gothic Revival.*

was already being rediscovered in the form of Gothic follies in fashionable landscape gardens, e.g. **Alfred's Hall** of *c.* 1725 at **Cirencester Park**, *Glos.* The romantic spirit of the age even created 'mournful ruines' in order to stimulate poetic reveries, e.g. at **Hagley Hall**, *W Mids*, where in *c.* 1740 a picturesque ruin was built with stones plundered from Halesowen Abbey, *W Mids*. In the realm of architecture proper Horace Walpole's **Strawberry Hill House, Twickenham, London**, of 1748 was highly influential. Here the Gothic elements are decorative and two-dimensional rather like stage scenery,

## GOTHIC REVIVAL continued

but Strawberry Hill captured the mood of the times and gave its name to this playful start to the Gothic Revival. The eighteenth-century spelling 'Gothick' is still used to describe the phenomenon, examples of which include the interior of **St John the Evangelist, Shobdon,** *Heref & Worcs*, which was converted in the 'Gothick' manner in 1753 by Walpole's friend Lord Bateman. Sanderson Miller's work, e.g. at **Lacock Abbey**, *Wilts*, and James Wyatt's **Slane**

**Castle,** *Meath*, Ireland, are notable 'Gothick' creations of the late eighteenth century.

The full-blooded Gothic Revival of the nineteenth century was given a decisive stimulus by the rebuilding of the Houses of Parliament in the 1830s where the serious Gothic detailing was designed by A.W.N. Pugin (1812–52), the chief campaigner for the cause of Gothic architecture in the fight against Classical taste which was dubbed the Battle of the Styles. The main architects of the triumphant Gothic Revival, which held sway for the rest of

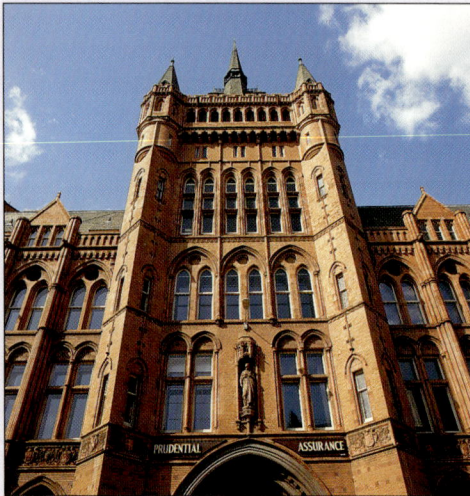

163 *The Prudential Assurance in Holborn, London, presents a fairytale façade to the street.*

164 *The Albert Memorial in Kensington Gardens, London, is a typically Victorian piece of Gothic Revival.*

## GOTHICK [see GOTHIC REVIVAL]

## GRANARY

Building for the storage of grain. Granaries were often raised structures, either lofts above a stable or barns resting on staddle stones. During the nineteenth century a new type of dockside granary was evolved which was in effect a multi-storey warehouse, e.g. the **Welsh Back Granary** of 1869 in **Bristol**, *Avon*.
[see BARN, GRANGE, STADDLE STONES]

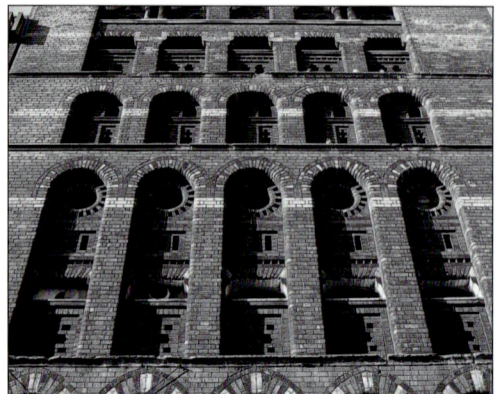

the century, were George Gilbert Scott (1811–78), George Edmund Street (1824–1881), Alfred Waterhouse (1830–1905), William Butterfield (1814–1900), William Burges (1827–81) and John Loughborough Pearson (1817–97). The major works of the Gothic Revival in London are Scott's **St Pancras Station** and **Albert Memorial**, Street's **Royal Courts of Justice** and Butterfield's **All Saints, Margaret Street**. Elsewhere, there are Waterhouse's **Manchester Town Hall**, Scott's **University of Glasgow**, Scotland, and a plethora of country houses, e.g. **Knightshayes Court**, *Devon*, by Burges. By the end of the nineteenth century, the mainstream of the Gothic Revival had run its course, but the occasional echo was still to be felt in the twentieth century, e.g. the **University Tower, Bristol**, *Avon*, of 1925. [see BATTLE OF THE STYLES, RUSKINIAN, 51, 268, 370]

**165** *St Pancras Station, London: a most intricate design. Among many other features note the dormer windows in the roof.*

## GRANGE

From the French '*grange*', meaning a barn. However, the word is now generally associated with a traditional type of rural residence consisting of a house with farm buildings attached. Many of the older granges were farming establishments which once belonged to a monastery.

**166** OPPOSITE *The Welsh Back Granary, Bristol, Avon, is reminiscent of an Italianate palazzo.*

## GRANITE

Extremely tough and durable igneous rock of crystalline structure containing quartz, felspar and mica, occurring in the upland areas of south-west England, Cumbria, Wales, Scotland and Ireland. Its chief properties as a building material are its resistance to water penetration and atmospheric pollution and its ability to take a high degree of polish.

Accordingly, it is used for cladding and decorative purposes, e.g. in memorials and

167 *A brave attempt to carve sculpture in granite on the church of St Mary Magdalene, Launceston, Cornwall.*

tombs. However, granite has been employed for a whole variety of purposes from field walls to churches. The traditional buildings of Cornwall are particularly noted for the ubiquitous use of granite, e.g. **St Mary Magdalene, Launceston**; **Godolphin House** and **Antony House**, as well as Celtic crosses and megalithic dolmens. At **Haytor** on **Dartmoor**, *Devon*, a novel railway was constructed out of granite blocks in the nineteenth century to facilitate the transport of granite from the local quarry. The colour of granite can vary from red and pink to green and grey depending on the felspar content. Grey granite has been used so extensively in **Aberdeen**, *Grampian*, Scotland, that it has been nicknamed 'Granite City'. Prominent use of granite is made in **London** along the **Embankme**nt. [see **138**]

**GREAT HALL** [see HALL]

**GREEK CROSS**
A cross in which all four arms are of equal length. Christopher Wren had hoped to build St Paul's Cathedral, London, in the plan of a Greek cross, but he was obliged by the Dean to revert to the more traditional form of the Latin cross. The original design was recorded in the form of the Great Model which is on display in the crypt of St Paul's. [see CRUCIFORM, LATIN CROSS]

**GREEK KEY** [see FRET]

## GREEK REVIVAL

As Neo-Classical architecture matured in the course of the eighteenth century, so there evolved a growing concern for its archaeological correctness. Of seminal importance was the rediscovery of the authentic buildings of ancient Greece from the impressive remains in southern Italy and Sicily as well as in Greece itself. Hitherto, Greek architecture had been considered an imperfect and primitive preliminary phase leading up to the later glories of the Roman era. A number of highly influential publications in the 1750s and 1760s, notably *The Antiquities of Athens* in 1762 by James Stuart and Nicholas Revett, argued convincingly that it was in fact in the buildings of the Greeks that the pure and true spirit of Classicism resided; and James 'Athenian' Stuart was among the first to provide examples of the Greek Revival, e.g. his **Doric Temple of**

**Theseus** at **Hagley Hall**, *W Mids*, in 1758.

Grecian temples rapidly became the height of fashion. In particular, replicas of the Athenian Tower of the Winds were adopted both as an eye-catcher, e.g. at **Shugborough**, *Staffs*, of 1764–70, and at **Mount Stewart**, *Down*, N. Ireland, of 1782–5, as well as the crowning feature of a larger building, e.g. the **Radcliffe Observatory, Oxford**, *Oxon* of 1772–94. The orders of Greek Doric and Ionic were assiduously applied to many a country house, court house, museum and art gallery. Among the most noted buildings of the Greek Revival are **St George's Hall, Liverpool**, *Mers*, of 1839–54, by Harvey Lonsdale Elmes; the **British Museum, London,** of 1823–47, by Robert and Sidney Smirke; **St Pancras New Church, London,** of 1819–22, by William and Henry William Inwood; **Manchester City Art Gallery** of

**168** *Mighty Greek Doric columns flank these modest front doors in Belgravia, London.*

**169** *All Saints, Camden Town, London: Classical steeple and portico. The order is Ionic.*

**GREEK REVIVAL continued**

1824–35 by Charles Barry; and **Belsay Hall**, *Northum* of 1806–17 by Charles Monck.

The most concentrated experience of the Greek Revival is to be had in **Edinburgh**, 'The Athens of the North', where an attempt was made to transform Calton Hill into a Scottish acropolis with such buildings as the **Royal High School** of 1825–9 and the **National Monument** of 1822. Other Greek Revival buildings in Edinburgh include **Customs House** of 1812, **Royal Scottish Academy** of 1822–6, **Edinburgh Academy** of 1822–36 and **Surgeon's Hall** of 1832. The Greek Revival lingered on longer in Scotland than elsewhere, especially in the **Glasgow** churches designed by Alexander 'Greek' Thomson, e.g. **St Vincent Street** of 1859. [see BATTLE OF THE STYLES, CARYATID, CLASSICAL, ORDER, TEMPLE, **94, 234**]

**170** *The Royal High School, Edinburgh, Scotland: note the triglyphs and metopes on the frieze.*

**171** OPPOSITE *University College, London. Note the colossal Corinthian order.*

## GROIN VAULT

The crossing of two barrel vaults at right angles produces a pattern of groins or angles. Also known as cross-vaulting. [see TUNNEL VAULT, VAULT, 333]

## GROTTO

The romantic idea of an artificial cave to suggest a hermit's retreat or the abode of a pagan deity caught on in the eighteenth century, as a popular feature of landscape gardens, e.g. at **Stourhead**, *Wilts*; **Stowe**, *Bucks*; **Goldney House**, Bristol, *Avon*. Grottoes were often encrusted with shells and enlivened with Classical sculpture. Alexander Pope's grotto at **Twickenham, London**, helped to spread the fashion.

172 *The grotto at Goldney House, Bristol,* Avon, *reflects the eighteenth-century taste for romantic settings.*

## GUILDHALL

Building in which the various medieval guilds met to regulate the affairs of their individual trades and professions. The term has come to be applied to the hall of a city corporation which assumed overall control of the guilds and hence of the commercial and civic interests of an entire city. Although the administrative functions of the guildhalls have long since passed to the local authorities in their town halls, many old guildhall buildings survive and still play a practical

**173** *The half-timbered Guildhall at Lavenham,* Suffolk, *dates back to the sixteenth century.*

role. **London's Guildhall** dates back to 1411, but much of its fabric is from the eighteenth century and later. **Exeter Guildhall**, *Devon*, ranks as the oldest municipal premises still functioning in Britain, with a history extending back to 1160, but the present hall was built in 1330 and has undergone a number of radical modifications. Also in Exeter, the Hall of the Weavers, Fullers and Shearmen of 1471, now known as the **Tuckers' Hall**, is less altered. The **Norwich Guildhall**, *Norfolk*, dates back to the fifteenth century. Four of York's guildhalls have survived, of which the most authentic is the **Merchant Adventurers' Hall** of the mid fourteenth century. Two remain in **Lavenham**, *Suffolk*; the one now known simply as the **Guildhall** of *c.* 1529 is a *tour de force* of medieval carpentry. There are several guildhalls in the Classical manner of the eighteenth century, e.g. at **High Wycombe**, *Bucks*; **Worcester**, *Heref & Worcs*; and **Bath**, *Avon*. The **Middlesex Guildhall** of 1906–13 in **Parliament Square, London**, is a Tudor revival structure housing the Middlesex Crown Court. [see MARKET HALL or HOUSE]

## GUILLOCHE

Decorative indentation on a moulding in a pattern of alternating circles and curves.

# H

**H-PLAN** [see E-PLAN]

## HA-HA

Device to separate the park or garden adjacent to a country house from the countryside and fields beyond. It consists of a sunken ditch with a vertical wall faced in stone providing an effective barrier to animal livestock. The advantage of the ha-ha over a conventional wall or fence is that it does not interrupt the sweeping view enjoyed from the house: the distant landscape appears to be an unbroken continuation of the garden. The term derives from the expression of sur-

## HALF-TIMBERING

Popular term for timber-framing, a method of construction whereby a building is supported by a framework of timber. The term 'half-timbering' refers back to the early medieval period when the timbers were formed by the halving of logs. A half-timbered structure was often built on a solid foundation of stone or brick. The timber framework was jointed together according to a standard plan. Usually the timbers were prefabricated at the carpenter's workshop and reassembled on site. All the various elements, i.e. the studs, posts, wall-plates and braces, took their stability from the sill or plate which was a baulk of timber laid horizontally on the foundation. Houses constructed in this way could be jacked up and moved on rollers. The Tudor historian, John Stow, recorded that his father's house in London was removed all of a piece a distance of 20 ft (6·1 m) by Thomas Cromwell, his neighbour in Throgmorton Street, who wished to extend his own garden. Half-timbered buildings could also be dismantled and rebuilt. The infill between the timbers could be lath and plaster, wattle and

bargeboard

post
brace

jetty

studs

nogging    cill or sill

prise occasioned by unexpectedly coming across a ha-ha.

## HAGIOSCOPE [see SQUINT]

## HALL

Also known as the great hall, this was the principal chamber of a medieval castle or manor house, e.g. the Norman hall of *c.* 1180 at **Oakham Castle**, *Leics.*

**Westminster Hall, London**, though rebuilt in the late fourteenth century, goes back to the eleventh-century Norman foundation of the Palace of Westminster. Originally a baronial hall was used for sleeping as well as eating, entertainment and ceremonial purposes; but it became increasingly common in late medieval times for the lord and his family to spend most of their time in

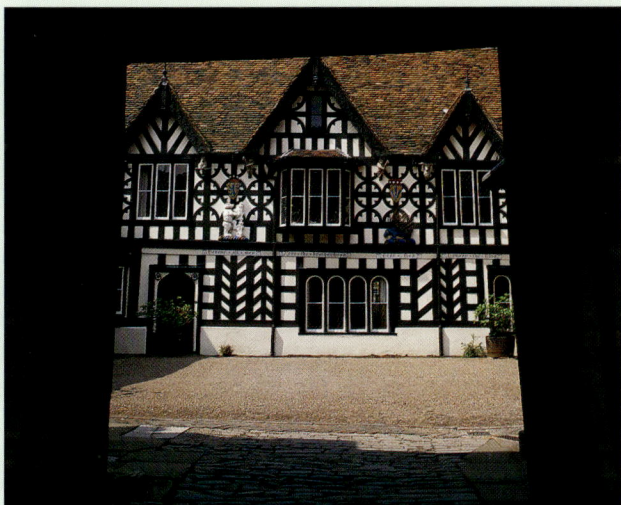

daub or brick nogging. Upper storeys were jettied out in an overhang. Exposed timbers could be carved to produce highly decorative ornamentation, e.g. at **Paycocke's, Coggeshall**, *Essex*. Half-timbering is generally associated with late medieval, Tudor and Jacobean times. A diminishing supply of timber, coupled with improved brick manufacture, contributed to the decline of half-timbering. Many fine examples survive in the Midlands and southern England. Excellent examples of original structures have been reconstructed at the **Avoncroft Museum of Building**, *Heref & Worcs*, and at the **Weald & Downland Open Air Museum**, *W Sussex*. [see BLACK AND WHITE WORK, CRUCK, JETTY, LATH, NOGGING, PARGETING, PLASTER, WATTLE AND DAUB, WEALDEN HOUSE, 125, 173, 215]

174 *The Lord Leycester Hospital* (ABOVE) *at Warwick*, Warw, *is a masterpiece of Tudor half-timbering.*
175 *The studs and jetties of the houses* (BELOW) *at Lavenham*, Suffolk, *create a bold decorative effect.*

**176** *The sixteenth-century Middle Temple Hall, London, has a magnificent double-hammerbeam roof.*

their private chamber or solar and even to take their meals in a room away from the rough communality of their household retainers in the hall. This trend was noted by William Langland in *Piers Plowman*: 'There in the hall the lord and lady liketh not to sit; now have the rich a rule to eat by themselves in a privy parlour'. An early example of this type of privy parlour may be seen at **Great Chalfield**, *Wilts*. The hall of an English noble residence was quite commonly, according to the early sixteenth-century account by Erasmus, an insanitary affair: 'strewed with rushes, beneath which lies an ancient collection of beer, grease, fragments, bones, spittle, excrement of dogs and cats, and everything that is nasty'. Nevertheless, the hall remained a prestigious setting with its carved screen, oak panels and painted beams, e.g. **Crosby Hall, London**; **Athelhampton House**, *Dorset*; **Cotehele**, *Cornwall*. The form of the hall was ideally suited to the colleges of Oxford and Cambridge, as it was to their legal counterparts in London, the Inns of Court, e.g. **Lincoln's Inn**, whose **Old Hall** dates back to 1490. The hall has since shrunk in importance as a feature of domestic architecture, and in a modern house the name denotes no more than a vestibule or passage. [see DAIS, GUILDHALL, SCREENS PASSAGE, SOLAR]

178 *The Old Hall of Lincoln's Inn, London, is a structure of red brick with white stone dressings.*

177 *Resplendent Crosby Hall in Chelsea, London, reflects the lifestyle of a wealthy medieval merchant.*

## HALL CHURCH

Type of church in which the nave and aisles are of the same height, e.g. the eastern part of the **Temple Church, London**, the enlarged chancel of 1240. The eastern end of **Bristol Cathedral**, *Avon*, of early fourteenth-century date, is a classic example of the hall church, described by Pevsner as being 'from the point of view of spatial imagination ... superior to anything else built in England and indeed in Europe at the same time'. The name and the form of the hall church are derived from the German *Hallenkirche*.

## HALL HOUSE

Medieval house consisting principally of a hall.

## HAMMERBEAM, HAMMERPOST

Horizontal wooden beam projecting from the top of the supporting wall which bears the weight of the roof rafters through arched braces. A hammerpost is a vertical timber at the inside end of the hammerbeam which supports a purlin. Where one hammerbeam carries a second hammerbeam, it is termed a double-hammerbeam, e.g. at **Middle Temple Hall, London**. [see TIMBER-TRUSSED ROOF, **176, 339**]

## HARLING

Scottish term for roughcast or pebbledash. [see ROUGHCAST]

## HATCHMENT

Panel, usually diamond-shaped, featuring the armorial bearings of the squire and hung in the church. [see ESCUTCHEON]

## HEADER [see BRICKWORK]

**179** *The hammerbeam roof in the Great Hall of Eltham Palace, London, was commissioned by Edward IV in 1479.*

## HELM

Type of roof surmounting a square tower, with four sloping faces descending from an apex to gables. Helms are more commonly found in Germany, but a rare example exists at the Saxon church of **St Mary, Sompting**, *W Sussex*. [see ROOF]

## HENGE

In the context of prehistoric archaeology, a uniquely British type of monument consisting of a circular space enclosed by a bank with an internal ditch. Stone circles are often found within a henge, e.g. at **Avebury** and **Stonehenge**, *Wilts*; and the **Ring of Brodgar, Orkney**, Scotland. [see STONE CIRCLE]

## HERM

Sculpture of a human head and torso emerging from a square, tapering

180 *One of the noble herms outside the Sheldonian Theatre in Oxford,* Oxon. *The carving is of recent date.*

pedestal, e.g. as garden statuary at **Chiswick House, London**, or on a chimneypiece as at **Hopetoun House**, *Lothian*, Scotland. Also known as a term, which may portray an animal or mythical being. [see ATLANTES, CARYATID, **76**]

## HERRINGBONE

Decorative arrangement of bricks, stones, tiles etc. laid diagonally in rows so that they meet those in the neighbouring rows to form a V-shaped angle.

## HEXASTYLE

A portico with six columns on its front elevation.

## HIBERNO-ROMANESQUE [see CELTIC, NORMAN]

## HIGH CROSS

The art of the high cross evolved most splendidly in tenth-century Ireland. Also known as the Celtic cross, it consisted of a tall, squarish shaft with a round head from which three short arms extended. The most ornate specimens, e.g. **Muiredach's Cross, Monasterboice**, *Louth*, and the **Cross of the Scriptures, Clonmacnoise**, *Offaly*, have a carving on every available space. The main purpose of such crosses was didactic, namely to illustrate stories from the Bible. They represent the chief artistic survival *in situ* of the early monasteries of Ireland. High crosses of simpler style exist in Cornwall, e.g. at **Sancreed** and **St Buryan**, as well as in Wales, e.g. the **Nevern Churchyard Cross** and the **Carew Cross**, *Dyfed*. The **Margam Stones Museum**, *W Glam*, contains an impressive collection of early crosses from various parts of Wales. In Scotland, the seventh-century **Ruthwell Cross**, *Dumfr & Gall*, is a masterpiece of Anglian art. During the Middle Ages the high cross evolved into an architectural monument in the Gothic

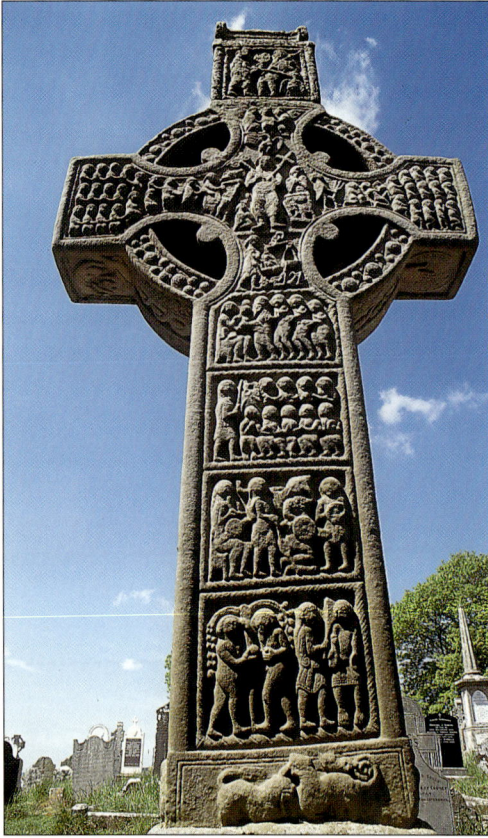

181 *Muiredach's Cross at Monasterboice*, Louth, *Ireland, shows the typical form of the Celtic high cross.*

182 *The High Tech Lloyd's Building in London displays a bold assortment of its functional components.*

style in which statues perched in canopied niches, e.g. the **Bristol High Cross**, which was removed to the landscape garden at **Stourhead**, *Wilts*, in 1765. [see CROSS PILLAR, ELEANOR CROSS, MARKET CROSS, **321**]

## HIGH-RISE [see STEEL-FRAME]

## HIGH TECH
Popular name for the futuristic style which first emerged in the 1970s and boomed in the 1980s. It celebrates the apparatus as well as the spirit of technology with a dramatic external display of naked engineering, e.g. the new **Lloyd's Building** of 1986 in **London** by Richard Rogers. The **Sainsbury Centre for Visual Arts,**

**Norwich**, *Norfolk*, of 1977 by Norman Foster first made an impact in Britain with the modern design technology that really constitutes the essence of High Tech rather than any specific architectural style.

## HILLFORT
Earthwork of prehistoric date built as a fortification around the summit of a hill by digging a series of ditches and ramparts. A hillfort can be univallate, bivallate or multivallate (from the Latin *'vallum'* meaning 'ditch') depending on the number of ditch-and-rampart combinations. The sites of some hillforts were previously occupied in the New Stone Age; but the most spectacular fortifica-

tions belong to the Iron Age. Dorset is the English county *par excellen*ce of the hillfort with such magnificent examples as **Maiden Castle** and **Hambledon Hill**. Some hillforts were reoccupied briefly in the immediate post-Roman era, e.g. **South Cadbury**, *Somerset*. **Old Sarum**, *Wilts*, housed a small township with castle and cathedral until the thirteenth century. But in general the hillforts of Britain have lain abandoned for almost two millennia, standing apart on their windswept uplands from the lowland sites favoured for subsequent settlement. [see EARTHWORK, PROMONTORY FORT, VITRIFIED FORT]

**183** *The Iron Age earthwork of Maiden Castle,* Dorset, *creates architecture out of the landscape itself.*

## HIPPED ROOF

Pitched roof with sloping gable ends. [see ROOF]

## HOOD-MOULD

Stone moulding above a window or doorway to channel off rainwater. Sometimes called a dripstone. A rectangular hood-mould may be called a label. [see LABEL STOP, RETURN, 67]

## HOSPITAL

In the Middle Ages the term denoted any charitable foundation for the care of the poor and infirm, e.g. an almshouse, school or institution for the sick. In modern usage, it is the last sense which has prevailed, although the name still adheres to

184 *The Old Operating Theatre in Southwark, London, shows the style of hospitals two centuries ago.*

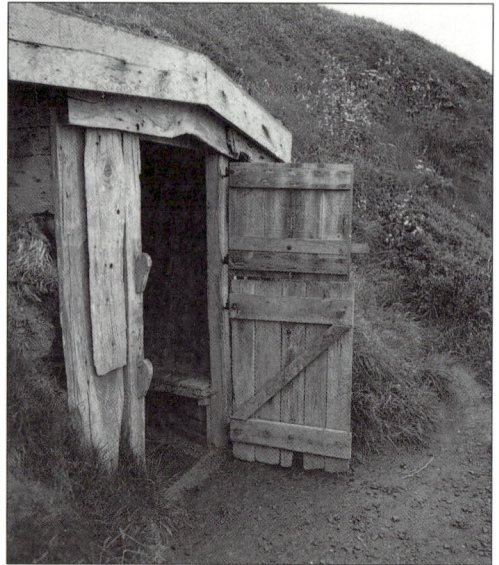

185 *Hawker's Hut at Morwenstow,* Cornwall: *even a simple structure can have architectural quality.*

many ancient foundations. The first purpose-built medical hospitals of the post-monastic era date from the eighteenth century; and some fine buildings have survived at **Guy's** and **St Bartholomew's Hospital, London**. The **Old Operating Theatre** at **Southwark, London** – once shared by the students of Guy's and St Thomas's – has survived intact and represents the primitive state of surgical practice in the early nineteenth century. The **Rotunda Hospital, Dublin**, Ireland, of 1751–5 was the first maternity hospital in the British Isles. During the Victorian era huge hospital establishments were built in every major town and city, most of which are still in service, e.g. **University College Hospital, London**, of 1897 by Alfred Waterhouse. [see ALMSHOUSE]

## HUT

In the context of prehistoric archaeology, the term is used to describe the simple dwellings now recognizable only from the traces of their foundations on the ground which are known as hut rings.

## HYPAETHRAL

Indicates that a building has no roof.

## HYPERBOLIC PARABOLOID [see ROOF]

## HYPOCAUST

Heated space beneath the floor of a Roman villa. The hot air circulated in the hypocaust before being drawn up through flues in the walls. A Roman hypocaust is exposed to view at **Chedworth Villa, Glos.** [see BATH HOUSE, ROMAN]

## HYPOSTYLE

Hall whose roof is supported by several rows of columns. **Westminster Hall, London**, was originally built in this manner, but it was remodelled at the end of the fourteenth century by the mason Henry Yevele and spanned by the hammerbeam roof of Hugh Herland which did not require any support from columns.

# I

## IMBRICATION

The term is derived from '*imbrex*' in Latin, i.e. a convex tile used for covering the joint between two adjacent roof tiles, which were usually of concave shape. It now means the arrangement of overlapping tiles.

186 *Iron Bridge at Coalbrookdale*, Shrops, *represents an early instance of industrialized building.*

## IMPOST

Stone which marks the point whence the arch springs. [see ARCH]

## INDENT

Recess carved out in a stone slab for the placing of a brass effigy. Indents are in evidence in many churches where the brasses have been removed. [see BRASSES]

## INDUSTRIALIZED BUILDING

Refers to the mass production of prefabricated building components for any type of structure, e.g. Abraham Darby's **Iron Bridge** at **Coalbrookdale**, *Shrops*, of

1779 whose parts were manufactured in a factory and assembled on site. Joseph Paxton's Crystal Palace for the Great Exhibition of 1851 in London demonstrated in most spectacular fashion that industrialized building was faster and cheaper than traditional methods. The firm of Thos. Cubitt, the builders of Belgravia and parts of Bloomsbury, London, brought the same approach to house construction in the early nineteenth century. Perhaps the ultimate in industrialized building was achieved by the crash building programme immediately after the Second World War (1939–45) when thousands of prefabricated homes were put up in record time. Some of these prefabs are still occupied. Nowadays, nearly all elements of a building are prefabricated; and there is an increasing trend to modular design based on units of standard dimensions, known as modules.

## INGLENOOK

Cosy niche or recess for a bench or seat forming an integral part of a fireplace.

## INN

Originally a hostelry built around a galleried courtyard, e.g. the **New Inn** at **Gloucester**, *Glos*, of 1457. Other fine medieval inns include the **Mermaid** of 1420 at **Rye**, *E Sussex*; the **George & Pilgrim's Inn, Glastonbury**, *Somerset*, of *c.* 1475 and the **George Inn** at **Norton St Philip**, *Somerset*. The Inns of Court in London owe their title to the fact that law students were once based in hostels known as inns, e.g. **Gray's Inn, Lincoln's Inn**. [see 148, 178]

## INTERLACE

Pattern created by intersecting lines.

## INTERSECTING TRACERY [see TRACERY]

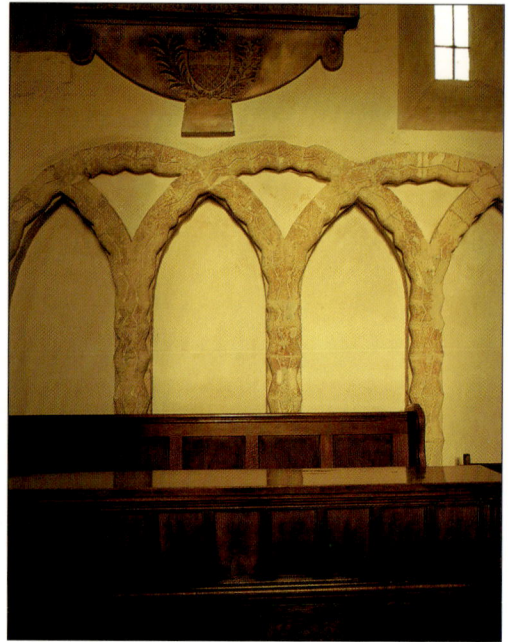

187 *Intersecting blind tracery in the church of St Mary, East Ham, London, creates a simple interlace pattern.*

## INTRADOS [see SOFFIT]

## IONIC ORDER [see ORDER]

## IRONWORK

Many examples of wrought iron, i.e. iron hammered into shape on an anvil, survive from the Middle Ages, ranging from bolts, hinges, knockers and grilles to the noble screen surrounding the tomb of Edward IV in **St George's Chapel, Windsor**, *Berks*. Decorative and structural use of wrought iron was greatly advanced in the seventeenth century in such guises as the staircase balustrade at the **Queen's House, Greenwich, London**, as well as in the inspired creations of Jean Tijou at **Hampton Court** and **St Paul's Cathedral, London**. The greater convenience of cast iron, i.e. molten iron poured into a mould,

188 OPPOSITE *The ironwork at Liverpool Street Station, London, makes architecture out of engineering.*

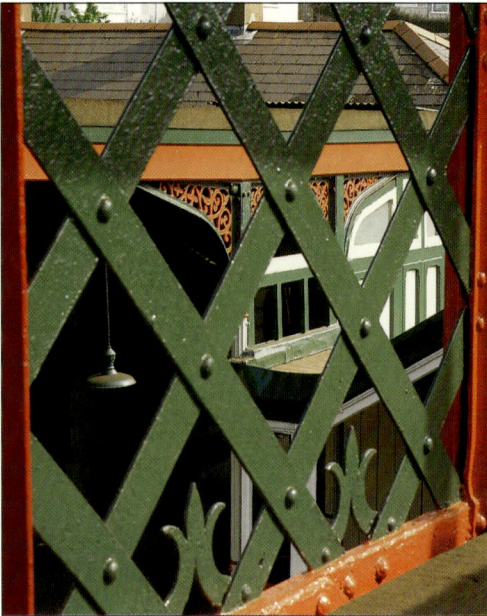

**189** *Torre Station in Torquay*, Devon, *makes an attractive use of painted ironwork and wood.*

recommended itself for a variety of purposes in the eighteenth and nineteenth centuries from balconies and fanlights to railings and canopies. As a building material combined with glass, a method sometimes described as ferrovitreous, iron made a substantial contribution to a new range of buildings such as railway stations and covered markets, conservatories and art galleries. Since it could be set in any given shape cast iron was often disguised, e.g. to resemble bamboo wood in a mock-Chinese staircase at the **Royal Pavilion, Brighton**, *E Sussex*, or Gothic columns and capitals at the **University Museum, Oxford**, *Oxon*. Iron also provided the structural support for the mills and warehouses of the Industrial Revolution and for the bridges of the railway era. From the 1890s steel came to replace iron as a structural material. [see BRIDGE, CONSERVATORY, COVERED MARKET, GATE, GLASS, RAILINGS, STATION, STEEL-FRAME, **186, 220, 243**]

## ISLAMIC

Islamic architecture made a significant impact on European architecture in the immediate aftermath of the Crusades and not just in the design of castles. The pointed arch, the hallmark of the Gothic style, probably originated in the Orient. However, it was not until the eighteenth century that travellers to the Near East and India consciously tried to imitate at home buildings which they had admired on their travels. Parodies of India's Islamic

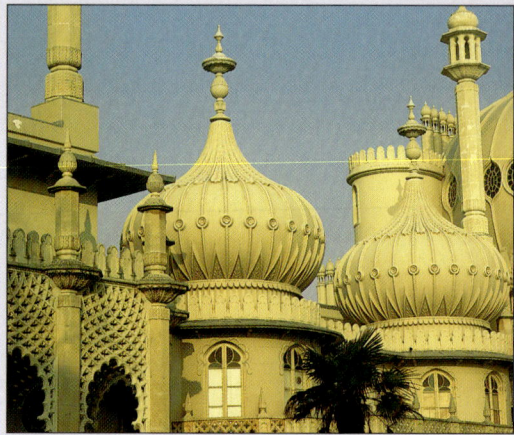

**190** *The domes of the Royal Pavilion, Brighton, E Sussex, were inspired by the Islamic style of India.*

## ITALIANATE

Term indicating that a building is in the Italian manner, usually because it has borrowed some of the features of Renaissance Italy, e.g. **Osborne House**, *Isle of Wight*. An entire Italianate village, modelled on Portofino, was created at **Portmeirion**, *Gwynedd*, Wales, from 1925 by the Welsh architect Clough Williams-Ellis. [see CLASSICISM, PALLADIANISM, **37, 166**]

**192** *The underpass* (RIGHT) *at the High Level Station at Crystal Palace, London, was built by Italian craftsmen.*
**193** *The Italianate villa* (FAR RIGHT) *in Park Village, London, was part of Nash's Regent's Park scheme.*

buildings, e.g. **Sezincote House**, *Glos*, were erroneously styled as 'Hindoo'. In Ireland, the gatehouse of **Dromana House**, *Waterford*, of 1840 was inspired by the same source. Since the underlying spirit and principles of Islamic architecture were not properly understood – and there was no Oriental Palladio available in translation to spell them out – British versions of Islamic style were pastiches composed of the most obvious external features, e.g. onion-shaped domes and cusped arches. The nineteenth-century taste for the exotic found many pleasing elements in Islamic design, and there resulted some striking creations, e.g. the **Arab Hall** at **Leighton House, Kensington, London**, of 1879; another **Arab Room** of 1880 within **Cardiff Castle**, *S Glam*, Wales; and the **Moorish Staircase** at **Kilkenny Castle**, *Kilkenny*, Ireland. In the early twentieth century a fanciful Hollywood version of Islamic, derived largely from the romantic vision of the Al Hambra in southern Spain, left its mark on some outlandish interiors, e.g. the **Tooting Granada** of the 1920s in **London**. [see MOSQUE, ORIENTALISM]

**191** *The Arab Room at Cardiff Castle, S Glam, Wales, is an attempt to reproduce the effect of an Islamic ceiling.*

# J

## JACOBEAN

The brief reign of James I (1603–25) gave its name to an architectural style, which although it was in many respects a continuation of the Elizabethan style, did add its own distinctive contribution. Increasingly, Classical motifs came to grace sumptuous entrance porches and noble carved screens and doorways. The strapwork of plaster ceilings became more elaborate, while exotic-looking Dutch gables created fanciful façades,

194 *Charlton House, Greenwich, London, of 1612 is a fine Jacobean mansion with a prominent porch.*

often surmounted by pepper-pot turrets, to create the essential image of the great Jacobean mansions, e.g. **Hatfield House**, *Herts*, of 1607–11; **Blickling Hall**, *Norfolk*, of 1619–25; **Charlton House, Greenwich, London**, of 1607–12; **Aston Hall, Birmingham**, *W Mids*, of 1618–35. **Audley End**, *Essex*, was built by Thomas Howard from 1605 to receive James I and his queen; the surviving Jacobean parts – the north porch and the great hall with its strikingly carved screen – are palatial indeed. A most intriguing Jacobean creation was Charles Cavendish's **Bolsover Castle**, *Derbys*, of 1612–21, a fairytale mansion which looks back to the Middle Ages while

## JACOBETHAN

Word invented to describe the curious fusion of Jacobean and Elizabethan styles which were mixed and adapted in

various hybrid nineteenth-century revivals such as **Harlaxton Manor, Lincs**, of 1831–55 by Anthony Salvin and the **Town Hall, Oxford**, *Oxon*, of 1893–7 by Henry T. Hare. The term is rarely encountered except in the commentaries of a few architectural writers.

195 *Queen's House, Greenwich, London: Jacobean in date but not of typical Jacobean appearance. The Palladian influence is clear.*

196 *The plaster ceiling in Prince Henry's Room, London, displays the intricate strapwork that was popular in the Jacobean period.*

embracing much of the spirit of the Renaissance.

The Jacobean era marked a watershed in British architecture. Half-timbered houses in the Elizabethan mode were still being built, e.g. **Prince Henry's Room** of 1610 in **Fleet Street, London;** but already the first strict essays in the austere Palladian style were being designed by Inigo Jones, e.g. the **Queen's House, Greenwich, London**, from 1616 and the **Banqueting House, Whitehall, London**, of 1619–22.

In both these buildings Inigo Jones demonstrated a pure Classicism far ahead of his time which contrasted sharply with the more casual use of Mannerist motifs which are the hallmark of most Jacobean buildings. Also epoch-making was Inigo Jones's Classical church of **St Paul** and the adjacent piazza of 1631–3 at **Covent Garden, London**, which introduced the formal square as the new model for urban planning. However, the exuberance and invention of the Jacobean era were to be overshadowed by the looming conflict between Crown and Parliament during the reign of Charles I and the outbreak of the Civil War in 1642. [see ELIZABETHAN, JACOBETHAN, MANNERISM, PALLADIANISM, RENAISSANCE]

## JAMB

The vertical sides of a window or doorway. The exposed external part of the jamb is known as a reveal. In Georgian terrace architecture the reveal is sometimes rendered and painted in a light colour. This can he highly decorative when an entire street of houses catches the oblique rays of the sun, e.g. in some of the squares of **Dublin**, Ireland.

## JESSE WINDOW

Church window in which the tracery represents the spreading branches of the Tree of Jesse, which is a symbol of the genealogical tree of Christ's ancestors. There is a fine fourteenth-century Jesse window at **Dorchester Abbey**, *Oxon*; and at **Waltham Abbey**, *Essex*, one of 1861 by the Pre-Raphaelite artist Edward Burne-Jones.

## JETTY

1) Projecting upper storey of a half-timbered building. This device provided

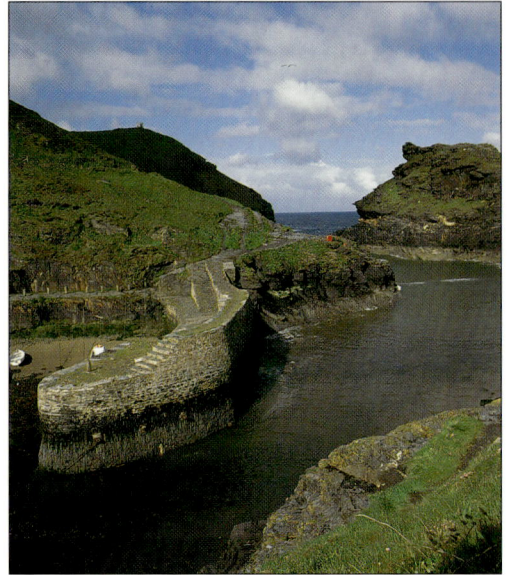

**198** *Even a sea wall can have architectural merit such as the jetty at Boscastle*, Cornwall, *built in the 1580s.*

extra floorspace, protected the lower part of the building from rain and also contributed to the cohesion and stability of the structure. [see HALF-TIMBERING, **377**]

2) Pier protecting a harbour.

## JIB DOOR

Concealed door, usually in a stately apartment, which is discreetly disguised to match the wallpaper or other decoration.

## JOGGLE OR JOGGING

Mason's device for preventing two stones from slipping against one another by means of a groove in one stone corresponding to a projection in the other. When not exposed to view, it is known as a secret joggle.

## JOISTS

Parallel timbers laid horizontally to support the floorboards of a room. Their underside can be left visible as a ceiling feature in the room below.

**197** *The long jetty of these buildings in Ledbury,* Heref & Worcs, *creates an interesting streetscape.*

# K

## KEEL
Moulding resembling in section the profile of a ship's keel. [see MOULDING]

## KEEP
Central stronghold of a castle where the lord 'kept' or lodged. The characteristic square tower-keep of the Normans may be seen at **Rochester Castle**, *Kent*; **Castle**

*199 The White Tower, keep of the Tower of London.*

Hedingham, *Essex*, and the **Tower of London**. Round keeps feature at **Conisbrough Castle**, *S Yorks*, and **Orford Castle**, *Suffolk*. [see CASTLE, DONJON, TOWER HOUSE, 62]

**KENTISH RAGSTONE** [see RAGSTONE]

**KENTISH TRACERY** [see TRACERY]

**KEY PATTERN** [see FRET]

## KEYSTONE
Central stone of an arch which may be given prominence by being made larger or projected. [see ARCH, GIBBS SURROUND]

## KILN
Structure containing a furnace or oven for burning lime, baking bricks or firing pottery. It evolved its round, tapering shape, aptly known as the bottle-oven, in the potteries district of Staffordshire, e.g. at the **Gladstone Pottery Museum, Longton, Stoke-on-Trent**, *Staffs.*

## KING POST
Vertical timber in a central position on a tie-beam or collar beam which supports the ridge at the apex of the roof. [see QUEEN POSTS, TIMBER-TRUSSED ROOF]

## KIOSK
Small pavilion of Oriental origin, characterized by a tent-like roof which has been adapted for structures such as a summerhouse or bandstand. The term is also used to describe small shops selling over the counter, even when these are no longer housed in a kiosk-like structure. [see PAVILION, TELEPHONE KIOSK]

## KIRK
Scottish term for church.

**200** *Scottish kirk at Staffin, Isle of Skye.*

## KITCHEN
The kitchen lay at the heart of daily life in a medieval castle. Huge open fireplaces large enough to roast an ox on a spit were not uncommon. Some medieval kitchens were located in a building of their own, e.g at the fourteenth-century manor house of **Stanton Harcourt**, *Oxon*, and the **Abbot's Kitchen** at **Glastonbury Abbey**, *Somerset*. A most evocative late-medieval kitchen has been preserved at **Gainsborough Old Hall**, *Lincs*. The kitchen at **Warkworth Castle**, *Northum*, was a model of culinary convenience in the fifteenth century. The cavernous kitchen at **Burghley House**, *Cambs*, shows the palatial lifestyle of a Tudor grandee in the sixteenth century. Thereafter, the kitchen evolved to accommodate the introduction of built-in cooking ranges. Occasionally, the kitchen of a grand establishment received special architectural treatment, e.g. at the **Royal Pavilion, Brighton**, *E Sussex*, where an exotic interior is dominated by four lofty iron columns disguised as palm trees.

## KNAPPED FLINT [see FLINT]

## KNEELER
Stone block mounted on the top of a wall or at the base of a gable. Also known as a kneestone, padstone, skew or template.

## KNEESTONE [see KNEELER]

## KURSAAL
The German word for a building or assembly room used by the visitors at a health resort. It has been borrowed in English to denote a casino or ballroom, usually at a seaside resort. [see ASSEMBLY ROOMS]

**201** OPPOSITE *The finely constructed medieval kitchens of Warkworth Castle, Northum, as they appear today.*

# L

## LABEL [see HOOD-MOULD]

## LABEL STOP
Decorative boss to mark the end of a hood-mould. [see HOOD-MOULD]

## LACED WINDOWS
Visual device to enhance the alignment of a series of windows on a façade by vertical parallel lines of bricks of a contrasting colour. This enjoyed limited popularity in England in the early eighteenth century.

## LADY CHAPEL
Chapel dedicated to the Blessed Virgin who was more familiarly known as Our Lady. Such chapels were usually prominent extensions to the east end of the chancel. In most cathedrals the Lady Chapel amounts to a church within the church, e.g. at **Bristol**, *Avon*; **Chester**, *Cheshire*; **Chichester**, *W Sussex*; **Exeter**, *Devon*; **Gloucester**, *Glos*; **Lichfield**, *Staffs*; **Salisbury**, *Wilts*; **Winchester**, *Hants*, and **Worcester**, *Heref & Worcs*. At **Ely**, *Cambs*, the Lady Chapel is located in a separate but linked building to the north of the cathedral. At **Durham**, *Durham*, the Lady Chapel is the Galilee at the west end.

## LAMP POST
The architectural treatment of lamp posts as an aesthetic contribution to the streetscape became widespread from the late eighteenth and early nineteenth centuries. As the Classical constraints of the Georgian era receded so there appeared some more florid Victorian designs, none more elaborate than that on the **Chelsea Embankment, London**, a dynamic piece of sculpture depicting two boys climbing

202 *Dolphin lamp post on the Embankment, London.*

the column of the lamp post which is rendered dramatic by spiral fluting and a horn of plenty disgorging its fruits. The ultimate in urban style was achieved by the installation in the 1870s of the rows of lamp posts adorned with dolphins along the **Embankment** in **London**.

## LANCET
Slender, pointed shape of arch or window which was the hallmark of the Early English phase of Gothic. Also known as an acute arch. [see ARCH, GOTHIC]

## LANTERN
Circular or polygonal structure on a roof or dome for the admittance of air and light. The lantern could be an important architectural feature, e.g. the great octagonal lantern of **Ely Cathedral**, *Cambs*,

built after the collapse of the crossing tower in 1322. [see 112]

## LATH
Thin strip of wood used for anchoring slates on a roof, or in combination with plaster to form a wall or ceiling of the type known as lath and plaster. [see LATTICE]

## LATIN CROSS
Cross consisting of one long and three short arms. [see CRUCIFORM, GREEK CROSS]

## LATTICE
Composition of diagonally intersecting laths to create a screen, usually in a garden. It also describes any pattern of dia-

203 *Leaded lights at Little Moreton Hall,* Cheshire.

mond shapes, e.g. a lattice window. [see LATH, 380]

## LAVABO or LAVATORIUM
The washing place in a medieval monastery, sometimes distinguished by special architectural treatment, e.g. at the Benedictine abbey (now the cathedral) at **Gloucester**, *Glos*, where the lavatorium is located in the fan-vaulted cloister; and at the Cistercian **Mellifont Abbey**, *Louth*, Ireland, where there is the ruin of an octagonal lavabo dating back to *c.* 1200. [see MONASTERY]

## LEADED LIGHT
Window consisting of small panes of glass held together by lead cames in lieu of glazing bars. A feature of Tudor and

mock Tudor. [see CAME, GLAZING BARS, WINDOW]

## LEAF AND DART
Convex moulding bearing alternating shapes resembling a leaf and a dart. [see MOULDING]

## LEAN-TO
Structure leaning for support on a larger one, e.g. an ancillary farm building.

## LEPER WINDOW [see LOWSIDE WINDOW]

## LESENE
Decoration consisting of a narrow, flat, raised band, known also as a pilaster-strip, which is characteristic of Saxon church exteriors e.g. **All Saints, Earl's Barton**, *Northants*, and **St Mary, Sompting** and **St Nicholas, Worth**, *W Sussex*. [see SAXON]

## LEVELLING COURSE
Course of brickwork which defines a horizontal level in a rubblestone wall. [see OPUS LISTATUM]

*204 The levelling courses in this fragment of Roman wall on Tower Hill, London, are clearly visible.*

## LIBRARY

The earliest collections of books and manuscripts belonged to the great monasteries of the Middle Ages. However, the oldest purpose-built library is reckoned to be that of **Merton College, Oxford**, *Oxon*, which dates back to 1373–8, although it underwent an internal refitting in 1623. It was built on the first floor to protect the books from rising damp. **Duke Humfrey's Library**, part of the Bodleian Library in Oxford, was built above the Divinity School in 1488, and was remodelled from 1598 by Thomas Bodley. Its layout of a long gallery with bookcases positioned at right angles, to form secluded bays with writing desks, remained the prototype for college libraries for several centuries. The **Chained Library** at **Hereford Cathedral**, *Heref & Worcs*, contains the largest num-

*205 Marsh's Library, Dublin, Ireland, was designed as a working library to house as many books as possible.*

**206** *The sumptuous library at Kenwood, London, by Robert Adam appears to be more concerned with putting on a fine show than with housing books.*

ber of ancient volumes still chained to their oak bookcases, a medieval security device.

Classical architecture made a powerful impact on the design of libraries. One of the first was the stately library of 1695 at the **Queen's College, Oxford**. **Marsh's Library, Dublin**, of 1701 was Ireland's first public library; it has retained its authentic fittings and fixtures of the period, e.g. cage-like compartments in which the reader would be locked while studying. **Trinity College Library** of 1719–32, also in Dublin, contains a magnificent Long Room some 209 feet (63·7 m) in length. Magnificent private libraries became a standard feature of the new generation of country houses in the Classical style of the eighteenth century, e.g. at **Kenwood, London**, designed by Robert Adam. The library at **Downhill**, *Derry*, N. Ireland was lodged in a spectacular rotunda called the **Mussenden Temple**. The form of the rotunda was also used for the **Radcliffe Camera, Oxford**, of 1737–49 by James Gibbs,

which is part of the Bodleian Library. The **Signet Library, Edinburgh**, Scotland, designed by William Playfair in 1819 and modified by William Burn in 1833, consists of two principal rooms, one above the other, linked by a grand staircase; the **Upper Library** is among the most splendid Neo-Classical interiors in the British Isles. The **Round Reading Room** at the **British Museum, London**, of 1852–7 was designed by Sydney Smirke. The Gothic Revival is best represented by the **John Rylands Library, Manchester**, of 1890–9 by Basil Champneys.

The Edwardian era witnessed a proliferation of public libraries which were generally imposing in style. Grand visions of the library continued into the 1920s and 1930s, e.g. **Manchester City Library** by E. Vincent Harris and the **Cambridge University Library** by Giles Gilbert Scott. The **University Library, Edinburgh**, Scotland, by Basil Spence was a significant contribution of the 1960s. The new **British Library** of the 1990s at **St Pancras, London**, by Colin St John Wilson has been described by the Prince of Wales as 'a dim collection of brick sheds groping for some symbolic significance'. In truth, this building lays greater stress and importance on its internal technology than on external display. [see CARREL, **307**]

207 *The nave vault of Winchester Cathedral*, Hants, *is like a web with small liernes linking ribs and tiercerons.*

## LIERNE

Tertiary rib in a vault, i.e. one which links ribs other than the main springers or the central boss. A lierne vault is one which makes use of liernes as a stylistic device, e.g. in the presbytery of **Ely Cathedral**, *Cambs*, and the nave of **Winchester Cathedral**, *Hants*. [see FAN VAULT, TIERCERON, VAULT]

## LIGHT

Denotes the space between the mullions of a window. Thus it is possible to refer to a window having a number of separate lights. [see MULLION WINDOW]

## LIGHTHOUSE

The idea of erecting lights or beacons to provide a landmark for shipping was introduced to Britain by the Romans, e.g. the **Pharos** at **Dover Castle**, *Kent*. During the Middle Ages such navigation

**208** *Smeaton's Tower, Plymouth,* Devon, *set the style for modern lighthouse design over two centuries ago.*

lights were usually mounted on a church tower, e.g. at **St Nicholas** on **Lantern Hill, llfracombe,** *Devon,* to mark the narrow harbour entrance. It was not until the eighteenth century that a purpose-built lighthouse prototype was developed. Most influential was John Smeaton's lighthouse of 1756–9, on the dangerous Eddystone Rocks off the south Devon coast. This pioneered the characteristic tapering shape and the practice of pegging the foundation stones together in order to withstand the constant pounding of the ocean. **Smeaton's Tower** was re-erected in 1884 on **Plymouth Hoe,** *Devon,* when it became due for replacement. There are many lighthouses around the coasts of the British Isles from **Muckle Fluga** on **Shetland,** Scotland, to the **Bishop's Rock** off the **Isles of Scilly**.

## LIMESTONE

Sedimentary type of rock which provides a diverse range of fine building stones. The Jurassic limestone belt in England extends in a broad curve from Yorkshire in the north-east down to Dorset in the south-west, with various outliers in the west such as the Cotswold Hills. There are many subtle regional variations, from the honey-coloured Bath stone and the golden limestone quarried at **Ham Hill,** *Somerset,* to the bleached white of the **Isle of Portland,** *Dorset,* and the greyish tones of the Blue Lias so powerfully in evidence at **Somerton,** *Somerset.* The finest limestones are known as oolites (hence the adjective 'oolitic') on account of their rounded granular structure resembling fish eggs, e.g. Ketton stone which was much used in the colleges of **Cambridge,** *Cambs.* The most widely used of the oolites is Portland stone which is both durable and easy to carve. The mountain limestones of northern England have created a distinctive regional identity in many towns and villages. Subterranean limestone quarries may be visited at **Beer,** *Devon,* and at **Corsham,** *Wilts.* [see CAEN STONE, FLAGSTONE, FREESTONE, MARBLE, RAGSTONE]

## LINENFOLD [see PANELLING]

## LINTEL

Horizontal piece of stone or wood which bridges the opening for a door or window. The lintel is characteristic of Classical architecture and megalithic building. [see TRABEATED, **138**]

## LISTEL [see FILLET]

## LODGE

1) During the Middle Ages the word denoted a temporary structure adjacent to a building under construction. This was

**209** *The hunting lodge could be a magnificent affair as in the case of Kinloch Castle, Isle of Rhum, Scotland.*

usually a hut in which the masons carried out part of their work, stored the tools and instruments of their trade and took their meal breaks. In the course of time the masons' lodge at a major project such as a cathedral, where the work continued for several generations, became an important institution which regulated the administrative aspects of masonry.

2) Nowadays, the word 'lodge' is more commonly associated with a small dwelling serving as a gatehouse located at the entrance to a country estate. Such lodges are often given special architectural treatment in line with the style of the great house inside the gates, e.g. a

210 *Queen Elizabeth's Hunting Lodge at Chingford,* Essex, *was built high to provide a grandstand view.*

miniature castle for a Baronial mansion or a small temple for a Neo-Classical residence. Occasionally, the lodge may be a cottage orné, or even something approaching a folly, e.g. at **Rushton**, *Northants*, where the lodge of the 1590s is a unique triangular structure symbolizing the Holy Trinity. **Rendlesham Hall,** *Suffolk*, has an impressive castellated lodge in the Gothic style complete with a crown formed by flying buttresses. [see GATEHOUSE ]

3) The word is also used in the sense of a hunting lodge to accommodate sporting guests. **Queen Elizabeth's Hunting Lodge** at **Chingford**, *Essex*, which dates back in fact to the reign of Henry VIII, was sited in order for the monarch to enjoy a view of the hunt in progress. Some more recent hunting lodges are veritable mansions, e.g. the Edwardian **Kinloch Castle,** on the **Isle of Rhum**, Scotland.

## LOFT
An upper room over a stable for the storage of hay or the space immediately

below the roof of a church tower or house. [see ATTIC]

## LOGGIA
A feature of Renaissance architecture consisting of a gallery open on at least one side and usually colonnaded. An early use of the loggia was by Inigo Jones *c.* 1616 at the **Queen's House, Greenwich, London**. [see BALCONY]

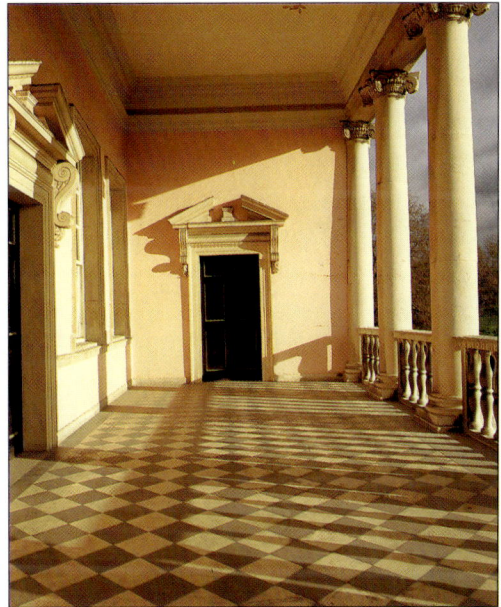

211 *Loggia of the Queen's House, Greenwich, London.*

## LONG AND SHORT WORK
Saxon method of arranging quoins as alternating long and short stones, e.g. on the church tower at **St Mary, Deerhurst**, *Glos.* [see QUOIN, SAXON]

## LONG BARROW [see BARROW]

## LONGHOUSE
The switch from the native round house of the Celts to the rectangular longhouse may have been the result of Norse influence. At any rate, the longitudinal plan

212 *Cratloe Woods House*, Clare, *Ireland, is a long house on the grand scale. The projecting element of the dwelling is small, hardly amounting to a wing.*

just one room deep and with the byre attached remained until very recently the most common type of rural dwelling in Ireland and western Scotland. The longhouse principle on a grander scale may be seen at **Cratloe Woods House**, *Clare*, Ireland, of the seventeenth century. [see BYRE, BLACK HOUSE, CROFT]

## LOOP [see ARROW LOOP]

## LOUVRE
Aperture in the roof of a medieval hall, usually crowned by a turret with slanting slates on the sides, to allow smoke to escape from a hearth below. Even when a fireplace with flues is installed a louvre provides useful ventilation.

## LOWSIDE WINDOW
A small window, occasionally found in a parish church in the south wall of the chancel, which appears to have been intended to permit outsiders to observe the officiating priest. It is thought that this was for the convenience of lepers – hence the alternative term of leper window – but this interpretation is uncertain.

## LOZENGE
Diamond-shaped segment, e.g. of a window. [see LEADED LIGHT]

## LUCARNE [see DORMER]

## LUNETTE
Semicircular opening or flat surface. [see TYMPANUM]

## LYCH GATE
Covered wooden gateway, usually open-sided, at the entrance to a churchyard and used as a resting place for the coffin: '*lych*' was the Saxon word for corpse. The lych gate is still a feature of many parish churches, e.g. at **St George, Beckenham,** *Kent,* **All Saints, Wing,** *Bucks.*

# M

## MACHICOLATION

Defensive contrivance of medieval castles and fortified houses, consisting of a projecting parapet with openings in the floor through which missiles, quicklime or boiling pitch could be dropped on any assailants, e.g. at **Guy's Tower, Warwick Castle,** *Warw.* [see BATTLEMENT, CASTLE, 152]

## MANNERISM

Loose and unconventional imitation of the appearance or manner of Classical architecture. Mannerism is also associated with the carefree Elizabethan and Jacobean handling of Classical motifs. [see ELIZABETHAN, JACOBEAN, RENAISSANCE]

*214 County Hall, London. Mannerism was also a strong feature of Edwardian Baroque.*

## MANOR HOUSE

Residence of the lord of the manor in medieval times under the feudal system. Manor houses in England abandoned serious defensive arrangements around the

*213 Athelhampton, Dorset: this medieval manor house has mock battlements but it is essentially undefended.*

215 *The manor house of Lower Brockhampton,* Heref & Worcs. *The smaller structure is the gatehouse.*

beginning of the fifteenth century, but many retained a token display of martial strength. In the course of time manor houses were overtaken in importance by the new country houses of the landed gentry. Among the earliest manor houses is the stone structure of Norman vintage at **Boothby Pagnell**, *Lincs*. Fine fifteenth-century examples include **Cotehele**, *Cornwall*; **Great Chalfield**, *Wilts*; and **Lower Brockhampton**, *Heref & Worcs*. Most manor houses were extensively rebuilt in the sixteenth century. In Scotland the tower house remained the favoured residence of the lairds. [see 363]

## MANSARD ROOF
Named after the French architect François Mansart, this form of roof is in two parts,

the lower part being longer and steeper than the upper part. The mansard usually has dormers or lucarnes. [see ROOF]

## MANSE
Residence of a minister of religion, especially of the Scottish Presbyterian Church.

## MANSION
A residence of substance and quality. The **Mansion House** in the **City of London** is the official home of the Lord Mayor.

## MANSION BLOCK [see APARTMENT HOUSE]

## MANTELPIECE [see CHIMNEYPIECE]

## MAQSURA [see MOSQUE]

## MARBLE
Metamorphic crystalline form of limestone. True marble occurs on Iona and

216 *The Marble Arch, London, originally stood in front of Buckingham Palace. Note the Roman-style carving.*

Skye in Scotland as well as in Connemara, *Galway*, Ireland; but Purbeck marble from Dorset is technically a misnomer, since it is merely a hard limestone capable of a high degree of polish. Purbeck marble makes a dramatic appearance in **Salisbury Cathedral**, *Wilts*, in the columns of the arcades, and it was shipped as far afield as **Beverley Minster**, *Humbs*. Lesser-known English 'marbles' include Derbyshire Fossil, Ashford Black, Hopton Wood, Bethersden and Sussex. **London's Marble Arch** is made from Italian marble quarried at Seravezza; and Italy has been the main source for most of the true marble used in the British Isles.

## MARKET CROSS

In the Middle Ages the market-place of a town was distinguished by a prominent cross of carved stone, known in Scotland as the mercat cross. Often the cross itself was but a small finial on the top of an imposing Gothic monument, which sometimes took the form of an open-sided structure beneath which it was possible to shelter from the rain, e.g. at **Malmesbury**, *Wilts*, and **Chichester**, *W Sussex*. The Scottish mercat cross, e.g. at **Prestonpans**, *Lothian*, and **Culross**, *Fife*, was often a simple column bearing a heraldic sculpture such as a unicorn. [see ELEANOR CROSS, HIGH CROSS]

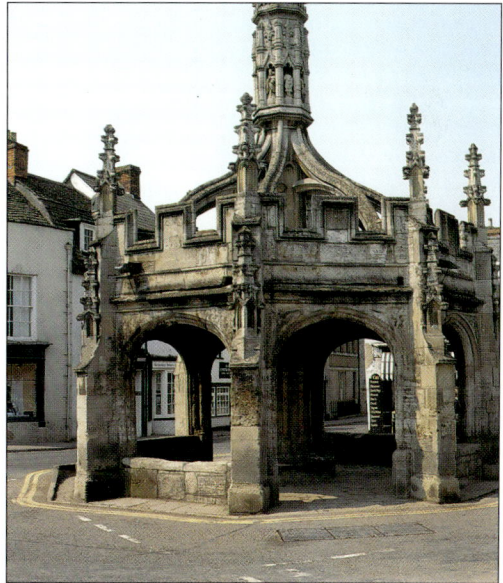

217 *The medieval market cross at Malmesbury*, Wilts, *is a Gothic structure which serves as a shelter.*

## MARKET HALL or HOUSE

Structure of wood or stone providing beneath a main room on the upper storey a covered space at ground-floor level open to the street via an arcade or colonnade, e.g. at **Shrewsbury**, *Shrops*, and **Rothwell**, *Northants*, both of Elizabethan date. The half-timbered market house at **Ledbury**, *Heref & Worcs*, of 1633 is supported by sixteen oak pillars. That at **Tetbury**, *Glos*, built in *c.* 1700 sits on a colonnade of robust stone columns. Many such structures still shelter the local markets. [see COVERED MARKET]

## MARTELLO TOWER

Type of coastal fortification consisting of a sturdy three-storey round tower some 26ft (7·9m) in diameter and with guns mounted on its flat roof. Martello towers were built from 1804 in great numbers, mainly along the south coast of England, in response to the perceived threat of a Napoleonic invasion. The form and the name of the Martello were derived from a French prototype on Mortella Point on Corsica. So urgent was the need for strengthening coastal defences that seventy-four Martello towers were built in Kent and Sussex alone, many of which have survived, e.g. at **Dymchurch**, *Kent*, and at **Eastbourne**, *E Sussex*. Martello towers were also built in the Channel Isles; and there are several in Ireland, including one at **Sandycove** near **Dublin,** once occupied by James Joyce. The Martello towers on the **Orkney** island of **Hoy**, Scotland, were actually built as a defence not against the French but

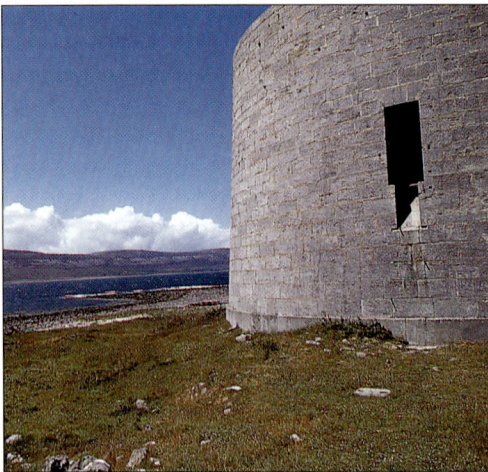

**218** *A martello tower on the coast of* Clare, *Ireland, typical of many built elsewhere in the British Isles.*

against the United States which declared war on Britain in 1812 as a result of British harassment of American ships trading with Napoleon's allies. [see FORT]

## MASK STOP [see STOP]

## MASONRY

The term embraces all that is involved in the art and craft of stone construction and decoration, from cutting in the quarry to carving in the workshop as well as the finished product. [see ASHLAR, BOASTED WORK, CAEN STONE, CAPSTONE, CHEQUER-WORK, CHERT, CORNERSTONE, COURSE, CYCLOPEAN, DIAPER WORK, DRESSINGS, DRYSTONE, FLAGSTONE, FLINT, FREESTONE, GRANITE, KEYSTONE, LIMESTONE, LONG AND SHORT WORK, MARBLE, MEGALITHIC, PARPEN, QUOIN, RAGSTONE, RUBBLESTONE, RUSTICATION, SANDSTONE, SARSEN, STONE CIRCLE, VERMICULATION]

## MASON'S MARK

Symbol, initial or monogram carved in the stone of a building by an individual mason as a personal signature. The precise function of these masons' marks is not fully understood, but they can help to define the various construction phases of a Gothic cathedral by identifying various parts of the work with the masons who completed them.

## MATHEMATICAL TILE

Tile nailed externally to a wall through a concealed flange. Mathematical tiles were designed to give a passing resemblance to brickwork, e.g. at the **Royal Crescent, Brighton**, *E Sussex*. Also known as a brick tile or a weather-tile. [see TILE]

## MAUSOLEUM

A general definition of a monumental tomb or burial, deriving its name from the Mausoleum of Halicarnassos erected

**219** *The Dashwood Mausoleum at West Wycombe,* Bucks, *is an open structure on the summit of a hill.*

in *c.* 350 BC in Asia Minor by Artemisia to commemorate her husband King Mausolus. Prehistoric Britain, by contrast, had built collective tombs rather than monuments to individuals. During the Middle Ages the desire of the rich and powerful to make their grave a lasting and noble memorial found expression in the tomb effigies and chantry chapels located in churches and cathedrals. It was not until the eighteenth century that the idea of the Classical mausoleum was taken up by noble families in order to create ancestral vaults which expressed the permanence of their social position from generation to generation. Such mausolea were designed by the leading archi-

tects of the day, e.g. at **Castle Howard**, *N Yorks*, of 1729 by Nicholas Hawksmoor for the Earl of Carlisle; and the **Templetown Mausoleum**, A*ntrim*, N. Ireland of 1783 by Robert Adam for the Hon. Arthur Upton. The **Dashwood Mausoleum** at **West Wycombe**, *Bucks*, is a roofless hexagonal enclosure on the top of a hill. The **Dulwich Picture Gallery, London**, of 1811–14 by John Soane incorporates a mausoleum for the benefactors of the gallery. The idea of the family mausoleum appealed to a broad spectrum of Victorian society, and many were built in the new metropolitan cemeteries. Some were lavish affairs, e.g. that of 1880 in **Highgate Cemetery, London**, designed by John Oldrid Scott for the millionaire Julius Beer. Following the death of the Prince Consort in 1861, Queen Victoria

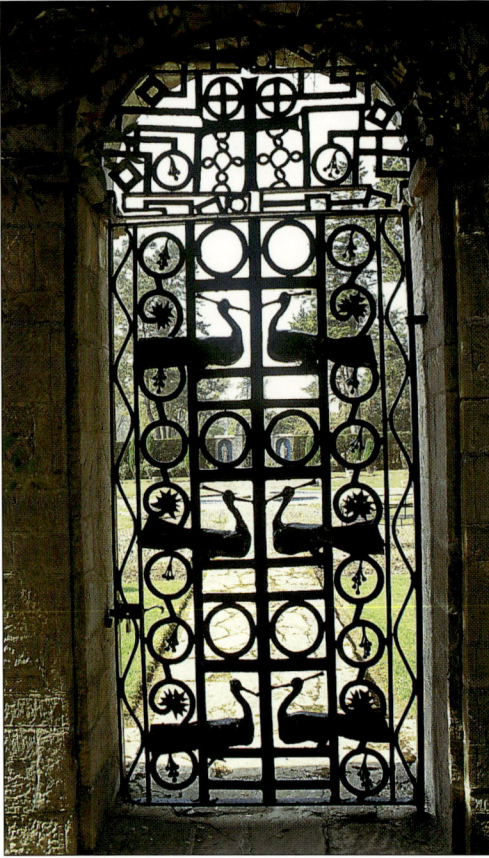

**220** *The mausoleum at Mount Stewart, Down, N. Ireland. The gate is a fine piece of wrought ironwork.*

built the ultimate mausoleum at **Frogmore**, near **Windsor Castle**, *Berks*. Except for a few isolated examples, e.g. **Tir Nan Og** in the 1920s at **Mount Stewart**, *Down*, N. Ireland, mausoleum building has been neglected in the twentieth century. [see CATACOMB, CEMETERY, CHANTRY CHAPEL, MEMORIAL, PYRAMID, TOMB SCULPTURE, WAR MEMORIAL]

## MEDIEVAL

The term is generally applied to an individual building to indicate that it belongs to the period of the Middle Ages, which may extend – according to different viewpoints – as far back as the early Saxon period immediately following the withdrawal of the Romans at the beginning of the fifth century AD or merely to the Norman Conquest of the late eleventh century. The end of the Middle Ages was a gradual transition which commenced in 1485 with the accession of the Tudors in the person of Henry VII. As a stylistic label, the term 'medieval' is far less meaningful than the precise definitions of Saxon, Norman and the three major phases of Gothic, i.e. Early English, Decorated and Perpendicular which together make up the medieval period. [see GOTHIC, NORMAN, SAXON]

## MEETING HOUSE

The Nonconformist sects, which first made an impact in the seventeenth century, brought an entirely new approach to the design of their places of religious devotion. The process of rejection of the ritual and symbolism of the Church of England manifested itself in the meeting house, which was a modest auditory structure, austerely fitted out with pews or benches, and oriented around readings from the Bible, not the celebration of the Mass. The prohibition of Nonconformism, not repealed until 1688, also contributed to a secular style of architecture which did not wish to attract unwelcome attention, e.g. the **Loughwood Meeting House**, *Devon*, established by the Baptists in 1653 in a remote corner of the county. The meeting house of the Quakers at **Come-to-Good, Feock**, *Cornwall*, of 1710 presents a homely, domestic face to the world: more like a cottage than a church. John Wesley's **New Room, Bristol**, *Avon*, of the 1740s, the oldest Methodist house in the world, provided accommodation for the minister and his family in an apartment above the meeting house. Gradually the designation 'meeting house' has been replaced by that of 'chapel' by Baptists

221 *Interior of the Loughwood Meeting House*, Devon.

and Methodists, but it is still used by the Quakers. [see AUDITORY CHURCH, CHAPEL]

## MEGALITH

Term derived from Greek, meaning 'big stone', to describe structures composed of large, rough blocks of stone. [see CHAMBERED TOMB, CYCLOPEAN, DOLMEN, MONOLITH, PREHISTORIC, STANDING STONE, STONE CIRCLE, 138]

222 OPPOSITE *Trethevy Quoit*, Cornwall, *exhibits the heavy monumental character of megalithic structures.*

# MEMORIAL

The commemoration of the dead or of past events assumes many different forms, from simple tombs in country churches to great monuments in city centres. [see CENOTAPH, MAUSOLEUM, MONUMENT, TOMB SCULPTURE, WAR MEMORIAL]

# MERCAT CROSS [see MARKET CROSS]

# MERLON

The raised, solid part of a battlement. [see BATTLEMENT, CRENELLATION]

# METOPE

In Classical architecture, the square space in a frieze of the Doric order located between two triglyphs. When carved, the term 'metope' applies to the sculptures themselves, e.g. the Parthenon metopes in the **British Museum, London**. [see 170]

# MEURTRIÈRE [see MURDER HOLE]

# MEWS

Narrow street originally consisting of a row of stables with living accommodation above for the grooms, e.g. in parts of Georgian and Victorian London such as **Belgravia** and **Kensington**.

# MEZZANINE

Low storey located between two of greater height. The mezzanine is usually between the ground and first floor, also known as an entresol. In a theatre it may denote the floor beneath the stage.

# MIDDEN

Archaeological term denoting a mound of ancient domestic rubbish. Sites of Mesolithic (Middle Stone Age) occupation can often only be detected through their associated middens, e.g. those on **Oronsay,** Scotland, which date back to the middle of the fifth millennium BC.

# MIHRAB [see MOSQUE]

# MILL [see FACTORY, WATERMILL, WINDMILL]

# MINARET [see MOSQUE]

# MINSTER

Denotes a church once belonging to a monastery, e.g. **Southwell Minster,** *Notts.*

# MINSTRELS' GALLERY [see GALLERY]

# MISERICORD or MISERERE

Hinged wooden seat in a choir stall with a wooden bracket fitted to the underside, on which, when the seat was up, the priest could rest while appearing to remain standing. These brackets were often magnificently carved with all manner of subjects, often secular and profane. They may be seen in many a medieval church, e.g. **Beverley Minster,** *Humbs;* **St George, Anstey,** *Herts;* **New College Chapel, Oxford,** *Oxon.* The largest and finest collections of misericords are in the cathedrals of **Chester,** *Cheshire;* **Exeter,** *Devon;* **Lincoln,** *Lincs;* and of **Wells,** *Somerset.*

223 *A medieval misericord in the church of the Holy Trinity, Stratford-upon-Avon,* Warw.

224 *The wide moat at Bodiam Castle*, E Sussex.

## MOAT

Defensive ditch, usually filled with water, surrounding a castle or manor house, e.g. at **Ightham Mote**, *Kent*; **Bodiam Castle**, *E Sussex*; and **Beaumaris Castle** on **Anglesey**, *Gwynedd*, Wales. The word is a corruption of 'motte' which originally denoted the mound of a castle. [see **103**]

## MOCK TUDOR

Popular name for the revival of Tudor-style half-timbered exteriors where the timbers are bolted to the façade for decoration, rather than being an integral part of the structure.

**MODEL VILLAGE** [see PLANNED VILLAGE]

225 *The half-timbering at Plas Newydd in Llangollen, Clwyd, Wales, is deceptive: it is pure mock Tudor.*

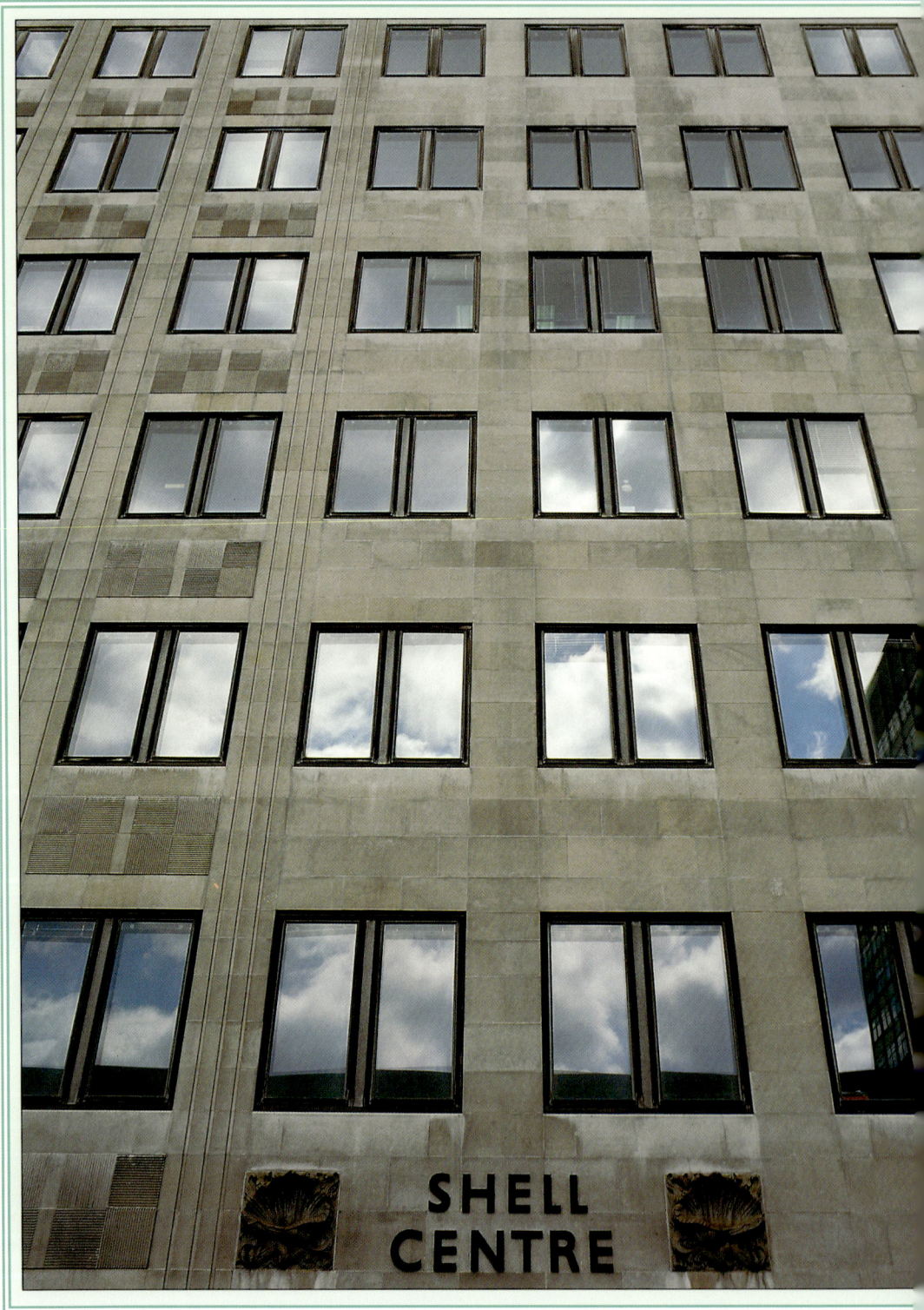

## MODERN, MODERNISM

The essence of Modernism lies in the rejection of historicism, i.e. the imitation of traditional architecture notably Classical and Gothic. It was helped along by the new structural possibilities of steel, concrete and glass. The initial impetus came in the 1920s and 1930s from a small number of Continental architects, of whom the most influential was the German, Walter Gropius, whose architectural school the Bauhaus promoted the concept of functionalism and the disdain of gratuitous ornamentation. Gropius spent some time in Britain and collaborated with Maxwell Fry on **Impington Village College**, *Cambs*, of 1936–9. Erich Mendelsohn and Serge Chermayeff designed the **De la Warr Pavilion** at **Bexhill-on-Sea**, *E Sussex*, of 1935–6. Maxwell Fry built the **Sun House, Hampstead, London** in 1935. Berthold Lubetkin founded the architectural firm Tecton which built the **Finsbury Health Centre** and the **Highpoint** flats at **Highgate, London**, characterized by sleek lines and unadorned geometrical form, imparting an air of functional efficiency. Modernism influenced the design of many commercial buildings in the 1950s and 1960s, which are now loosely considered as 'modern'. However, this latterday 'Modernism' generally produced uniform buildings with little claim to artistic merit. In recent years alternative solutions are being sought in High Tech and Post-Modernism; and there is even a return to the traditional values of Classicism. [see ART DECO, BRUTALISM, FUNCTIONALISM, HIGH TECH, POST-MODERNISM]

**226** OPPOSITE *The legacy of Modernism inspired the design of the Shell Centre, London. The façade achieves elegance through the pairing of the windows and spacing between the storeys.*

## MODILLION

In Classical architecture, a small console or bracket usually in a series supporting the top element of the cornice in an entablature. [see ENTABLATURE]

## MODULE [see INDUSTRIALIZED BUILDING]

## MONASTERY

The word is derived from a Greek root, meaning 'to live alone', reflecting the original monastic ideal of the desert hermits of Egypt and Syria. Gradually, such hermits came together in small communities, though they continued to seek out remote locations far from towns and cities. These early monks provided the inspiration for the monastic movement in Europe several centuries later.

Among the first monasteries to be established in the British Isles were those in Ireland from about the fifth century.

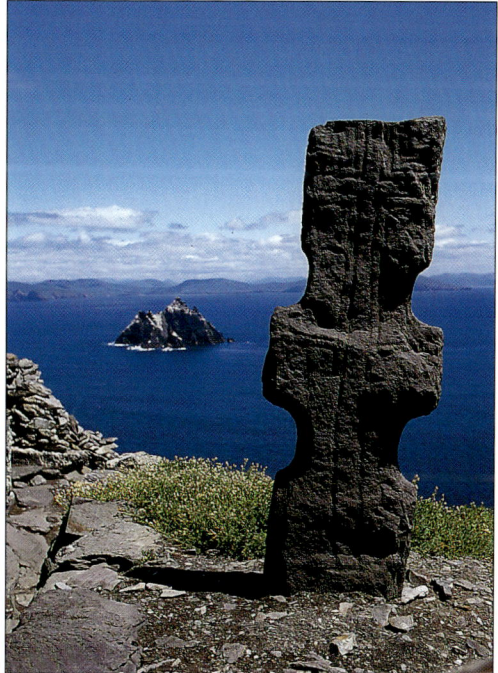

**227** *A roughly hewn cross in the burial ground of the ancient monastery of Skellig Michael, Kerry, Ireland.*

**228** *Chapter-house of Jervaulx Abbey, N Yorks. Note the stone bench and the central column which supported the vaults.*

Some were communities which gathered to venerate a hermit of great renown, e.g. St Kevin at **Glendalough**, *Wicklow*, Ireland. Ancient monastic sites abound in Ireland, and some amounted to small cities, e.g. **Clonmacnoise**, *Offaly*. Such places were rebuilt many times in the course of the years, but a few of the island monasteries have remained very much as they must have appeared when first built, e.g. **Skellig Michael** off the coast of Kerry. Irish monasticism reached Scotland via St Columba's foundation on the island of **Iona,** off Mull; and from there it extended to northern England via **Lindisfarne**, *Northum.*

Irish monks visited parts of southern England, but English monasticism also had its own Saxon founding fathers, e.g. as at **Malmesbury Abbey**, *Wilts*, by St Aldhelm in 676; **Shaftesbury Abbey**, *Dorset*, in 888 by Alfred the Great. However, the real impetus to build new abbeys and priories was to come from France in the aftermath of the Norman Conquest. At first, the Benedictines enjoyed a virtual monopoly. By contrast to the reformed orders which followed, the followers of the original rule of St Benedict did not eschew wealth and the

**229** *Saxon sculpture in the porch of Malmesbury Abbey,* Wilts, *a monastery founded in the seventh century.*

fine buildings it could provide, e.g. **St Mary's Abbey, York**, *N Yorks*; **Tewkesbury Abbey**, *Glos*; and **Glastonbury Abbey**, *Somerset*. From the twelfth century a reform movement was spearheaded by the Cistercians who upheld the ideal of an arduous existence living off the land on the outer fringes of human society and who promoted an architecture of noble austerity without undue ostentation. The Cistercians were soon to abandon their erstwhile simplicity as they amassed great wealth through their efficient management of the vast acreages with which they were endowed. It was mainly the profits of sheep farming which financed their magnificent rebuilding programmes, e.g. at **Fountains Abbey** and **Rievaulx Abbey**, *N Yorks*. Of the various orders of medieval monasticism in the British Isles, only the Carthusians followed a rule of solitary living in individual cells, e.g. at **Mount Grace Priory**, *N Yorks*. As a general statement of fact, the wealth and influ-

ence of the monasteries in the Middle Ages can hardly be overstressed. According to a contemporary saying, 'if the Abbess of Shaftesbury were to wed the Abbot of Glastonbury, their heir would own more land than the King'.

The Dissolution of the Monasteries in the 1530s and 1540s by Henry VIII was much more than an act of ecclesiastical reform, since it amounted to the most radical redistribution of land ownership since the Norman Conquest. Henry VIII's policy of destroying monastic buildings was partly motivated by his desire to strip them of their valuable fittings such as lead roofs, but more importantly he intended to make them uninhabitable, 'for fear the birds should build therein again'. However, it was not possible to wipe from the map the hundreds of abbeys, priories and friaries which had been built in durable stone over so many centuries; and even in their present ruinous state the beauty and majesty of monastic architecture may still be appreciated. Indeed, the romance of the ruins endows them with an added poignancy. But not all monasteries were physically

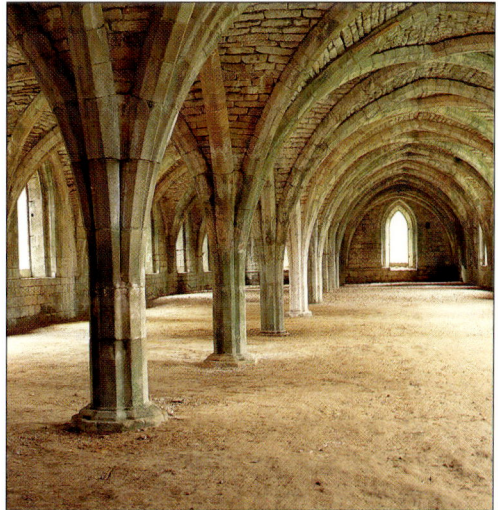

**230** *The dormitory undercroft at Fountains Abbey*, N Yorks, *served as the refectory of the lay brethren.*

**231** *The fan-vaulted lavatorium at Gloucester Cathedral,* Glos, *was originally built for the Benedictine monks.*

destroyed: some survived for use as church or cathedral, e.g. **Selby Abbey**, *N Yorks*; **Bristol Cathedral**, *Avon*; and **Gloucester Cathedral**, *Glos*. Others were converted into country houses, e.g. **Lacock Abbey**, *Wilts*; **Buckland Abbey**, *Devon*.

The revival of the monasteries in England began in 1814 with the refoundation of **Downside Abbey**, *Somerset*, and continued with the building of **Buckfast Abbey**, *Devon*, in 1907. In 1948 a small Benedictine community reoccupied the ruins of **Pluscarden Priory**, *Grampian*, Scotland. Ireland has many thriving monastic communities, but the medieval abbeys are mainly in ruins, albeit with some notable exceptions, e.g. **Holycross**, *Tipperary*. [see ABBEY, ALIEN HOUSE, ALMONRY, BARN, BEEHIVE CELL, CALEFACTORY, CELL, CHAPTER HOUSE, CLOISTER, CONVENT, DORTER, FRATER, FRIARY, GARTH, GATEHOUSE, LAVABO, MINSTER, NIGHT STAIR, NUNNERY, ORATORY, PRIORY, QUADRANGLE, REREDORTER, ROUND TOWER, SCRIPTORIUM, SLYPE]

232 *The Tristan Stone near Fowey,* Cornwall, *is a prehistoric monolith of unknown significance.*

233 *The Glenfinnan Monument,* Highland, *Scotland, with a statue of an anonymous Highlander.*

## MONOLITH

Term derived from Greek, meaning 'single stone', and usually applied to prehistoric standing stones. [see MEGALITH, STANDING STONE, TRILITHON]

## MONOPTERAL

Classical temple, usually circular, having a single row of columns on all sides in lieu of solid walls, e.g. the **Rotondo** at **Stowe**, *Bucks*, designed in 1721 by John Vanbrugh [see PERIPTERAL, ROTUNDA]

## MONUMENT

The general definition of ancient monument embraces a wide range of creations, from stone circles to castles; but a narrower definition applies to structures which commemorate a person or an event. After the Roman withdrawal from Britain at the beginning of the fifth century AD, the notion of erecting purpose-built monuments such as triumphal arches was immediately abandoned. During the Middle Ages tomb sculpture was the most prolific form of monument. It was not until the late seventeenth century that the Classical idea of the monument, in the form of the triumphal column, was revived, and in dramatic fashion, with the **Monument** by Christopher Wren to mark the Great Fire of London in 1666. This consists of a single Classical stone column 202 feet (61·6m) high with a flaming urn on top. Monumental columns were built elsewhere, e.g. the **Glenfinnan Monument**, *Highland*, Scotland, of 1815 commemorating the Jacobite rising of 1745, and the **Nelson Column** in **Trafalgar Square, London**, of 1843. The **National Monument** of 1822, on the summit of **Calton Hill, Edinburgh,** Scotland, was originally conceived as a copy of the Parthenon, but the money ran out in 1829

234 *The uncompleted National Monument in Edinburgh, Scotland, is a potent expression of the Greek Revival.*

when only twelve columns had been built; dubbed 'the pride and poverty of Scotland', it remains a striking silhouette on the Edinburgh skyline. The Gothic Revival produced elaborate works such as the **Scott Monument, Edinburgh**, Scotland, of 1844 and the **Albert Memorial, London**, of 1872. The **Wallace Monument** of 1870, near **Stirling**, *Central*, Scotland, is a massive 220 feet (67·1m) high tower with a crown spire and a colossal bronze statue of Wallace perched on a corner ledge. The Edwardian era turned for inspiration to the Baroque, e.g. as in the **Ashton Memorial, Lancaster**, *Lancs*, of 1909 and the **Victoria Memorial** of 1911 in front of Buckingham Palace, **London**. [see ARCH, CENOTAPH, ELEANOR CROSS, OBELISK, TOMB SCULPTURE, WAR MEMORIAL, **164**]

## MOORSTONE

Block of stone lying on the surface of a moor, which provided a convenient source of stone for many uses from the megaliths of prehistory to modern drystone walling. [see SARSEN, **48**]

## MORTAR

Compound of lime or cement with sand and water used for bonding stones or bricks. The name derives from the mortar in which the mixture was originally prepared. [see CONCRETE]

## MOSAIC

Decorative surface of small pieces of glass or stone set in concrete to produce abstract or figurative designs. Roman mosaics are well preserved at a number of sites, e.g. **Littlecote**, *Wilts*; **Lullingstone**, *Kent*; **Rockbourne**, *Hants*; **Fishbourne**, *W Sussex*; **Chedworth**, *Glos*. The art died out after the departure of the Romans. Mosaic pavements were an exception in the Middle Ages, and the thirteenth-century **Great Pavement** in **Westminster Abbey, London**, was probably executed by Italian craftsmen. The full rediscovery of mosaics in Britain did not occur until the nineteenth century, e.g. when the internal decoration of **St Paul's Cathedral, London,** was completed. The Byzantine Revival favoured extensive use of mosaics, e.g. at **Westminster Cathedral, London**, of 1895–1903 and the surprising interior of **Debenham House, Kensington, London,** of 1913. Modern mosaics made an appearance in some stations of the London Underground in the 1980s, e.g. at **Tottenham Court Road**. [see OPUS ALEXANDRINUM, OPUS SECTILE, TESSELLATED, **305**]

## MOSQUE

Place of communal prayer for Muslims. It is only in recent decades that the distinctive Islamic style of mosque has made an appearance in Britain, notably in **Birmingham**, *W Mids*; **Cardiff**, *Wales*; **Glasgow**, Scotland, and **London**. These mosques employ modern materials but

235 *Dazzling mosaic* (ABOVE) *at Debenham House, Kensington, London.*
236 *The dome and minaret* (LEFT) *of the London Mosque use modern materials in a traditional design.*

adhere to the traditional dome and the minaret which is a slender tower, from which the call to prayer is given. The main internal feature of a mosque is the *mihrab*, the focal point for prayer, which is a niche set in the *qibla*, i.e. the wall facing towards Mecca. The *minbar* is a type of pulpit, and the *maqsura* is a screen.

## MOTTE AND BAILEY [see CASTLE]

## MOUCHETTE
Motif of curvilinear tracery in the form of a curved dagger. [see TRACERY]

193

# MOULDING

Decorative profile given to a continuous projection, e.g. on an entablature or arch. There are many types of moulding. [see ASTRAGAL, BEAD, BOLECTION, BOWTELL, CABLE, CAVETTO, CHEVRON, COVING, CYMA RECTA, CYMA REVERSA, DENTIL, DOGTOOTH, EGG AND DART, FILLET, KEEL, NEBULE, OVOLO, ROLL, SCOTIA, TORUS, WAVE]

Bead moulding

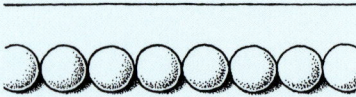

Billet moulding

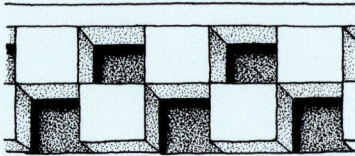

Keel moulding

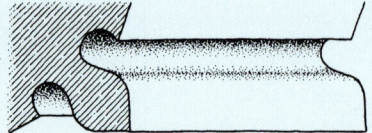

Bolection moulding

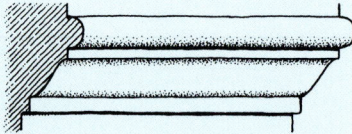

Leaf and dart moulding

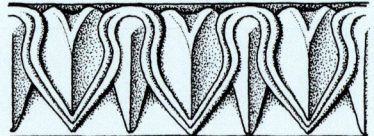

Bowtell or edge roll moulding

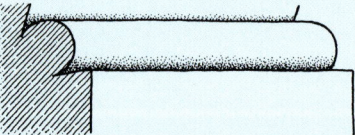

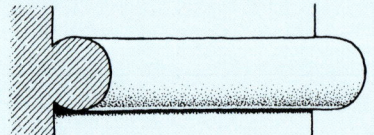

Ovolo moulding

Cable moulding

Roll moulding

Cavetto moulding

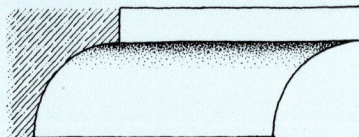

Scotia moulding

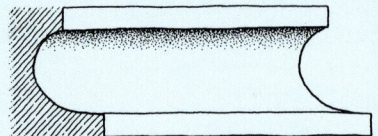

Egg and dart moulding

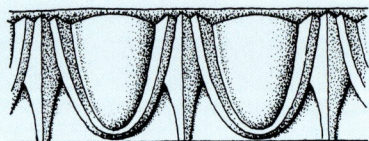

Torus moulding

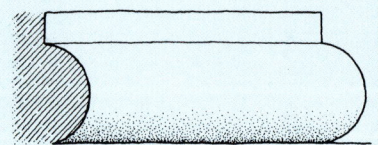

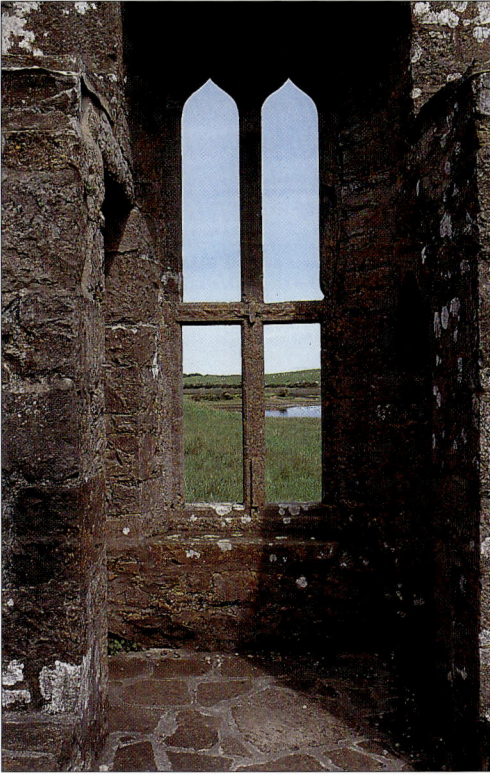

237 *A single mullion and transom combine to create a pleasing window at Rosserk Friary, Mayo, Ireland.*

# MULLION

Upright element of wood, stone or iron which divides a window into separate lights. [see LIGHT, TRANSOM, WINDOW, 96]

# MULTIVALLATE [see HILLFORT]

# MUNICIPAL BUILDINGS

The first town halls evolved from the market-house tradition of the Middle Ages. Even Christopher Wren's magnificent **County Hall** at **Abingdon**, *Oxon*, of 1677–80 followed the old idea of a building raised on an arcade above a covered market area. Among the earliest of municipal buildings designed exclusively for administration was the Palladian **Liverpool Town Hall**, *Mers*, of 1748–55 by the Woods of Bath. The town halls of

the nineteenth century divide fairly equally between Neo-Classical and Gothic Revival. In the former category are the Baroque Revival **Leeds Town Hall**, *W Yorks*, of 1855–9 by Cuthbert Brodrick and the Italianate **Halifax Town Hall**, *W Yorks*, of 1859–62 by Charles Barry. Notable Gothic designs include **Manchester Town Hall**, of 1864–7 by Alfred Waterhouse and the Scottish Baronial **Town House** in **Aberdeen**, *Grampian*, Scotland, of 1868 by Peddie and Kinnear. Grandiloquence became the order of the day towards the end of the nineteenth century, e.g. **Sheffield Town Hall**, *S Yorks*, of 1891–6 by E.W. Mountford and **Glasgow City Chambers**, Scotland, of 1883–8 by William Young.

The taste for Baroque monumentality was carried forward into the twentieth century by **Belfast City Hall**, N. Ireland, of 1906 by Brumwell Thomas. Among many town halls built around this time by the London boroughs, **Deptford Town Hall** of 1902 by Lanchester, Stewart & Rickards stands out. The same firm designed the **City Hall** of 1901–5 at **Cardiff**, Wales, centrepiece of a huge scheme which has been nicknamed the 'Welsh Washington'. Perhaps the most powerful of the Baroque Revival municipal buildings was the

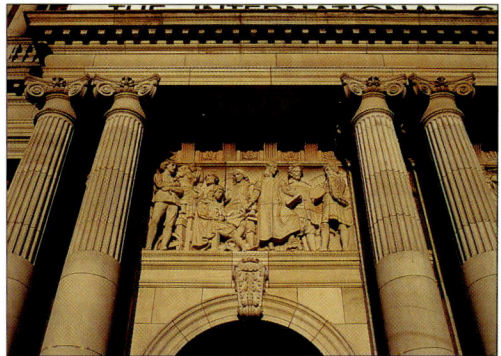

238 *Sculptured panel in full relief over the entrance to Glasgow City Chambers, Scotland.*

**239** *The Baroque dome and clocktower of Cardiff City Hall, Wales, crown a grand complex of municipal buildings.*

**London County Hall** of 1912–22 by Ralph Knott. Thereafter a simpler Classicism was preferred, e.g. **City Hall, Swansea**, *W Glam*, Wales, of 1930–4 by Percy Thomas; and there are buildings in similar style at **Bristol**, *Avon*; **Norwich**, *Norfolk,* and **Southampton**, *Hants*, also of the 1930s. In recent decades municipal buildings have shed any illusions of grandeur and have opted for an outward appearance hard to distinguish from the general run of office blocks. A much noticed departure from this trend was the **Hillingdon Civic Centre, London**, of 1977 by Robert Matthew and Johnson Marshall which borrowed freely from the pitched roofs and brickwork of suburban domestic architecture. [see **34, 214**]

## MUNTIN
Vertical element of a door or panel. [see DOOR, DOORWAY]

## MURAL
The practice of painting designs and

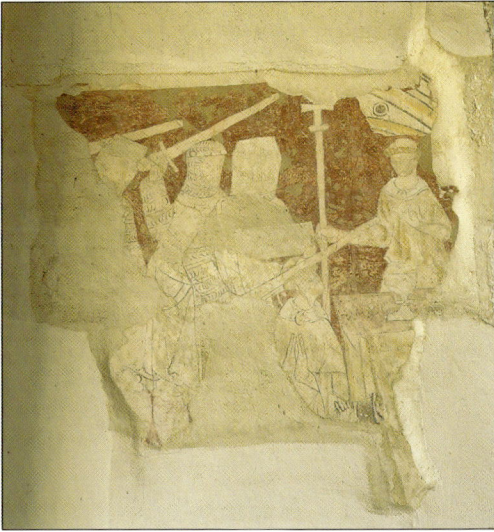

240 *A medieval mural at St Augustine, Brookland,* Kent, *portrays the assassination of Thomas à Becket.*

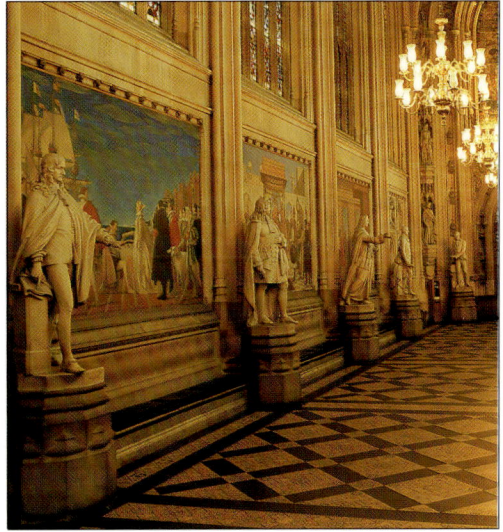

241 *Victorian murals adorn the walls of St Stephen's* Hall *in the Houses of Parliament, London.*

scenes on walls – introduced by the Romans – was revived in the Middle Ages. **Longthorpe Tower**, *Cambs*, contains the most complete set of medieval murals, from the fourteenth century, in a domestic setting. Parish churches of the period were embellished with Biblical scenes, partly as didactic aids for a largely illiterate congregation. The church of **St George, Trotton**, *W Sussex*, and **St Peter & St Paul, Pickering**, *N Yorks*, provide dramatic examples of the power of religious murals.

The rising tide of Puritanism in the sixteenth century brought this tradition to an abrupt end. Mural painting was taken up in a completely different context in noble Baroque interiors of the late seventeenth and early eighteenth centuries, e.g. the **Painted Hall** at the **Royal Naval College, Greenwich, London**; **Kensington Palace, London**; and **Blenheim Palace**, *Oxon*. These are compositions in the grand manner, but the trend was not followed by the more restrained Palladian and Neo-Classical style which held sway for the rest

of the eighteenth century. The Gothic Revival of the nineteenth century launched a new medievalism in mural painting, most notably exemplified by the twelve murals in **Manchester Town Hall** by Ford Maddox Brown between 1879 and 1893. They reflect the Victorian enthusiasm for murals previously promoted by Prince Albert and John Ruskin among others, which also left its mark from *c.* 1850 in the **Houses of Parliament, London**, and shortly afterwards in the **Oxford Union, Oxford**, *Oxon*. In recent years there has been a revival of illusionist murals in private houses. [see FRESCO, TROMPE L'OEIL]

## MURDER HOLE
Aperture in the masonry of a fortified dwelling or castle, through which projectiles could be dropped on assailants. At **Warwick Castle**, *Warw*, there are several murder holes located in the arch of the gatehouse. This contrivance is also known by the French name '*meurtrière*'. [see MACHICOLATION]

## MUSEUM

The golden age of the museum as an architectural genre occurred in the nineteenth century when it was conceived as a prestigious temple of culture worthy of standing alongside any palace of commerce. Prime examples in the Classical tradition are the **British Museum, London**, of 1823–47 by Robert Smirke; the **Ashmolean, Oxford**, *Oxon*, of 1841–5 by Charles Cockerell; and the **Fitzwilliam, Cambridge**, *Cambs*, of 1837–47 by George Basevi and Charles Cockerell. The Gothic Revival is best represented by the **University Museum, Oxford**, *Oxon*, of 1855–60 by the partnership of Deane and Woodward. The **Royal Scottish Museum, Edinburgh**, Scotland, of 1861 by Captain Fowke is a brilliant

242 *The Geffrye Museum, London, occupies a Georgian almshouse. Note the simple pediment and quoins.*

243 *The Royal Scottish Museum in Edinburgh admits plenty of light through its glass and iron structure.*

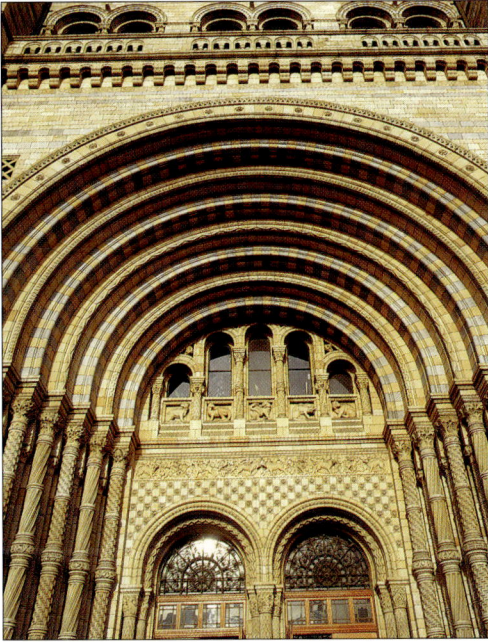

display of the building technology of glass and iron. In the aftermath of the Great Exhibition of 1851 in London a vast area of Kensington was earmarked for cultural projects which included the **Natural History Museum,** the **Science Museum** and the **Victoria and Albert Museum**. The **Horniman Museum, London**, of 1896–1901 by Charles Harrison Townsend is a stylish essay in the Art Nouveau manner. New museum buildings in London in recent decades include the **National Army Museum,** the **Museum of London**, and the **Design Museum**; but the most highly acclaimed modern museum in Britain is the **Burrell Collection** in **Glasgow**, Scotland, of 1983, an imaginative blend of old and new in an attractive woodland setting. [see ART GALLERY, **18**]

**244** *Doorway of the Natural History Museum, London. Note the Romanesque Revival terracotta façade.*

**245** *The Burrell Collection, Glasgow, Scotland, combines sandstone, steel and glass in an effective manner.*

# N

## NAILHEAD
Ornamental stone band composed of small pyramid-like shapes, e.g. in Early English Gothic.

## NARTHEX [see GALILEE]

## NAVE
Main body of a church, not including the choir. The word is derived from Latin 'navis', meaning 'ship', symbolizing the voyage of souls through life and into eternity. [see CATHEDRAL, CHURCH, 72]

## NEBULE
Moulding with an undulating or serpentine lower edge.

## NECROPOLIS [see CEMETERY]

## NEEDLE SPIRE [see SPIRE]

## NEOLITHIC [see PREHISTORIC]

## NEW TOWN
The practice of founding a new urban settlement on a green-field site was already much in evidence during the Middle Ages, e.g. at **Salisbury**, *Wilts*, where the squares of the original gridiron layout are still known by the ancient name of 'chequers'. Less successful was the foundation of **Winchelsea**, *E Sussex*, which failed to live up to the expectations of its creator, Edward I. Various new settlements were established by landlords and factory owners in the course of the eighteenth and nineteenth centuries; the workers' settlements at **Port Sunlight**, *Mers*, and **Bourneville**, *W Mids*, are of particular note. But the real impetus towards the idea of the new town was given by Ebenezer Howard's vision of the garden city as realized at **Letchworth** and **Welwyn**, *Herts*, by the 1920s. The New Towns Act of 1944 set the agenda for the creation of many new towns in recent decades, e.g. **Harlow**, *Essex*; **Milton Keynes**, *Bucks*; **Crawley**, *W Sussex*; **Corby**, *Northants*; and **Cumbernauld**, *S'clyde*, Scotland. [see GARDEN CITY, PLANNED VILLAGE]

## NEWEL
The central column around which a spiral staircase climbs. The term also denotes the prominent post located at the base of a staircase or on the landing; these were elaborately carved in the sixteenth and seventeenth centuries. [see STAIRCASE, 331]

## NICHE
Wall recess designed to accommodate an urn or statue. [see AEDICULE, 367]

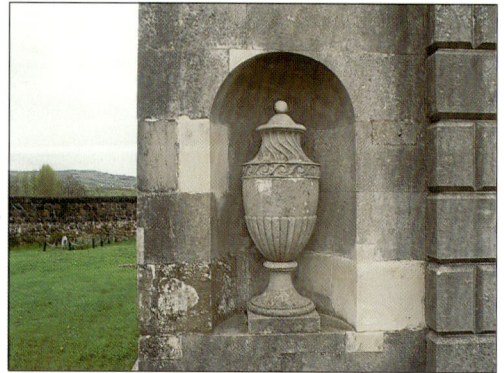

246 *Urn niche, Templetown Mausoleum*, Antrim, *N Ireland.*

## NIGHT STAIR
Staircase in a monastic establishment giving direct access from the dorter (dormitory) to the church of the abbey or priory. It was used by the monks or nuns

247 OPPOSITE *The imposing night stair at Hexham Abbey*, Northum.

when attending the holy offices which took place during the night hours. A splendid example survives in **Hexham Abbey**, *Northum.* [see MONASTERY]

## NISSEN HUT

Semicircular, tunnel-shaped structure formed by bending sheets of corrugated iron to make the walls and roof one continuous element. Named after Lt.-Col. P.N. Nissen (1871–1930) whose prototype was taken up by the armed forces for cheap and convenient accommodation. Some Nissen huts have been turned over to non-military use, e.g. one on **Orkney**, Scotland, converted in 1943 by prisoners of war to serve as their **Italian Chapel**, as it is still known.

## NODDING OGEE [see OGEE]

## NOGGING

A nog is a small block of wood which gave its name to the technique of infilling the spaces of a timber-framed building. Later, brick was more commonly used for the purpose, e.g. at the medieval market hall from **Titchfield**, *Hants*, now in the **Weald & Downland Museum**, *W Sussex*. [see HALF-TIMBERING]

## NOOK SHAFT

Shaft located in the angle of a window or doorway.

## NORMAN

Known on the Continent as Romanesque, this early medieval style of architecture employed the round arch after the manner of the Romans. It owes its designation of Norman in the British context to the fact that the style became widespread in the late eleventh and twelfth centuries in the aftermath of the Norman Conquest. By contrast to the ensuing phase of Gothic or pointed architecture, Norman buildings required bulky cylindrical columns and thick walls to support the sheer dead

**248** *Norman column, St David's Cathedral,* Dyfed, *Wales.*

## NORMAN REVIVAL

The nineteenth-century enthusiasm for Norman architecture owed much to Thomas Hopper, whose **Gosford Castle**, *Armagh*, N. Ireland, of 1819 ranks as the earliest specimen of the Norman Revival in the British Isles. His subsequent design for

**249** OPPOSITE *Norman Revival at Gosford Castle,* Armagh, *N. Ireland.*

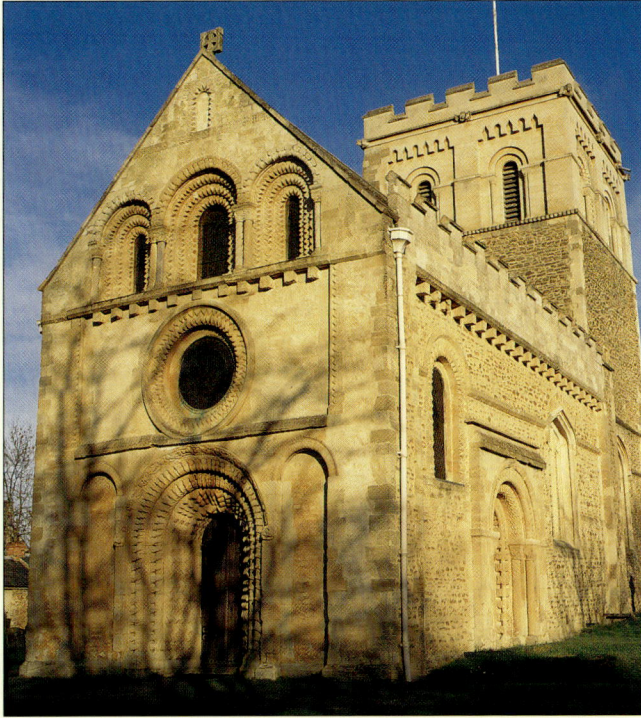

250 *The church of St Mary the Virgin, Iffley,* Oxon, *presents an exceptionally rich Norman exterior. The rose window was a later addition.*

weight of the structure. The prominent round arches were usually the object of powerful carvings of deeply incised chevrons and grotesque beakhead figures inspired by memories from pagan Norse mythology.

Apart from the great cathedrals of **Durham**, *Durham*; **Rochester**, *Kent*; **Southwell**, *Notts*; **Ely**, *Cambs*; and monastic churches such as **St Bartholomew-the-Great, Smithfield, London**, there are many parish churches which bear the distinctive imprint of the Norman style, e.g. **St Mary & St David, Kilpeck**, *Heref & Worcs*; **St Mary the Virgin, Iffley**, *Oxon*; and **St John the Evangelist, Elkstone**, *Glos*; as well as the Scottish parish churches at **Leuchars**, *Fife*, and **Dalmeny**, *Lothian*. The Norman interior of **St David's Cathedral**, *Dyfed*, Wales, is among the most impressive of its kind in the British Isles.

In the secular domain, the Normans excelled in castle building, e.g. the **White Tower, London**; **Rochester Castle**, *Kent*; and **Colchester Castle**, *Essex*. Some rare examples of a more modest domestic architecture survive, e.g. **Boothby Pagnell Manor**, *Lincs*, and in the city of **Lincoln**, *Lincs*, the **Jew's House** and the **Norman House**. As an expression of power and permanence, Norman architecture has yet to be surpassed. [see BEAKHEAD, CASTLE, CATHEDRAL, CELTIC, CHANCEL ARCH, CHAPEL, CHEVRON, CHURCH, FONT, KEEP, MANOR HOUSE, **110, 147, 364**]

**Penrhyn Castle**, *Gwynedd*, Wales of 1827–46 is the most impressive example of the genre. Also of great interest is the Norman Revival work at **Arundel Castle**, *W Sussex*, commissioned by the 15th Duke of Norfolk between 1870 and 1910.

## Nosing

Projecting front edge of a tread. [see STAIRCASE ]

## Nunnery

A monastic establishment for women. During the Middle Ages some notable nunneries were founded, e.g. the late ninth-century Benedictine **Shaftesbury Abbey**, *Dorset*, and the Augustinian **Lacock Abbey**, *Wilts* of 1232. Both were typically aristocratic institutions which accommodated the daughters of noble families. [see MONASTERY]

# O

## OAST HOUSE

Brick building, found especially in Kent and Sussex, designed for the drying of hops. The distinctive shape of the oast house is given by its windowless drum-like extension with a conical roof topped by a cowl which turns with the wind to ensure maximum ventilation. With the switch to oil-heated sheds most of the traditional oast houses have been converted for residential use.

## OBELISK

Form of monument, originating in Egypt, consisting of a lofty, tapering, four-sided stone shaft culminating in a small pyramid-shaped apex. **Cleopatra's Needle** in **London** is a genuine Egyptian antiquity, but there are many smaller imitations usually in cemeteries. Larger obelisks were used as novel eye-catchers in landscape gardens. The 197 feet (60m) high **Wellington Testimonial** in **Phoenix Park, Dublin,** Ireland, of 1817 by Robert Smirke is the tallest obelisk in Europe. [see **265**]

## OBSERVATORY

Structure designed for the housing of telescopes and other astronomical instruments. The **Old Royal Observatory** in **Greenwich Park, London**, designed by Christopher Wren, was founded in 1675 by Charles II 'for the finding out of places for perfecting navigation and astronomy'. A smaller observatory was built in 1776 in **Edinburgh**, Scotland, in a castellated Gothic style; it was super-

*251 The design of the Old Royal Observatory, Greenwich, shows a harmonious blend of art and science.*

*252 The octagon shape of the Old Royal Observatory, Greenwich, is reflected in the pattern of the ceiling.*

seded in 1818 by the **New Observatory**, a cruciform Neo-Classical temple with a central dome. A remarkable private observatory was built by the nineteenth-century Earls of Rosse at **Birr Castle**, *Offaly*, Ireland.

## OCTAGON

An eight-sided room or building, e.g. the medieval chapter house at **York Minster**,

*N Yorks*. The **Old Royal Observatory** at **Greenwich, London**, is crowned by its **Octagon Room**. The **Octagon** of 1720 by James Gibbs is all that remains of **Orleans House, Twickenham**, London. In the eighteenth century the octagon shape also appeared in several versions of the Tower of the Winds in Athens. [see TEMPLE]

## OCTASTYLE

A portico with eight columns on its front elevation.

## OCULUS
Latin meaning 'an eye', it denotes a round aperture in a wall or at the apex of a dome.

## OEIL DE BOEUF [see BULL'S EYE WINDOW]

## OEILLET
French meaning 'small eye', it denotes in medieval architecture a narrow opening in a fortification for the discharge of projectiles. [see ARROW LOOP, BALISTRARIA]

## OGEE
A pointed arch with a sinuous double curve composed of concave and convex elements, a favourite feature of Decorated Gothic. A nodding ogee is one which projects and leans forward, usually supporting a canopy, e.g. in the **Lady Chapel, Ely Cathedral**, *Cambs.* [see ARCH, 56, 269]

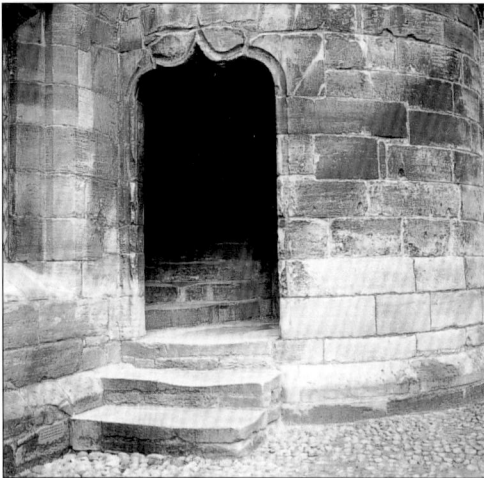

253 *Flat ogee arch in Linlithgow Palace, Scotland.*

## OOLITE, OOLITIC [see LIMESTONE]

## OPEN PEDIMENT [see PEDIMENT]

## OPEN-TIMBERED
Describes a wooden roof whose beams and rafters are exposed to view. The halls of medieval houses were open-timbered. [see TIMBER-TRUSSED ROOF]

## OPERA HOUSE [see THEATRE]

## OPUS ALEXANDRINUM
Combination of mosaic and opus sectile in paving work. [see MOSAIC, OPUS SECTILE]

## OPUS INCERTUM
Roman walling technique consisting of irregular stones set in concrete.

## OPUS LISTATUM
Roman walling technique consisting of alternating courses of rubblestone and levelling courses of brick, e.g. at **Tower Hill, London**, and **Richborough Castle**, *Kent.* [see LEVELLING COURSE]

## OPUS QUADRATUM
Roman walling technique using squared stones.

## OPUS RETICULATUM
Roman walling technique, with stones set diagonally in concrete.

## OPUS SECTILE
Paving of pieces of marble of various shapes and sizes. [see MOSAIC]

## ORANGERY
Garden building with large south-facing windows to provide a warm environment for exotic plants, especially oranges. It has been suggested that the building of orangeries may have been motivated partly as a political tribute to William of Orange around the end of the seventeenth century when the vogue first caught on. However, the underlying purpose of the orangery was to create an airy but sheltered place for informal encounters away from the confinement of a grand house. Niches for stat-

254 *The Orangery at Wrest Park,* Beds, *has large windows on the same principle as a greenhouse or conservatory.*

ues and urns were to be found among the orange trees. The **Orangery** at **Kensington Palace, London**, of 1704 was designed by Nicholas Hawksmoor and John Vanbrugh. There are also orangeries at **Powis Castle**, *Powys*, Wales; **Dyrham Park**, Avon; **Hanbury Hall**, *Heref & Worcs*; **Saltram House**, *Devon*; and **Tatton Park**, *Cheshire*. In the nineteenth century the orangery was passed over in favour of the new conservatories of glass and iron. [see CONSERVATORY]

## ORATORY

From Latin '*oratorium*', meaning a place for prayer, such as the churches of the early Christian period, e.g. the **Gallarus Oratory**, *Kerry*, Ireland. The Roman Catholic Church has retained the word to denote such grand structures as the **Brompton Oratory, London**, of 1878–84 modelled on the Chiesa Nuova in Rome.

255 *The Gallarus Oratory,* Kerry, *Ireland, is a drystone structure resembling the shape of an upturned boat.*

## ORDER

In Classical architecture this denotes the style and disposition of the various elements of a building from the plinth supporting the base of the column to the capital and the entablature above. Classical theory and practice recognized a number of different orders or modes of design which followed specific rules of proportion and ornamentation. The Doric, Ionic and Corinthian orders were evolved by the Greeks and later modified by the Romans who added the Composite order, a cross between Ionic and Corinthian, to their repertoire. The more utilitarian Tuscan order may have its origins in the ancient architecture of the Etruscans. Greek Doric, once held in low repute as primitive and archaic, is now considered to embody the purest expression of the Classical spirit. Knowledge of the Classical orders was an essential part of an architect's repertoire from the late seventeenth century until the 1920s. After decades of neglect, more interest is now being shown. [see CLASSICAL, ENTABLATURE, GREEK REVIVAL, MANNERISM, PALLADIANISM]

CLASSICAL ORDERS

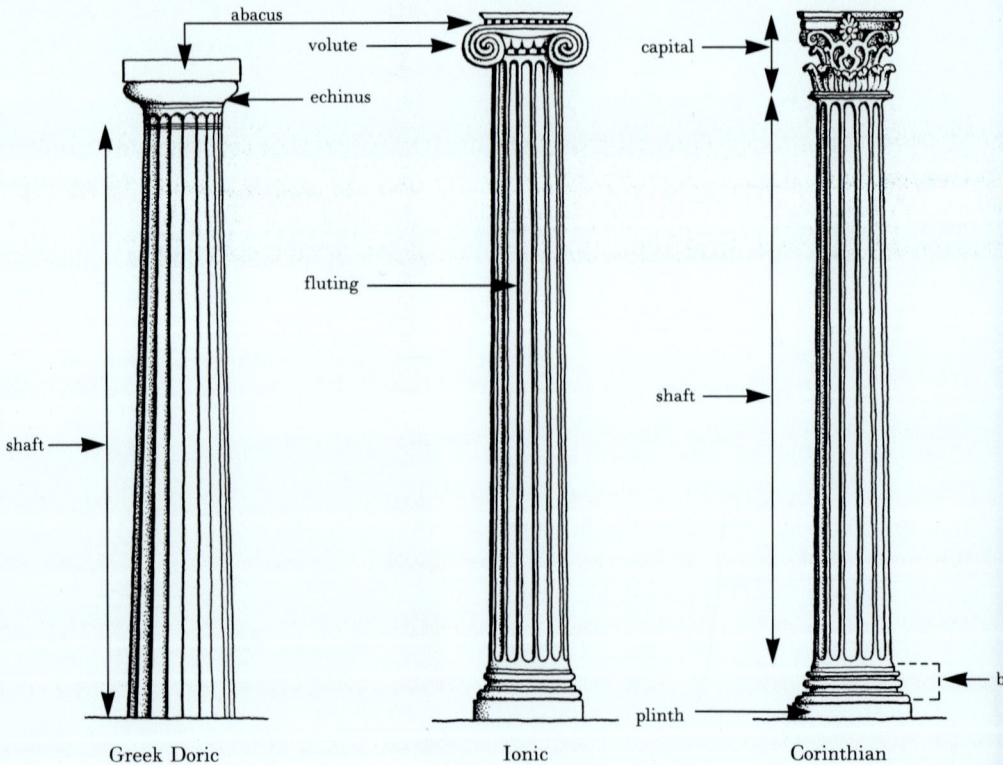

Greek Doric     Ionic     Corinthian

ENTABLATURE

A  architrave
B  astragal
C  cornice
D  corona
E  cyma recta
F  cyma reversa
G  dentils
H  fascia
I  frieze
J  listel or fillet
K  metope
L  modillion
M  triglyph

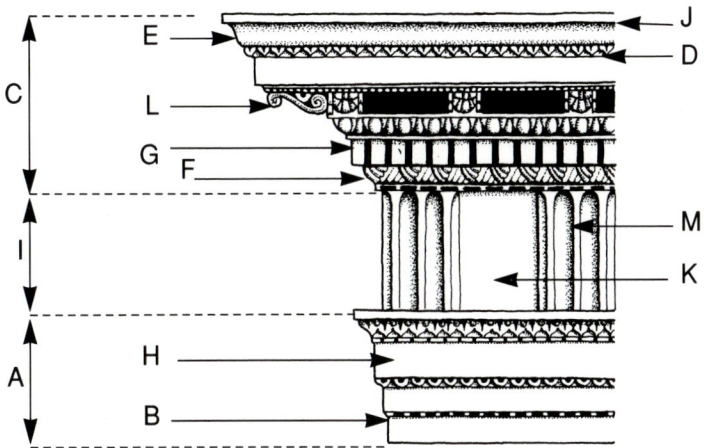

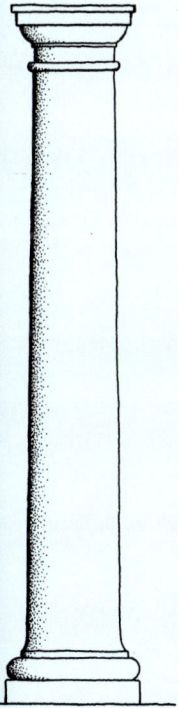

Tuscan

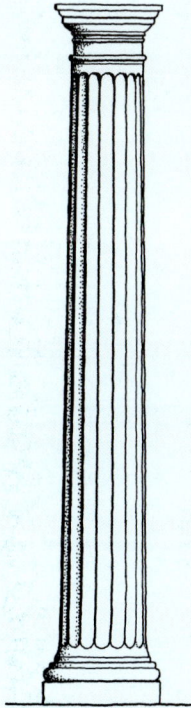

Roman Doric

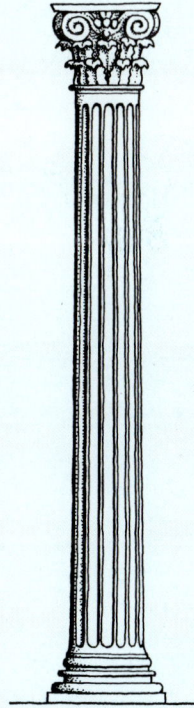

Composite

## ORIEL

Projecting upper storey window, a characteristic feature of medieval architecture

256 *This Gothic oriel at Lincoln Castle,* Lincs, *shows that medieval masons took delight in decorative detail.*

257 *An oriel in the revived 'Queen Anne' style over the front door of Old Swan House, Chelsea Embankment, London.*

e.g. at **Lincoln Castle**, *Lincs*, and the **Banqueting Hall** of **Sudeley Castle**, *Glos.* The name is derived from Latin '*oratoriolum*', meaning 'a small place for prayer'. The medieval oriel has been adopted and widely imitated in a variety of recent Post-Modernist buildings. [see **280**]

## ORIENTALISM

In the context of architecture and design 'orientalism' denotes the imitation of building styles from a vast area extending from the Middle East to India and the Far East, e.g. the **Durbar Room, Osborne House**, *Isle of Wight.* [see CHINOISERIE, ISLAMIC, KIOSK, MOSQUE, PAGODA]

## ORMOLU

From French '*or moulu*', meaning 'ground-up gold', denotes a gilded form of bronze or brass which was used, especially in the eighteenth century, for decorating walls, doors and furniture.

## ORTHOSTAT

Upright stone, usually in the context of the megalithic tombs of prehistory. [see STANDING STONE, **138**]

## OSSUARY

A structure, usually a vault or undercroft, for the storage of human bones, e.g. at **St Leonard's Church, Hythe**, *Kent*, which contains thousands of skulls and thigh bones of medieval date. [see CATACOMB, CHARNEL HOUSE, CRYPT]

## OUBLIETTE

Small cell, dark and unventilated, in a medieval castle which could be entered only via a trapdoor from above, e.g. at **Warwick Castle**, *Warw.* As the French name implies, a prisoner in an oubliette was usually forgotten and left to rot. This was known in Scotland as the pit, e.g. at **Neidpath Castle**, *Borders.* [see DUNGEON]

258 *The exotic North Gate to the Royal Pavilion, Brighton, E Sussex, could have been taken directly from India. It was built in 1832 for William IV.*

## OVERSAIL

Part of a structure projecting outwards beyond the part below it, e.g. courses of stone in a corbel supporting a bartizan or an oriel as at the **Earl's Palace, Kirkwall, Orkney,** Scotland. [see CORBEL, JETTY, **260**]

## OVOLO

A convex moulding, often decorated with an egg and dart pattern. [see MOULDING]

# P

PADSTONE [see KNEELER]

## PAGODA
Traditional Buddhist temple of China and Japan, usually multi-storeyed with pro-jecting roofs. The form was borrowed in England in the eighteenth century as an exotic item to ornament a landscape garden. The **Kew Gardens Pagoda, London**, of 1761 was designed by William Chambers from sketches made during a visit to China. The nineteenth-century pagoda at **Alton Towers**, *Staffs*, is a replica of the To Ho pagoda in Canton. The **Peace Pagoda** of 1985 in **Battersea Park, London,** is of Japanese inspiration, as is the slightly earlier structure at **Milton Keynes**, *Bucks*.

259 *The Peace Pagoda in Battersea Park, London, is an example of Japanese-inspired Orientalism.*

**260** *Earl's Palace, Orkney. Note the corbelling.*

## PALACE

A stately mansion, or more specifically, the residence of a monarch, duke or bishop. Any royal abode may be described as a palace, even the Saxon hall of Alfred the Great at **Cheddar**, *Somerset*, of which only the post-holes remain. The **Palace of Westminster, London**, was originally built in the eleventh century by Edward the Confessor and subsequently enlarged by William Rufus, who remarked that it was 'too big for a chamber and not big enough for a hall'. Westminster Hall – as the great hall of the Palace of Westminster is now known – accommodated the court of the English monarchy throughout the Middle Ages until 1512 when Henry VIII removed the royal household to Whitehall Palace near by. Henry maintained several palaces, including that of **Hampton Court, London**, where he added the magnificent great hall to the palatial residence which he graciously consented 'to receive' from its original creator, Cardinal Wolsey. After Whitehall Palace was destroyed by fire in 1698, the royal court was transferred to **St James's Palace, London**. William and

261/262 *Hampton Court Palace, London. To the Tudor palace* (OPPOSITE) *Wren added Fountain Court* (ABOVE). *Note the arcade and the row of bull's-eye windows.*

Mary, however, preferred the more salubrious air of Kensington a few miles to the west, where they commissioned Christopher Wren to convert the Jacobean mansion of Nottingham House into **Kensington Palace**, and they took up residence in 1690. The Hanoverians added a touch of grandeur to Kensington Palace with the lavish decoration of the **Cupola Room,** designed in 1722 by William Kent to glorify George I in the guise of a Roman emperor. Distinctly unpalatial, by contrast, was the modest brick house in Kew Gardens, rented in 1728 by Queen Caroline, which thereby acquired the name of **Kew Palace.** The

move from Kensington Palace to **Buckingham Palace** was made in 1837 by Queen Victoria. Although George IV had previously spent enormous sums of money on it, the definitive identity of Buckingham Palace was created by the remodelling of the main front in 1913. The **Palace of Holyrood House, Edinburgh**, which has retained much of its ancient character, is the official residence of the monarch in Scotland.

But the most palatial structure in the British Isles is not royal: **Blenheim Palace**, *Oxon*, was built early in the eighteenth century for the Duke of Marlborough. The Baroque design by John Vanbrugh sought to outdo the grandiloquent court architecture then in vogue on the European mainland. [see BISHOP'S PALACE, STATELY HOME, **179**]

## PALAZZO

The Italian word for 'palace' defines a type of grand residence, often in an urban context. The Italianate *palazzo* was promoted above all by Charles Barry as a fitting idiom for gentlemen's clubs, e.g. the **Travellers'** of 1829 and the **Reform** of 1830 in London. The *palazzo* style, with its solid and stately aspect standing tall and dignified, was especially favoured by banks and commercial houses in the nineteenth century, notably in **Bradford**, *W Yorks*, and in **Manchester.** [see RUSTICATION]

**263** *Spencer House, London. Note the rusticated basement and the tall* piano nobile *of this elegant palazzo.*

## PALLADIANISM

The theory and practice of the Palladian style originated in the writings and buildings of the Italian architect Andrea Palladio (1508–80). Although he designed palaces and churches, Palladio's enduring international repute resulted from his distinctive designs for villas or country houses in the Veneto region of Italy. In these he applied principles of symmetry and harmonious proportion culled from his analysis of ancient Roman buildings; and he added elements of temple architecture, e.g. the pediment, to grace and dignify many a noble residence. The success of the original Palladian formula was that it could transform an ordinary house in the country into a veritable temple of apparent Classical authenticity.

The first true disciple of Palladianism in England was Inigo Jones (1573–1652), whose buildings are particularly in evidence in London, e.g. the **Banqueting House, Whitehall**, from 1619; the **Queen's House, Greenwich**, from 1616; the **Queen's Chapel, St James's**, from 1623; and the church of **St Paul,**

**264** *The east front of Chiswick House, London. A grand staircase leads up to the portico of the villa.*

**Covent Garden**, from 1631. The Palladian enthusiasms of Inigo Jones are also much in evidence in his work at **Wilton House**, *Wilts*, where he devised some magnificent

## PALISADE

Defensive wall of wooden stakes, e.g. as built by the Normans to enclose their motte and bailey castles. [see CASTLE, RATH]

## PALM HOUSE [see CONSERVATORY]

## PANEL TRACERY [see TRACERY]

## PANELLING

The lining of interior walls with timber in the form of overlapping boards dates back to the thirteenth century. The art of panelling or wainscoting as it was originally known had evolved further by the fifteenth century when the panel-and-frame method became widespread. This involved a framework of vertical stiles and horizontal rails which had narrow grooves to receive the individual panels. In this fashion even ceilings could be covered with panelling. In the later medieval period panels were painted or carved with a linenfold pattern which imitated the folds of a length of cloth when hung vertically. The Elizabethan era brought to the art of panelling its delight in a variety of motifs ranging from heraldic devices to columns and arches loosely derived from Classical architecture. Typical of the period is the **Great Oak Room** of *c.* 1590 in the **Red**

265 *The west elevation of Chiswick House. The dome rests on an octagonal drum. The chimneystacks are disguised as obelisks.*

apartments based on the exact proportions of a cube. But his example was not taken up by the next generation of architects after the hiatus of the Civil War in the 1640s.

In the 1720s Lord Burlington and a group of supporters launched a serious revival of Palladianism which was to dominate the architectural scene for more than half a century. During this time and beyond there arose in all parts of the British Isles a host of stately country houses with porticos and pediments, e.g. **Houghton Hall**, *Norfolk*, by Colen Campbell. Lord Burlington's own 'villa' of **Chiswick House, London**, is remarkable for the fact that it was designed not for occupation but as a cultural showcase. In Ireland, the Palladian formula was applied to a new generation of elegant country houses, e.g. **Strokestown Park**, *Roscommon*; **Russborough**, *Wicklow*; and **Castletown House**, *Kildare*. In these artfully contrived designs, elegant colonnades link the main house to flanking pavilions which contain the service facilities of stables and kitchens. [see CUBE, PIANO NOBILE, VENETIAN DOOR or WINDOW, VILLA, 49, 126, 129, 195, 211]

**Lodge, Bristol,** *Avon.* The trend for fanciful ornamentation continued into the Jacobean age, e.g. at **Audley End,** *Essex.* The French term '*boiserie*' refers to elaborately carved panelling from the seventeenth century, e.g. in the **Cedar Drawing Room, Warwick Castle,** *Warw.* By the nineteenth-century panelling had become more uniform and the old craft skills were increasingly mechanized. But a rich man was still able to indulge a taste for ornate panelling, e.g. William Waldorf Astor's refurbished **Hever Castle,** *Kent,* from 1903.

## PANTILE

Curved roofing tile of S-shaped section, introduced from the Low Countries in the 1630s. It is a marked regional feature of the eastern counties of England, especially Norfolk. [see TILE]

## PARABOLIC or PARABOLOID [see ROOF]

## PARADISE

Open courtyard in front of a church, or the garden of a monastery. The word is little used, but the cloister garth of **Chichester Cathedral,** *W Sussex,* is called a paradise. [see PARVIS or PARVISE]

## PARADOS

In medieval military architecture, a bank of earth or low wall on the inner side of a fortification.

## PARAPET

Low wall, often battlemented, along the roof of a house or on a curtain wall.

## PARAPET SPIRE [see SPIRE]

## PARCLOSE

Screen within a church which provides a division between a shrine or chapel and the main body of the church. [see ROOD SCREEN]

266 *The parapet of the medieval city wall which still encircles York,* N Yorks.

## PARGETING

External decorative plasterwork in low relief, applied to half-timbered houses; it was especially popular in the sixteenth and seventeenth centuries, e.g. at the **Old Sun Inn, Saffron Walden,** *Essex*; and the **Priest's House, Clare,** *Suffolk.*

267 *Impressive pargeting on a gable end of the Old Sun Inn, Saffron Walden,* Essex.

**268** *The rich medievalism of the Gothic Revival lavishly displayed in the House of Lords, Westminster, London.*

## PARLIAMENT HOUSE

Throughout the Middle Ages and right up to 1834, when destroyed by fire, the Palace of Westminster, London, was the principal home of first the English and then the British parliament. The new **Houses of Parliament** by Charles Barry and A.W.N. Pugin were a successful symbiosis of Gothic ornamentation and Classical planning, of which Pugin remarked: 'All Grecian, sir; Tudor details on a classic body'. The opulent interior of the House of Lords is a particularly evocative expression of the Gothic Revival. The House of Commons was rebuilt after bomb damage during the Second World War (1939–45).

Scotland's former **Parliament House** in **Edinburgh** of *c.* 1640 possesses a fine hammerbeam roof with a 49 feet (14·9m) span; but its parliamentary career came to an early end in 1707 with the Treaty of Union between Scotland and England. In Dublin, the **Irish Parliament House** of 1729 was a grand Neo-Classical building by Edward Lovett Pearce and far superior to its rival at Westminster at that time; but it was rendered redundant in 1801 when the the Act of Union with Britain came into force. It was then sold to the Bank of Ireland and modified in order to 'reconcile the citizens' to the changed circumstances. The present Irish Parliament meets in **Leinster House, Dublin**, a town mansion of 1745 designed by Richard Castle.

## PARLIAMENTARY CHURCH

Denotes the churches built in the Scottish Highlands following Acts of Parliament of 1823–4. Standard designs were used for these plain edifices, including one by Thomas Telford, e.g. at **Staffin, Isle of Skye**, which is typically austere. [see **200**]

## PARPEN

Block of masonry which passes through the entire thickness of a wall, and thus has two exposed faces.

## PARTERRE

The ground floor of a theatre auditorium behind the orchestra.

## PARVIS or PARVISE

Term more commonly used in France which denotes an area in front of a cathedral or church. In the British context the word is sometimes used to describe the upper chamber of a church porch. [see PARADISE, PORCH]

## PASSAGE GRAVE [see CHAMBERED TOMB]

## PAVEMENT [see MOSAIC]

## PAVILION

Ornamental type of structure which may be used as a summerhouse in a garden or by spectators and players at a cricket field. In the latter context, a pavilion can be anything from a wooden hut to a multi-storeyed building with imposing balconies, e.g. at **Lord's Cricket Ground, London**. The word may also be applied to subsidiary blocks flanking a larger building. Elegant stone pavilions mark the corners of the formal garden at **Montacute**, *Somerset*; their pointed roofs suggest the canopy of a medieval tent, which is the original meaning of *'pavillon'* in French. The idea of the pleasure pavilion as a building of light-hearted fantasy was taken to the extreme from about 1811 by John Nash's rebuilding of the **Royal Pavilion, Brighton**, *E Sussex*, for the Prince Regent. However, the term was also used at **Wrest Park**, *Beds*, for the **Pavilion** of 1709–11 by Thomas Archer, which is a garden building in the Classical manner. [see CASINO, GARDEN BUILDINGS, **190**]

## PEABODY BUILDINGS

The American philanthropist George Peabody devoted much of his energies and fortune 'to ameliorate the condition of the poor and needy of this great metropolis (London) and to promote their comfort and happiness'. He pursued this aim through the construction of decent housing at affordable rents; and between 1862 and 1897 the Peabody Trust managed to rehouse some 20,000 people from the London slums. The distinctive architecture of the Peabody Buildings, mainly

**269** OPPOSITE *Garden pavilion at Montacute House, Somerset. Note the ogee-shaped roof and stone finial.*

**270** *Typically dour exterior of one of London's Peabody Buildings. This one is in Bloomsbury.*

designed by Henry Darbishire, has a prison-like quality, with its spartan inner courtyards and forbidding exteriors which strike a defensive note. This was probably the intent, since Peabody Buildings were implanted in the middle of slum areas as bastions of respectability. Inner London abounds in impressive specimens, e.g. **Old Pye Street, Westminster; Peartree Court, Clerkenwell; Greenman Street, Islington**; and a vast complex between the **Barbican** and **Old Street**. Grim as they now appear, the Peabody Buildings were a considerable improvement on the squalid housing which they replaced.

## PEBBLEDASH [see ROUGHCAST]

## PEDESTAL

In Classical architecture, a supporting element of a column, consisting of a plinth, a die or dado and a cornice. A pedestal may also support an ornamental urn or statue.

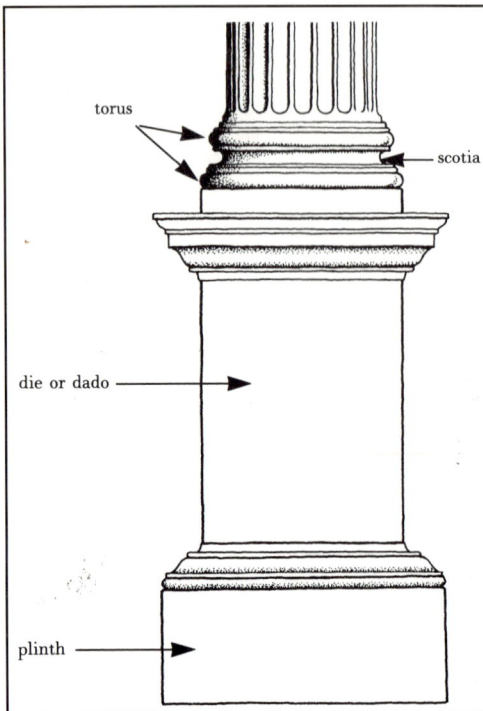

## PEDIMENT

In Classical architecture, the triangular frame or gable resting on the entablature above a portico. The pediment came to be used in Neo-Classical buildings as a purely decorative feature over doors and windows. An open pediment dispenses with the apex of the triangle; a broken pediment has an opening in its base; and a segmental pediment replaces the two upper members of the triangle with one continuous arc or segment. [see ENTABLATURE, **242, 282, 300, 310**]

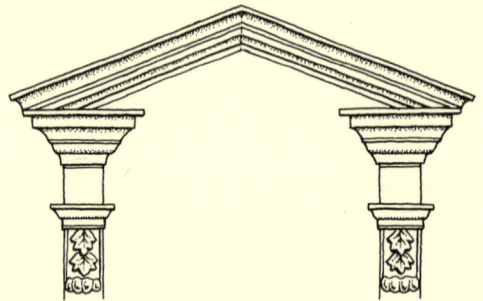

Broken pediment

## PELE or PEEL TOWER

Tower house of modest proportions, like a fortified farmhouse arranged vertically. Many were built in the troubled border area of England and Scotland, e.g. at **Elsdon**, *Northum*; and **Smailholm Tower**, near **Kelso**, *Borders*, Scotland. [see BASTLE HOUSE, TOWER HOUSE]

## PENDANT

Literally, a hanging element in a roof or ceiling, e.g. in the fan vaults of the **Henry VII Chapel, Westminster Abbey, London**; and the **Divinity School, Oxford**, *Oxon*.

Regular or triangular pediment

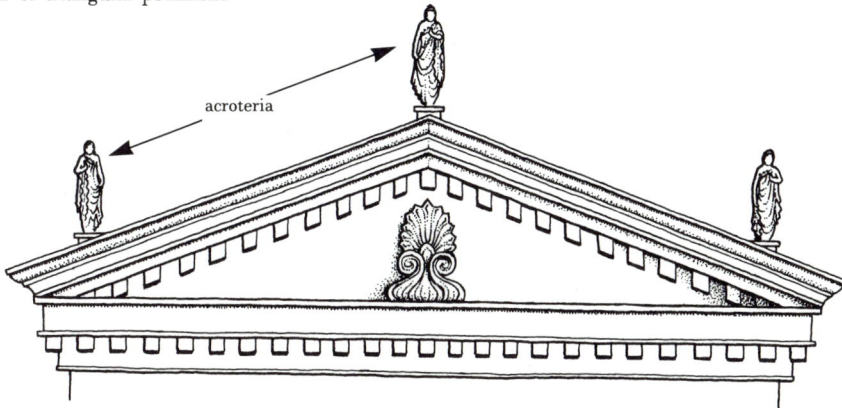

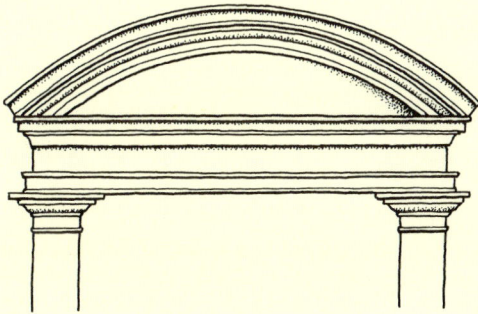

acroteria

Segmental pediment

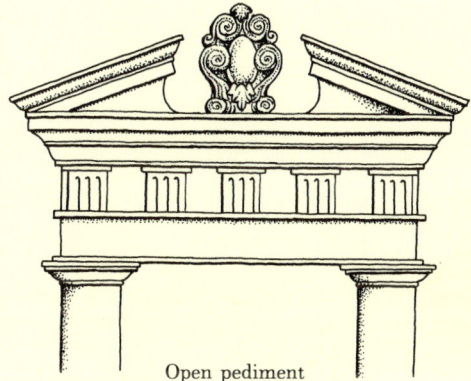

Open pediment

[see FAN VAULT, PLASTERWORK, 161]

## PENDENTIVE
Triangular transitional element with concave sides between a right-angled structure and a circular drum or dome. [see SQUINCH]

## PENTHOUSE
Ancillary structure with sloping roof, leaning on the wall of a larger building; or an additional structure on the roof of a hotel, apartment house or office block. [see LEAN-TO]

## PERGOLA
Item of garden architecture consisting of a covered walk formed by parallel rows of columns connected by overhead beams, and usually adorned with climbing plants, e.g. at **Polesden Lacey,** Surrey.

## PERIPTERAL
In Classical architecture, a type of temple in which the cella is surrounded entirely by columns. Imitations were popular features in landscape gardens, e.g. the **Temple of Ancient Beauty** at **Stowe,** *Bucks,* designed in 1734 by William Kent. [see MONOPTERAL]

271 *The box pews of St Mary-at-Hill, London, are an integral part of Wren's design. Note the big reredos.*

## PERISTYLE

In Classical architecture, a single row of columns surrounding an open courtyard. [see EGYPTIAN HALL]

## PERPENDICULAR GOTHIC [see GOTHIC]

## PEW

Fixed wooden bench arranged in rows in a church to seat the congregation and choir. Pews were introduced in the fourteenth century and became increasingly elaborate in the later Middle Ages when carpenters demonstrated their prowess by carving ornate bench ends, sometimes topped by finials known as poppyheads. In the post-Reformation era, and especially in the seventeenth century, high box pews with hinged doors became common in churches and the meeting houses of the Nonconformists. Many of Christopher Wren's churches in the **City of London** were originally fitted out with box pews which completely filled the nave, e.g. at **St Mary-at-Hill**. In many parish churches family pews were private enclaves set apart from the rest of the congregation, rather like a box at the theatre. Sometimes these were sumptuously furnished, e.g. the **Scrope Pew** at **Holy Trinity, Wensley**, *N Yorks*, and the **Bateman Pew** at **St John the Evangelist, Shobdon**, *Heref & Worcs*. [see BENCH END, MISERICORD, POPPYHEAD, STALLS]

## PIANO NOBILE

Italian term, meaning the 'noble storey' in the sense of the principal floor of a *palazzo*, set above a modest basement and containing the most prestigious rooms. The *piano nobile* was a marked feature of the Palladian style with its range of tall windows dominating the façade. The importance of the *piano nobile* was often stressed by a triumphal external staircase, e.g. at **Chiswick House, London**. [see PALLADIANISM]

## PIAZZA

The urban square of Renaissance Italy was introduced to London in 1631 by the **Covent Garden** scheme designed by Inigo Jones. This piazza gave birth to the many London squares subsequently laid out, although these frequently substituted an enclosed private garden for the open public space of the Italian original. [see SQUARE]

## PICTISH STONES [see CROSS SLAB]

## PIER

Solid vertical support of brick or masonry, also known as a pillar. In Gothic architecture a pier is usually surrounded by a number of attached circular shafts and is known as a compound or clustered pier. [see PILASTER, RESPOND, SEASIDE PIER]

## PILASTER

In Classical architecture, a pier of rectangular section projecting from a wall, and belonging to one of the orders. [see **272, 279**]

## PILASTER STRIP [see LESENE]

272 *Lindsey House, London. The* piano nobile *is evident in the tall first-floor windows. Note the pilasters.*

273 *Piazza at Covent Garden, London. The false portico of St Paul's is for scenic effect. Note the entasis.*

## PILLAR [see PIER]

## PINEAPPLE

The emblem of the pineapple carved in stone commonly occurs as a finial on gateposts and balustrades. It may well owe its popularity to its symbolism as a token of welcome. The cult of the pineapple was given its most splendid monument in 1761 at **Dunmore Park**, *Central*, Scotland, where Lord Dunmore built himself an exquisite banqueting house, a folly in the form of a pineapple 50 feet (15·2m) in height.

## PINNACLE

Ornamental spire-like structure, usually decorated with crockets, which occurs on medieval buttresses and towers e.g. at **Magdalen College, Oxford**, *Oxon*. [see 55]

## PISCINA

Carved stone basin set in a niche of the chancel wall of a church, used for washing the Communion vessels.

## PIT [see OUBLIETTE]

## PITCHED ROOF [see ROOF]

## PLANNED VILLAGE

Planned or model villages have been inspired by a wide variety of motives, from the landscaping ideals of country gentlefolk and the social theories of philanthropists to the practical ambitions of industrialists. Some of the earliest planned villages were laid out as unimaginative rows of cottages on either side of a main street, e.g. **Nuneham Courtenay**, *Oxon*, in the 1760s by Lord

274 *Saltaire*, W Yorks. *Note the cobblestones.*

Harcourt and **Milton Abbas**, *Dorset*, from 1773 by the future Earl of Dorchester. Such uniformity and regimentation in the village scene was condemned as unEnglish by the proponents of the Picturesque who advocated schemes offering variety and surprise. More adventurous in this respect were the eighteenth-century planned villages of **Selworthy Green**, *Somerset*; **Old Warden**, *Beds*; and **Blaise Hamlet**, *Avon*. Notions of social reform underlay the model villages of **Ford**, *Northum*, and **Talbot Village**, *Hants*.

The industrial era of the late eighteenth century gave birth to the factory village. **New Lanark**, *S'clyde*, Scotland,

**275** *Milton Abbas*, Dorset (ABOVE) *was a village built by the local landowner.*
**276** *New Lanark* (BELOW) *was a Scottish factory village where the planning resulted from the social philosophy of the founders.*

grew out of the utopian vision of the textile manufacturers David Dale and Robert Owen. The industrial magnates Titus Salt and Edward Akroyd gave their names to their mid-nineteenth-century factory villages of **Saltaire** and **Akroydon** in Yorkshire. The Irish landscape is full of villages and even small towns planned by the local landowner, e.g. **Strokestown**, *Roscommon*; **Westport**, *Mayo*; and **Birr**, *Offaly*. The village of **Adare**, *Limerick*, is a picturesque collection of English-style thatched cottages, built around the middle of the nineteenth century by the 3rd Earl of Dunraven. In Wales, in 1925, the architect Clough Williams-Ellis began at **Portmeirion**, *Gwynedd*, a planned village loosely modelled on Portofino in Italy. [see GARDEN CITY & SUBURB, NEW TOWN, PLANTATION TOWN]

### PLANTATION CASTLE
Type of castle, often of the Scottish tower-

*277 Monea, a plantation castle, Fermanagh, N Ireland.*

house type, built in Ireland in the course of the planned colonial settlements known as 'Plantations' of the sixteenth and seventeenth centuries, e.g. **Monea Castle** and **Castle Balfour**, *Fermanagh*, N. Ireland. [see PLANTATION TOWN, TOWER HOUSE]

### PLANTATION TOWN
Planned urban settlement in Ireland, especially in Ulster, founded by settlers from Britain. Several were named after their founders, e.g. **Cookstown**, *Tyrone*, and **Irvinestown**, *Fermanagh*, N. Ireland. [see PLANTATION CASTLE]

### PLASTERWORK
Quality plaster, a mixture of burned gypsum and water which sets hard on drying, was introduced to England from France in the thirteenth century and was known as 'Plaster of Paris'. Lavish use of fanciful plasterwork really began with the Elizabethans, whose stylistic invention was followed by the Jacobeans. Fine seventeenth-century plaster ceilings have survived at **Lanhydrock**, *Cornwall*; **Levens Hall**, *Cumbria*; and **Craigievar Castle**, *Grampian*, Scotland. These were confident, hand-crafted productions which relied on the bold relief of strapwork and even dramatic pendants for their artistic effect, unaided by the addition of colour. In the eighteenth century, the Adam brothers revolutionized the appearance of plasterwork in England and Scotland, while in Ireland the Italian Francini brothers brought their dazzling Rococo plasterwork creations to many a country house, e.g. **Castletown House**, *Kildare*, and **Riverstown**, *Cork*. Robert West was among the most talented of plaster craftsmen, e.g. at **86 St Stephen's Green, Dublin**, and at **Newbridge**, *Dublin*, Ireland. At **Castle Ward**, *Down*, N. Ireland, there is a novel attempt in the **Gothick Boudoir** to reproduce in plaster the effect of fan vaulting. The result was

described by John Betjeman as being like 'standing under the udders of a cow'. [see ADAM STYLE, CEILING, PARGETING, ROCOCO, STRAPWORK, STUCCO, **196**]

278 *Elaborate foliage patterns adorn this seventeenth-century plaster ceiling at Ham House, Surrey.*

## PLATE [see HALF-TIMBERING]

## PLATE TRACERY [see TRACERY]

## PLINTH
In Classical architecture, the supporting element of the base of a column or pedestal. [see ORDER, PEDESTAL, PODIUM]

## PODIUM
1) In Classical architecture, the continuous plinth constituting the base of a building. A plinth supporting a colonnade is called a stylobate.

2) Raised platform in an auditorium.

## POINTED ARCHITECTURE
Alternative term for Gothic architecture, since the pointed arch was the determining feature of the style. It was often used in lieu of 'Gothic' in the nineteenth century, e.g. in A.W.N. Pugin's pamphlet of 1853, *The True Principles of Pointed or Christian*

*Architecture.* However, the pointed arch may ultimately have Islamic origins. [see ARCH, BATTLE OF THE STYLES, GOTHIC]

## POINTING
Mortar exposed to view between the joints of masonry or courses of brickwork.

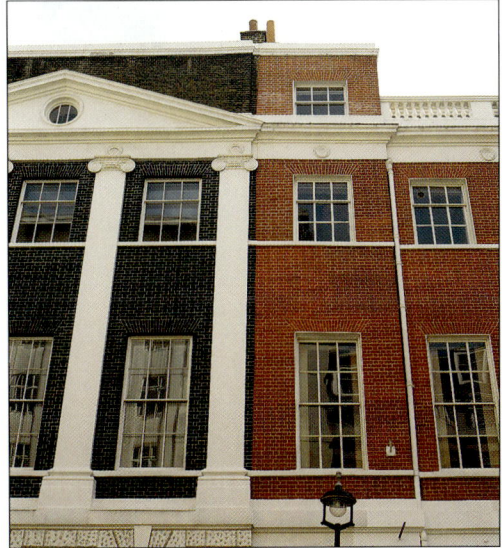

279 *The pointing shows up well in these façades in Stratford Place, London. Note the colossal pilasters.*

## POLYCHROMY
The practice of combining materials of various colour to create durable decorative patterns in the fabric of a building. It was promoted within the context of the Gothic Revival by John Ruskin in *The Seven Lamps of Architecture* and *The Stones of Venice*:

> The true colours of architecture are those of natural stone, and I would fain see these taken advantage of to the full. Every variety of hue, from pale yellow to purple, passing through orange, red and brown, is entirely at our command; nearly every kind of green and grey is also attainable; and with these, and pure white, what harmonies might we not achieve?

In practice, however, polychromy was generally achieved through the simpler combination of red, yellow and black brickwork with dressings of white stone, e.g. at William Butterfield's **Keble College, Oxford**, *Oxon*, of 1870 and at his **All Saints, Margaret Street, London**, of 1849. Spectacular polychromatic brickwork may be seen at **Templeton's Carpet Factory, Glasgow**, Scotland, of 1890. Polychromy is in favour among Post-Modernists. [see POST-MODERNISM, RUSKINIAN, **140, 289, 368**]

## POPPYHEAD
Type of finial of carved wood adorning a bench end, e.g. at **St Margaret, Cley-next-the-Sea**, *Norfolk*, and **St Mary, Ivinghoe**, *Bucks*. [see BENCH END]

## PORCH
Covered entrance to a building, especially of a church, where it might be fitted with benches and adorned with sculpture, e.g. at **Malmesbury Abbey**, *Wilts*. Sometimes a church porch may contain an upper storey, e.g. **St Mary Redcliffe, Bristol**, *Avon*. **St John the Baptist,**

**280** *The porch of St John the Baptist, Cirencester, Glos. Note the oriels arranged in bays.*

281 *The Adam portico at Osterley Park House, London.*

**Cirencester**, *Glos*, has a three-storey porch of *c.* 1490 in the Perpendicular style. [see GALILEE, PARVIS, PORTE COCHÈRE]

**PORTAL TOMB** [see DOLMEN]

**PORTCULLIS**
Defensive feature of a medieval gatehouse consisting of a heavy grille of iron, or wood and iron, which could be lowered by a windlass and secured by deep vertical grooves at the side. The defenders were able to fire at their attackers through the openings in the portcullis. Good examples remain at **Warwick Castle**, *Warw*, and at **Cahir Castle**, *Tipperary*, Ireland. [see YETT]

**PORTE COCHÈRE**
Porch designed to allow the passage of horse-drawn carriages.

**PORTICO**
Classical colonnade with pediment which provides a covered entrance and façade for a building of some consequence. [see 94, 264, 273]

**PORTICUS**
Shallow side chambers attached to the nave of a Saxon church. [see SAXON]

**PORTLAND STONE** [see LIMESTONE]

**POST**
Vertical timber of a roof or a half-timbered structure. [see HALF-TIMBERING, KING POST, QUEEN POSTS, TIMBER-TRUSSED ROOF]

**POST-AND-LINTEL** [see TRABEATED]

**POSTERN**
Small gateway, often a side or rear entrance to a walled enclosure such as a monastery, castle or fortified town. The remains of a thirteenth-century postern gate may be seen on **Tower Hill, London**. [see SALLY-PORT]

# POST-MODERNISM

Term first coined in the 1940s, but more widely used since the 1970s, to describe the styles which arose as a reaction against the worst excesses of Modernism. As the name implies, Post-Modernism can be better understood in terms of what it seeks to replace than of what it actually stands for. However, its approach and methods are distinctive: it is eclectic, promotes symbol and decoration such as poly-chromy, oriels and pediments, and it takes delight in whim-sical statements and historical references from Egyptian to Classical. Post-Modernist buildings aim to be enter-taining as well as utilitarian, e.g. the **Regatta Headquarters, Henley**, *Oxon*, of 1985 by Terry Farrell and the **Clore Gallery** at the **Tate, London**, of 1989 by James Stirling. The critics of Post-Modernism dismiss it as jokey and superficial, but it has produced some lively results e.g. the **Marco Polo Building** in **Battersea**, London. [see MODERNISM]

282 *Post-Modernism's talent for visual entertainment is conveyed by the Marco Polo Building, London* (ABOVE) *where the Neo-Classical open pedi-ment endows the structure with a mix-ture of tradition and bravado.*
283 *The Clore Gallery at the Tate, London,* (BELOW) *relies on colour and detail for its playful effects.*

284 *Grimspound, Dartmoor,* Devon, *once sheltered a small community. It contains the traces of some twenty round huts. The wall of the pound has been restored.*

## POUND

Prehistoric drystone walled enclosure built to afford protection against rustlers and animal predators, e.g. **Grimspound** on **Dartmoor**, *Devon*, which dates back to the Bronze Age. [see CAHER, CASHEL]

## POWER STATION

Some early power stations aspired to architectural grandeur, e.g. Giles Gilbert Scott's majestic **Battersea Power Station, London**, of 1929–33 which symbolizes the awesome potential of industrial energy. Modern power stations tend to concentrate on naked engineering, although their cooling towers do possess an austere kind of beauty.

## PRECEPTORY

Estate or building belonging to the Knights Templar in the Middle Ages. The fortified church of **Torpichen Preceptory**, *Lothian*, Scotland, later became the principal Scottish seat of the Knights Hospitallers of St John.

## PREFAB [see INDUSTRIALIZED BUILDING]

## PREHISTORIC

The residents of Britain during the Old Stone Age which ended in *c.*8300 BC left behind no architecture; but traces of their occupation have been discovered in natural caves, e.g. **Kent's Cavern**, *Devon*; **Creswell Crags**, *Derbys*; **Wookey Hole** and **Gough's Cave, Cheddar Gorge**, *Somerset*.

The Mesolithic or Middle Stone Age (*c.*8300 BC – *c.*4000 BC) was characterized by a nomadic society consisting of tribes of hunter-gatherers, whose mobility was largely determined by their endless quest for food supplies. Little remains of the Mesolithic peoples but the scant traces of their seasonal camp sites, e.g. at **Mount Sandel**, *Derry*, N. Ireland, and occasionally middens or mounds of domestic rubbish composed of bones or crustacean shells, e.g. on the Scottish Hebridean island of **Oronsay**.

The Neolithic or New Stone Age

285 *The oldest prehistoric housing in the British Isles is at Knap of Howar on Papa Westray, Orkney, Scotland.*

(*c.*4000 BC – *c.*2000 BC) witnessed the revolutionary transition to organized agriculture and permanent settlements with proper houses, e.g. the Neolithic villages of **Skara Brae** and **Knap of Howar** on **Orkney**, Scotland. The period also saw the beginnings of a sophisticated burial culture in chambered tombs and of ritual settings of standing stones, e.g. at **Avebury** and **Stonehenge**, *Wilts*, which achieved their full glory during the Bronze Age (*c.*2000 BC – *c.*700 BC). During this time individual interments came to replace collective burials. The Iron Age (*c.*700 BC – AD 43) was marked by increasing social and political tensions as tribes of warriors vied for supremacy and sought security in defensive strongholds, notably the hillforts and promontory forts which were eventually abandoned during the Roman occupation. It was the colonization of most of mainland Britain by the Romans from AD 43 which marked the end of the prehistoric era. [see AVENUE, BARROW, BROCH, CAHER, CAIRN, CASHEL, CAUSEWAYED CAMP, CELTIC, CHAMBERED TOMB, CHEVAUX DE FRISE, CIST, COURTYARD HOUSE, COVE, CRANNÓG, CUP-AND-RING MARKS, DESERTED VILLAGES, DOLMEN, DUN, EARTHWORK, FOGOU, HENGE, HILLFORT, HUT, MEGALITH,

MIDDEN, MONOLITH, ORTHOSTAT, POUND, PROMONTORY FORT, RATH, SARSEN, STANDING STONE, STONE CIRCLE, TRILITHON, VITRIFIED FORT, WHEELHOUSE]

## PRESBYTERY
Part of a church located east of the choir and containing the high altar. [see CHOIR, CHANCEL, RETRO-CHOIR]

## PRESTRESSED CONCRETE [see CONCRETE]

## PRINCIPAL RAFTERS [see RAFTERS]

## PRIORY
Monastic establishment under the authority of a prior or prioress. [see MONASTERY]

## PRISON or GAOL
In the Middle Ages prisoners were locked up in a variety of places ranging from castle dungeons to cells in market houses. Probably the earliest purpose-built prison in the British Isles was that at **Hexham**, *Northum* in *c.* 1330. However, prison architecture did not evolve as a specialized genre until the eighteenth century, e.g. with Newgate Prison, London, of 1770–8 by George Dance II, which was demolished in 1902. **Kilmainham Jail,**

286/287 *The forbidding architecture of penal confinement: Beaumaris Gaol* (ABOVE) *on Anglesey, Wales, and Kilmainham Jail* (OPPOSITE) *in Dublin, Ireland.*

**Dublin**, Ireland, of 1787–96 acquired a grim reputation as the 'Bastille of Ireland' and was left to rot from 1924 until 1960 when it was refurbished as a museum and memorial. **Beaumaris Gaol** on **Anglesey**, *Gwynedd*, Wales, was built in 1823 according to the improved standards of the Gaol Act of that year; it was closed in 1878 and is remarkably well preserved. In the Victorian era many large prisons were built, e.g. **Wormwood Scrubs** and **Pentonville, London**. **Belmarsh** in **Woolwich, London**, of 1991 marked a new approach to prison design. [see DUNGEON, OUBLIETTE, 74]

## PRODIGY HOUSE [see ELIZABETHAN]

## PROMONTORY FORT

Variant of the Iron Age hillfort which makes use of the natural defences provided by the headland of a cliff, leaving only the landward approach to be strengthened by ditches and ramparts. Cornwall bears the traces of some twenty-two promontory forts around its rugged coastline, e.g. at **Porth Island** at **St Columb Minor**. Also known as a cliff castle.

## PROSCENIUM

In Classical architecture, the stage of a Greek or Roman theatre. In modern usage, the term denotes that part of the theatre between the curtain and the orchestra or the stage arch facing the auditorium.

## PUBLIC HOUSE

The development of the public house as a specialized building belongs firmly to the Victorian era when the characteristic interiors lined with mahogany, brass and mirrors were created in order to provide a dignified and comfortable environment. Every item was embellished, from the painted porce-

288 *A fine example of Victorian pub architecture: the Crown Liquor Saloon, Belfast, N Ireland.*

lain handles of the beer pumps to the ornate cast iron legs of the tables and the etched designs on the window glass. From *c*. 1880 pub layouts favoured a proliferation of private booths or compartments, sometimes known as snugs. The **Crown Liquor Saloon, Belfast,** N. Ireland, of 1885 and the **Red Lion, Duke of York Street, London**, of 1880 are outstanding examples of the period. [see INN, 19]

## PUDDING STONE

Stone composed principally of an amalgam of sandstone fragments and usually smoothed by the passage of water. The result is a building stone of coarse texture. [see SANDSTONE]

## PULPIT

Elevated structure of stone or wood in a church or cathedral used for the preaching of the sermon. A medieval pulpit was usually carved in the Gothic style and often painted as well, e.g. in the collegiate church at **Fotheringhay**, *Northants*. The imposing appearance of a pulpit was sometimes heightened by the addition of a canopy or tester above. In the seventeenth century these could serve as acoustic sounding boards to project the voice of the preacher to optimum effect. The pulpits of Christopher Wren's churches are

289/290 *The Victorian pulpit of All Saints, Margaret Street, London,* (ABOVE) *and the medieval specimen at Fotheringhay, Northants,* (RIGHT) *show contrasting styles.*

particularly fine, e.g. at **St Stephen Walbrook, London** of 1672–9. Pulpits of the Georgian era were occasionally quite elaborate. The impressive triple-decker pulpit provided a seat for the clerk in the lowest section; the middle section was occupied by the priest when reciting prayers; and the top section was reserved for the preaching of the sermon. The pulpit was usually a permanent fixture, but some churches preferred a wheeled pulpit which could be moved according to

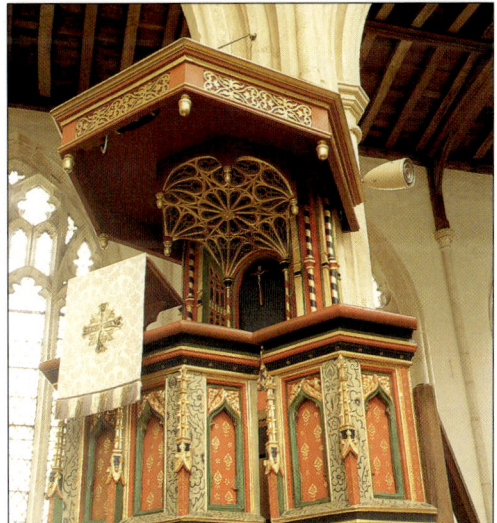

changing needs and circumstances, e.g. at **St Michan, Dublin**, Ireland. Victorian pulpits generally reflected the spirit of the Gothic Revival.

## PULPITUM

Stone screen dividing the choir from the nave of a cathedral, generally adorned with fine Gothic carving and with canopied niches for statues. The pulpitum of **York Minster**, *N Yorks*, of *c.* 1500 contains a sculpture gallery portraying the medieval kings of England. Many cathedrals have lost their pulpitum, but examples survive at **Canterbury**, *Kent*; **Exeter**, *Devon*; **Gloucester**, *Glos*; **Rochester**, *Kent* and **Southwell**, *Notts*. One of the functions of the pulpitum was to provide privacy for the choir stalls as well as a measure of protection from cold draughts. [see ROOD SCREEN]

## PUMPING STATION

Building which houses the great pumps required for the mains water supply or sewage disposal. Victorian architects often produced extravagant and exotic designs for these structures. The lofty standpipe tower of 1867 at **Kew Bridge Pumping Station, London,** is dressed up as an Italian campanile; **Abbey Mills Pumping Station** of 1869 at **West Ham, London,** is a fantasy of Orientalism; and the monumental specimen at **Papplewick**, *Notts*, of the 1880s is a bold composition of Renaissance inspiration. [see WATER TOWER]

## PURBECK MARBLE [see MARBLE]

## PURLIN

Longitudinal timber piece in a roof. [see TIMBER-TRUSSED ROOF]

## PUTLOCK or PUTLOG

Short piece of timber inserted into a wall for the purpose of supporting scaffolding. Putlog holes, the apertures in the masonry made to receive the putlogs, are a feature of many medieval buildings.

## PYLON

In the architecture of ancient Egypt, a flanking tower of pyramidal shape located by the entrance to a temple. The profile of the pylon has been adapted for the colossal metal structures which carry high-voltage electricity across the country.

## PYRAMID

This square-based monument with triangular sides meeting at a pointed apex was evolved by the ancient Egyptians for royal tombs. In the British Isles the pyramid appears mainly as a funerary monument, e.g. at the **Egyptian Mausoleum, Blickling Hall**, *Norfolk*.

**291** *The steeple of St George, Bloomsbury, London, presents a novel version of the pyramid form.*

# Q

QIBLA [see MOSQUE]

## QUADRANGLE

Square or rectangular courtyard enclosed by buildings, often in a unified style. The quadrangle established itself in the fourteenth century as the prototype for college architecture, e.g. the **Mob Quad** at **Merton College, Oxford**, *Oxon*; and the **Old Court** of **Corpus Christi College, Cambridge**, *Cambs*. Among the most elegant is the **Canterbury Quadrangle** of 1631–6 at **St John's College, Oxford**, *Oxon*. [see CLOISTER]

QUADRATURA [see TROMPE L'OEIL]

## QUADRIGA

Sculptural group composed of a chariot drawn by four horses, e.g. that of 1912 on the **Constitution Arch** at **Hyde Park Corner, London**.

## QUARRY

Small pane of glass, either square or diamond-shaped, used to glaze a window of leaded lights. The word is derived from French *'carré'*, meaning a square. [see LEADED LIGHT, WINDOW]

QUATREFOIL [see FOIL, TRACERY]

**292** *The Old Court, Corpus Christi, Cambridge*, Cambs.

## QUEEN ANNE

The reign of Queen Anne (1702–14) was not a neatly circumscribed stylistic period, although it did coincide with the brief flowering of the Baroque in England. The label of 'Queen Anne' was rediscovered in the late nineteenth century by architects such as Norman Shaw (1831–1912) and W. Eden Nesfield (1835–98) who found inspiration in the buildings of the beginning of the eighteenth century for the development of their own architecture. The characteristics of this Victorian 'Queen Anne' were a homely but exciting blend of decorative red brickwork, white window frames, fanciful oriels and a dramatic roofscape with prominent eaves and gables. Norman Shaw really made the style his own in the fashionable parts of London, e.g. at **Lowther Lodge, Kensington**, of 1875 and **Old Swan House, Chelsea**, of 1876. The 'Queen Anne' style was also taken up in the garden suburb of **Bedford Park** in **Chiswick, London**. [see 257]

294 *The revived 'Queen Anne' style of the nineteenth century at Bedford Park, London.*

293 *Early eighteenth-century urbanism at Queen Anne's Gate, London. Note the canopies over the doors.*

## QUEEN POSTS

Vertical roof timbers arranged in pairs on a tie beam, supporting side purlins. [see KING POST, TIMBER-TRUSSED ROOF]

## QUIRE [see CHOIR]

## QUIRK

Abrupt V-shaped indentation in a moulding or between two mouldings.

## QUOIN

Derived from French '*coin*', meaning 'corner', the term denotes the dressed stones displayed prominently and decoratively on the corners of a building. The practical use of quoins goes back to the Saxon era, but they became a more stylish feature from the Tudor until the Victorian era. [see LONG AND SHORT WORK, 242]

## QUOIT [see DOLMEN]

# R

## RADIATING CHAPELS

Series of chapels projecting from the apse or ambulatory of a church or cathedral, e.g. at **Norwich Cathedral**, *Norfolk*.

## RADIATING VAULTS

Vaults springing from a central column, a feature of Gothic chapter houses, e.g. at **Westminster Abbey, London** and, **Lincoln Cathedral**, *Lincs.*

295 *A central column supports the radiating vaults of the chapter-house at Lincoln Cathedral,* Lincs.

## RAFTERS

Roof timbers which extend from the wall-plate to the ridge of the roof. There are two basic types: principals and common rafters. [see TIMBER-TRUSSED ROOF]

## RAGGLE

Recess or groove incised in a stone wall to receive the roof edge of an adjacent structure. [see **313**]

## RAGSTONE

Durable, coarsely textured limestone used for rough construction work. Kentish ragstone, transported by barge, was used by the Romans in conjunction with levelling courses of brick for the city wall of Londinium, built in *c.* AD 200. The Normans used Kentish ragstone in the construction of **Rochester Castle**, *Kent.* [see LEVELLING COURSE]

## RAIL

Horizontal element within the framework of a door or panel. [see DOOR, PANELLING]

## RAILINGS

Vertical iron bars set in stone or concrete which serve as a boundary fence. Iron railings were a feature of Georgian and Victorian town houses, sometimes to prevent people from falling into the sunken area between the pavement and basement. [see AREA, **99, 332**]

## RAILWAY ARCHITECTURE [see BRIDGE, STATION, TUNNEL, VIADUCT]

## RAINWATER HEAD

Box-shaped receptacle made of lead or cast iron, located at the top of a drainpipe and serving to collect rainwater from a gutter. The rainwater head may be ornamented by a heraldic device, a decorative monogram or some figurative design bearing the date of construction. [see GARGOYLE]

## RAMPART

A defensive wall or embankment. [see CASTLE, EARTHWORK, HILLFORT]

## RANDOM RUBBLE

Masonry composed of stones of irregular size and shape. [see RUBBLESTONE]

## RATH

Also known as a ringfort, this was the most widespread defensive structure during the Iron Age and early medieval period in Ireland, where the remains of some 30,000 have been identified. In essence, the rath was a fortified farmstead, consisting of a circular earthwork, behind which several huts were built. The rath was strengthened by a palisade driven into the embankment. The fact that so many raths have survived in Ireland may be partly due to the respect of farmers towards these 'fairy rings'. [see CASHEL, DUN]

## RAVELIN

In military architecture, an outwork beyond the main fortifications in the shape of an angular rampart resembling an arrowhead. The ravelin was a feature of many artillery forts, e.g. at **Fort George**, *Highland*, Scotland. [see FORT, REDAN]

## RECTILINEAR TRACERY [see TRACERY]

## REDAN

A small ravelin. [see RAVELIN]

## REEDING

Decorative moulding composed of closely grouped vertical convex elements.

## RE-ENTRANT

Inward-pointing angle, e.g. in a fortification. The opposite of a salient, which points outwards.

## REFECTORY

Dining-hall of a monastery, also known as the frater. [see MONASTERY]

## REGENCY

The architectural style which provided the transition between Georgian and Victorian took its name from the Regency of the Prince of Wales (1811–20) who later reigned as George IV (1820–30). The use of a royal title to describe a chapter in architectural history is more justified in the case of the Prince Regent than in any other since he was a most prolific and enthusiastic patron of major building projects. These ranged from the **Royal Pavilion** in **Brighton**, *E Sussex*, to a radical remodelling of **Buckingham Palace, London**, and **Windsor Castle**, *Berks*. The most impressive achievement of the period was the redevelopment of **London's West End**, extending up Regent Street to Regent's Park, a scheme devised by John Nash (1752–1835), the Prince Regent's most favoured architect and the chief exponent of the Regency style.

296 *Bust of a prolific Regency architect at a church of his own design: All Souls, Langham Place, London.*

Although the rules of Classical proportion still prevailed, there was an eclecticism to the Regency which drew its inspiration from India and China as well as Greece and Rome. Regency architecture is also well illustrated by the terraces, squares and crescents at **Brighton**, *E Sussex*, and **Cheltenham**, *Glos*, with their bow windows and graceful iron balconies and verandas. [see CHINOISERIE, GREEK REVIVAL, ORIENTALISM]

**297/298** *The theatricality of John Nash's grand design for London is shown by Chester Terrace* (RIGHT) *and Cumberland Terrace* (BELOW).

## REINFORCED CONCRETE [see CONCRETE]

## RELIEVING ARCH
Arch designed to relieve the weight pressing down on another arch or opening.

## RELIQUARY
Receptacle for the relics of a saint, most usually in the form of a small embellished casket. [see SHRINE]

## RENDERING
Plaster covering of a brick or stone wall.

## REREDORTER
Latrine block of a monastery. [see MONASTERY]

## REREDOS
Wooden or stone screen located behind the altar in a church, usually carved and deco-

## RENAISSANCE

The term is French, but the 'rebirth' of the Classical culture of Rome was initiated in Italy in the fifteenth century and came to full bloom in the sixteenth century. Generally, the first influx of Renaissance ideas in architecture and design crossed the English Channel after having passed through the medium of France and the Low Countries. The direct Italian influence of the Renaissance may be said to have begun in London in 1512 with the tomb of Henry VII in **Westminster Abbey** by Pietro Torrigiani, and the Italianate terracotta medallions affixed to the courtyard walls of **Hampton Court Palace** in the 1520s by Cardinal Wolsey. It became extremely fashionable to graft Renaissance motifs on to medieval buildings as a token of modernity, e.g. at **Old Wardour Castle**, *Wilts*; **Crichton Castle**, *Lothian*, Scotland; **Kenilworth Castle**, *Warw*; and at **Caerlaverock Castle**, *Dumfr & Gall*, Scotland, where in 1634 the Earl of Nithsdale added a handsome range in the new Renaissance manner.

**299** *The Leweston tomb, Sherborne Abbey*, Dorset, *is a Renaissance blend of Classical and medieval.*

**300** *The Renaissance pediments at Caerlaverock Castle,* Dumfr & Gall, *Scotland, are improvised but attractive.*

rated. The reredos could amount to a work of monumental proportions, e.g. at **Winchester Cathedral**, *Hants*; **Durham Cathedral**, *Durham*; and **St Albans Abbey**, *Herts*. [see RETABLE, 271]

## RESPOND

Half-pier bonded into a wall and supporting one end of an arch, usually at the termination of an arcade.

**301** *The Tuscan colonnade at Godolphin House,* Cornwall: *a sturdy provincial vision of Renaissance style.*

However, it was not until Inigo Jones (1573–1652) returned to England after his stay in Italy at the very beginning of the seventeenth century that the true spirit of the Italian Renaissance, as exemplified by the architecture of Andrea Palladio, made itself felt in the more serious and correct Classical manner known as Palladianism. But the Renaissance in Britain was cut short by the outbreak of Civil War in the 1640s. [see ELIZABETHAN, MANNERISM, PALLADIANISM]

## RESTORATION

The Restoration of the Monarchy in 1660 in the person of Charles II released many pent-up ideas and much energy in the realm of architecture. Above all, the Restoration is significant for the career of Christopher Wren (1632–1723) who went on to dominate the scene for two more generations. The exuberant mood of the times is well expressed by the lively invention of the English Baroque. The obvious delight in charming decoration marks a complete contrast to the austerity of the Puritan outlook under Cromwell. The superlative wood-carving skills of craftsmen such as Grinling Gibbons were deployed on a dazzling array of swags, garlands, festoons and some miraculous three-dimensional renderings of fruit and flowers. Gibbons came to prominence in 1670 and later worked in close association with Wren. Some of his best work may be seen on the stalls and organ case of **St Paul's Cathedral, London**, and in the chapel of **Trinity College, Oxford**, *Oxon.* **Tredegar House**, *Gwent*, Wales, of 1665 is a fine example of a country house of the Restoration period. [see BAROQUE, STUART]

**302** *Characteristic post-Restoration façade at Drumlanrig Castle,* Dumfr & Gall, *Scotland.*

## RETABLE

Framework of decorative panels which stand on the rear of an altar or just behind it, e.g. at **St Mary, Thornham Parva**, *Suffolk*. [see REREDOS]

## RETICULATED TRACERY [see TRACERY]

## RETRO-CHOIR

Eastward extension of a major church beyond the high altar, e.g. at **Southwark Cathedral, London**. [see APSE, AMBULATORY, PRESBYTERY]

## RETURN

Abrupt change of direction at a right angle of a dripstone or hood-mould. The term also applies to a row of choir stalls running north-south connecting the main stalls at their western ends.

## REVEAL [see JAMB]

## REVETMENT

1) Decorative facing of a wall.

2) Retaining wall of an embankment.

## RIB

Raised band of stone which relays the weight of a vault to a wall or column. As Gothic architecture evolved, so the ornamental deployment of ribs went far beyond any structural necessity, especially in the highly decorative fan vaults of the Perpendicular phase. [see FAN VAULT, LIERNE, VAULT, 45, 91, 157, 365]

## RIBBON DEVELOPMENT

Controversial phenomenon of the 1920s and 1930s: the practice of building houses in a single line along a main road. This contributed substantially to the suburbanization of the countryside, for the semidetached was the most usual type of house in such developments. In 1935 restrictions were imposed by the Ribbon Development Act.

## RIDGE, RIDGE-PIECE

Horizontal timber running lengthways along the apex of a roof; it receives the upper ends of the rafters. [see TIMBER-TRUSSED ROOF]

## RINGFORT [see CASHEL, DUN, RATH]

## RISE

Vertical distance from the springing line of an arch or vault to the soffit at its crown. [see ARCH]

## RISER

Vertical front of an individual step. [see STAIRCASE]

## ROCOCO

Decorative style of the eighteenth century which contrasted to the heaviness of Baroque with its fanciful use of delicate ornament. Patterns were composed of swirling scrolls, ribbons and graceful curves dotted with representations of shells, animals and birds. Rococo is derived from two French words: *'rocaille'* or rock-work and *'coquille'* or shell. Rococo is most apparent in the plasterwork by the Italian Francini brothers in the country houses of Ireland and in the town houses of Dublin decorated by Robert West. In London, Rococo made a rare appearance inside the Georgian house at **1 Greek Street** in **Soho**. The ceiling of the late seventeenth-century library at the **Queen's College, Oxford,** *Oxon*, sports some elegant Rococo plasterwork. **Claydon House**, *Bucks*, contains some magnificent rooms of *c.* 1765 decorated in the Rococo style. [see PLASTERWORK]

**303** OPPOSITE *The Rococo plaster at Castletown House, Kildare, Ireland, was the work of Italian craftsmen.*

## ROLL
Semi-circular moulding, sometimes known as a scroll. [see MOULDING]

## ROMAN
The Roman presence in the British Isles (AD 43 to 410) covered most of England and Wales and extended for a while into the Scottish Highlands. The Antonine Wall in the Central Lowlands of Scotland marked for a brief period the northernmost frontier of the Roman Empire before it fell back to the more defendable **Hadrian's Wall** which may still be seen in impressive sections between **Newcastle**, *Tyne & Wear*, and **Carlisle**, *Cumbria*. The conquest of Ireland was contemplated but never attempted. The relics of Roman Britannia cover a wide range of buildings and monuments. [see AGGER, AMPHITHEATRE, AQUEDUCT, BASILICA, BATH HOUSE, BRICKWORK, CASTRUM, DISTANCE SLAB, FORT, HYPOCAUST, LIGHTHOUSE, MOSAIC, TEMPLE, VILLA, WALL]

**304** *Gorgon's Head from the Temple of Sulis, Bath, Avon.*

**305** *Roman mosaic pavement c. AD 362 at Littlecote, Wilts, which adorned a shrine dedicated to Orpheus.*

## ROMANESQUE
Continental revival in the early Middle Ages of the Roman or round-arched style of building, better known in Britain as Norman, and in Ireland as Hiberno-Romanesque. [see CELTIC, NORMAN]

## ROOD, ROOD LOFT, ROOD SCREEN
'Rood' was the Saxon word for the cross or crucifix which was set up in medieval churches at the eastern end of the nave, usually suspended from a beam spanning the chancel arch. Sometimes the rood was supported on a rood screen which separated the nave from the chancel. The more substantial rood screens incorporated a loft or gallery which could be reached via a staircase. Often the stairs were built into the masonry adjacent to the chancel arch where they remain as evidence of many a rood screen destroyed in the aftermath of the Reformation in 1530s. The rood screens gave medieval carpenters an opportunity to make a prominent display of their talents, and many sought to emulate the prowess of the masons by creating wooden versions of stone structures, e.g. at **St Michael the Archangel, Mere**, *Wilts*; **St Peter & St Paul, Lavenham**, *Suffolk*; at **St Andrew, Cullompton**, *Devon*; and at **St Mary the Virgin, Charlton-on-Otmoor**, *Oxon*. [see PULPITUM]

# ROOF

There are several variations on the basic pitched or sloping roof, e.g. hipped, mansard, helm and gambrel. Nowadays many roofs are flat; but the technology of reinforced concrete has produced some novel forms such as the paraboloid and the hyperbolic paraboloid. [see SADDLEBACK, TIMBER-TRUSSED ROOF, **345**]

Pitched roof

Gambrel roof

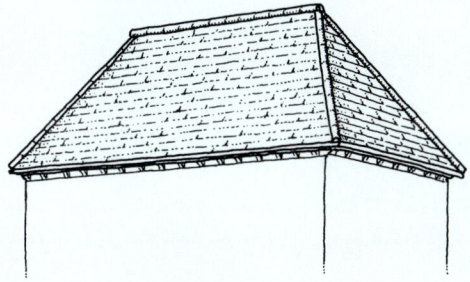

Hipped roof

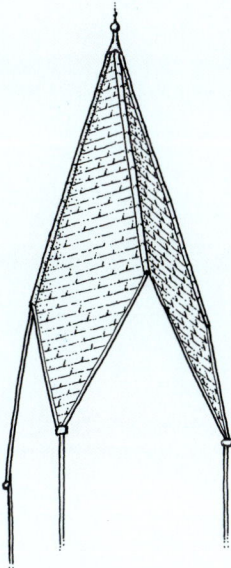

Helm roof

Mansard roof

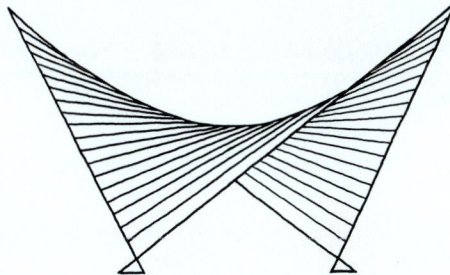

Hyperbolic paraboloid roof

306 *An unusual variant of the rose window at Winchester Palace, Southwark, London.*

## ROSE WINDOW

Circular window with ornate tracery, most commonly located in medieval cathedrals of the Early English and Decorated phases of Gothic, e.g. at **Westminster Abbey, London**; **York Minster**, *N Yorks*; **St Albans Abbey**, *Herts*; **Lincoln Cathedral**, *Lincs*. There is an impressive nineteenth-century rose window in the chapel of **Lancing College**, *W Sussex*. [see STAINED GLASS, WHEEL WINDOW, 250]

## ROTUNDA

Circular building of Classical origin. The type became popular in the eighteenth century as an eye-catcher in a landscape garden, e.g. the **Mussenden Temple** of 1785 at **Downhill**, *Derry*, N. Ireland. The great house at **Ickworth**, *Suffolk*, of 1794–1830 is in the form of an elliptical rotunda, connected by curving corridors to two flanking wings. [see MONOPTERAL, ROUND HOUSE, 89]

307 *The spectacular rotunda of the Mussenden Temple, Downhill, Derry, N Ireland, was built as a library.*

# ROUGHCAST

Durable external rendering composed of sand and cement with crushed stone, gravel or pebbles applied. Roughcast provides a building with a tough protective shell which prevents the penetration of water into the masonry joints. The technique is also known as pebbledash, and in Scotland as harling.

# ROUND CHURCH

In the early Middle Ages several churches were built with a circular nave in imitation of the Church of the Holy Sepulchre in Jerusalem, e.g. the much restored **Holy Sepulchre, Cambridge**, *Cambs*, of c. 1130 and the **Temple Church, London**, of *c.* 1240. Nothing remains of the round naves of **St John, Clerkenwell, London**, and the **Temple Church, Bristol**, *Avon*, whose present ruins date from the fifteenth century rebuilding. At **Orphir** on **Orkney**, Scotland, there is more to be seen of the round church of early twelfth-century date. The round church of the Knights Hospitaller at **Little Maplestead**, *Essex*, of *c.*1335 is well preserved and still in use.

308 *Remains of the round church at Orphir, Orkney, Scotland. The circular plan is marked on the ground.*

# ROUND HOUSE

Apart from the Classical rotunda, there are other types of structure which have adopted the circular ground plan. At **Veryan**, *Cornwall*, there are two pairs of round thatched cottages built in the early nineteenth century, which are said to owe their circular shape to an old superstition that the devil can only hide in corners. The imposing **Round House** at **Chalk Farm, London**, was built in 1847 to accommodate the turntable of the London and Birmingham Railway. [see ROTUNDA]

# ROUND TOWER

Characteristic structure of early Christian Ireland, which has been variously interpreted as a look-out, a refuge against Viking raids or a belltower – albeit without provision for a fixed bell. The sophisticated construction of the round tower represents a notable Irish contribution to the architecture of the period. The slender form with its conical roof is rendered elegant by the use of entasis, i.e. the slight swelling of the contour which counteracts the visual distortion that straight lines would have created. Irish round towers are invariably found in association with early medieval monastic sites, e.g. **Glendalough**, *Wicklow*; **Ardmore**, *Waterford*; **Monasterboice**, *Louth*; **Cashel**, *Tipperary*; **Kells**, *Meath*; **Devenish Island**, *Fermanagh*. The 112feet (34·1m) high round tower at **Kilmacduagh**, *Galway*, has developed a marked lean. The presence of two round towers in Scotland, at **Abernethy** and **Brechin**, *Tayside*, may be ascribed to Irish influence. The round towers span the tenth to twelfth centuries, but there was a renewed interest in the form of the round tower in the nineteenth century, e.g. the memorial to Daniel O'Connell in the **Glasnevin Cemetery, Dublin**, Ireland. Round towers of a different type, as fully integrated church towers, may be seen especially in **Suffolk** and **Norfolk**, where they evolved as a natural response

to the difficulty of building strong square corners with the local flint.

## ROUNDEL
Decorative panel of circular shape, made of wood, glass or stucco.

## RUBBLESTONE
Stone that is tough and durable but impossible to work. It is usually employed for walls, sometimes with freestone dressings, e.g. at **Farleigh Hungerford Castle**, *Somerset* of the fourteenth and fifteenth centuries. [see RANDOM RUBBLE]

## RUNNING DOG
Frieze ornament of Classical origin composed of a series of spirals like breaking waves.

## RUSKINIAN
One of the high priests of the Gothic Revival, John Ruskin (1819–1900) was not an architect, but his writings had a profound influence in their day. He promoted the honest use of building materials, i.e. not disguising them as something else. But it was his advocacy of polychromy and the forms of Venetian Gothic which established his reputation and created the Ruskinian style. However, Ruskin lived to regret the considerable impact of his successful propaganda:

> I would rather, for my own part, that no architects had ever condescended to adopt one of the views suggested in this book, than that any should have made the partial use of it which has mottled our manufactory chimneys with black and red brick, dignified our banks and drapers' shops with Venetian tracery, and pinched our parish churches into dark and slippery arrangements for the advertisement of cheap coloured glass and pantiles.

**309** OPPOSITE *Early Christian round tower at the monastic site of Glendalough, Wicklow, Ireland.*

(1874 preface to *The Stones of Venice*). [see POLYCHROMY, VENETIAN GOTHIC]

## RUSTICATION

This masonry technique originated from the fortified Italian *palazzo* which used large projecting blocks of rough-faced or 'rustic' stone to create a forbidding façade. Rustication is often applied only to the lower storey of a building in order to create the visual impression of a weighty and solid foundation. Several types of rustication evolved, e.g. vermiculated, diamond-pointed, and cyclopean, but the original concept has been extended to include smooth-faced and deeply chamfered masonry as well. [see **109, 263**]

**310** *Rustication on the lower façade of the Old Bailey, London. Note the segmental pediment.*

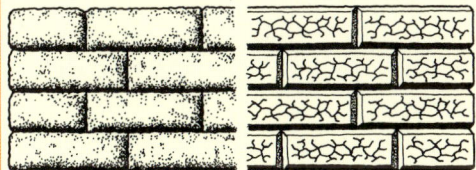

Cyclopean rustication    Vermiculated rustication

Smooth rustication

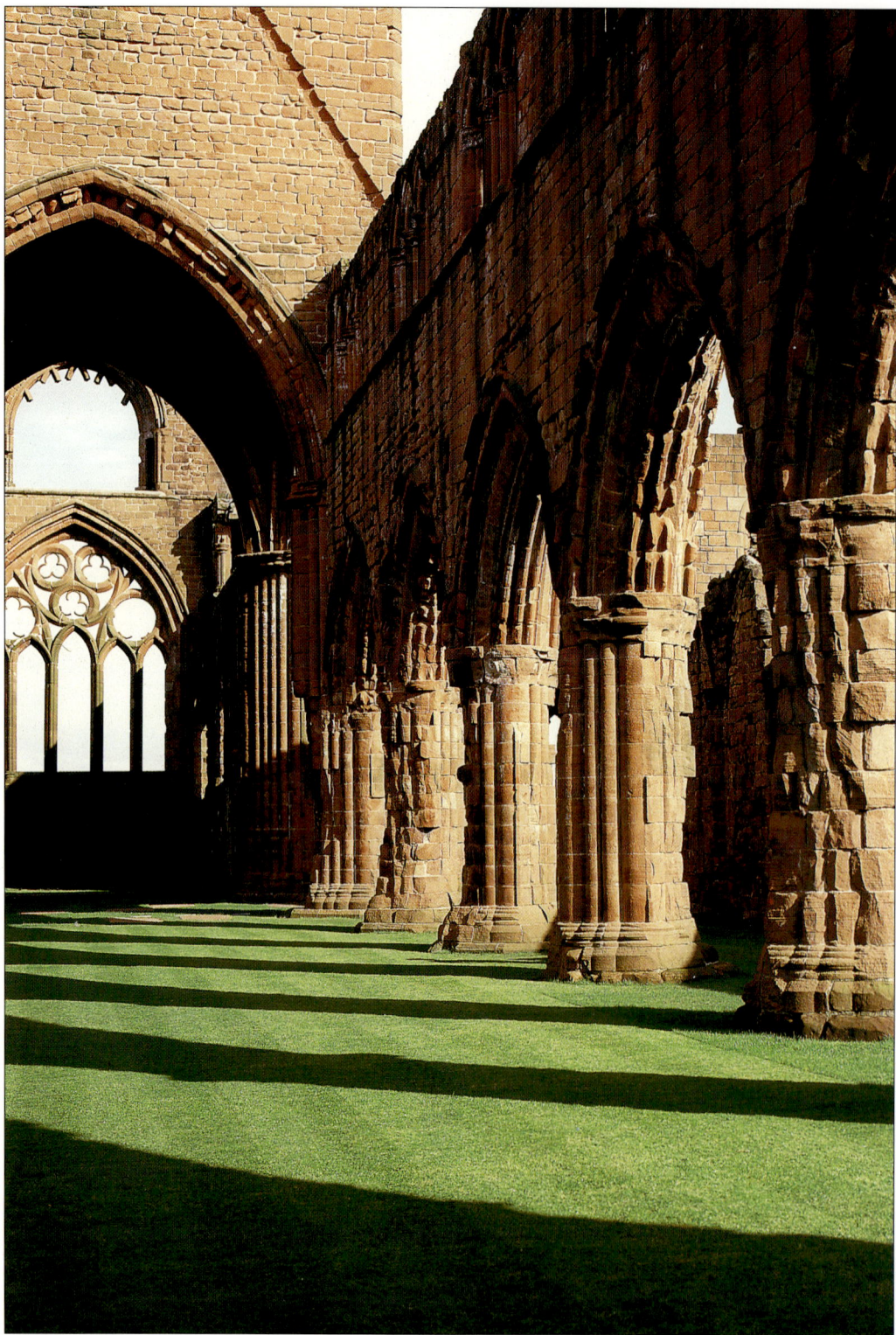

# S

**SACRISTY** [see VESTRY]

**SADDLEBACK ROOF**
Pitched roof located over a tower.

**SADDLE BAR**
Horizontal iron bar supporting the lead cames of a window. [see CAME, LEADED LIGHT]

**SALIENT** [see RE-ENTRANT]

**SALLY-PORT**
Small gate in a castle or town wall through which a tactical counter-attack could be launched. [see POSTERN]

**SANCTUARY**
Immediate surrounding of the main altar of a church, usually marked by a step and/or a low rail.

**SANDSTONE**
Sedimentary rock composed essentially of compressed sand, in which the grains of quartz and occasionally felspar or mica are bound together by something as strong as silica or as weak as clay. Sandstone occurs most plentifully in the northern counties of England and in southern Scotland, but also in the Midlands, Devon and Cornwall. Brownish colours predominate, but the best-known sandstones are the Old Red and the New Red. Many other hues are possible, from pink and grey to brown, yellow and deep purple. The cathedrals at **Chester**, *Cheshire*; **Carlisle**, *Cumbria*; **Hereford** and **Worcester**, *Heref & Worcs*, display a

variety of hues; as do **Sweetheart Abbey**, *Dumfr & Gall*, Scotland; and **Furness Abbey**, *Cumbria*. [see PUDDING STONE, SARSEN]

**SARACENIC**
Antiquated term for Islamic. [see ISLAMIC]

**SARSEN**
Boulder of grey siliceous sandstone which occurs on the surface of the land. The word 'sarsen' is derived from 'Saracen' since these stones were once considered to be foreign to the places where they are found. In fact, they are probably the remnants of rock strata which have long since been eroded. Sarsens were a convenient source of building stone for the megalithic structures of prehistory e.g. **Avebury** and **Stonehenge**, *Wilts*. [see MOORSTONE]

**SASH WINDOW**
Type of window which opens vertically in fixed grooves, introduced from Holland in the late seventeenth century. It has since generally replaced the casement type. [see CASEMENT, WINDOW]

**311** OPPOSITE *Sweetheart Abbey*, Dumfr & Gall, *Scotland*, shows the brilliant colour that sandstone can achieve.

**312** *A pair of elegant sash windows in Royal York Crescent, Bristol*, Avon.

## SAXON

Saxon (or Anglo-Saxon) culture prevailed in England from AD 410 to 1066 and made some inroads into southern Scotland and the Welsh borders. The Celtic realm of Ireland remained entirely untouched. The architectural remains of Saxon England are essentially of churches modest in scale and sparing in decoration. Beneath the later medieval structures of **Hexham Abbey**,

**313** *The late Saxon church of St Laurence, Bradford-on-Avon,* Wilts, *has a finely sculpted exterior.*

*Northum,* and **Ripon Cathedral**, *N Yorks,* are the remarkable Saxon crypts of churches founded in the 670s by St Wilfrid. The crypt at Hexham uses Roman masonry from the nearby ruins of Corstopitum. Some Roman stones were also incorporated into the Saxon church of **St John the Evangelist, Escomb**, *Durham,* of *c.* 675 which is a strikingly intact example of the basic square-ended, nave-and-chancel plan without aisles. There is also impressive Saxon work from *c.* 685 in the chancel of **St Paul, Jarrow**, *Tyne & Wear.* The Saxon crypt of **St Wystan, Repton**, *Derbys,* noted for its stylish twisted columns, has been

314 *Saxon sculpture of Christ dating back to c. 800 at St Mary, Breedon-on-the-Hill*, Leics.

315 *The solid Saxon crypt beneath Ripon Cathedral,* N Yorks, *was built in the late seventh century.*

dated to *c.* 760. There is a fine example of later Saxon architecture of the tenth century at **St Laurence, Bradford-on-Avon**, *Wilts*.

Triangular-headed windows, a Saxon speciality are in evidence in the tenth-century nave of **St Mary, Deerhurst**, *Glos*, where the tower displays excellent long and short work that is also typical of the period. The basilican plan was widely adopted for the Saxon churches of southern England, e.g **St Peter, Bradwell juxta Mare**, *Essex*, of *c.* 654 and **All Saints, Wing**, *Bucks* of eighth-century origin. Impressive eleventh-century Saxon churches survive at **St Mary, Sompting**, and **St Nicholas, Worth**, *W Sussex*; the latter retains the arches which once gave access to the porticus or side chambers which were often found as extensions to the basilican plan. The Romanesque style reached southern England during the late Saxon period. The last but one Saxon king of England, Edward the Confessor, built the Benedictine abbey at **Westminster** in the Romanesque style just prior to the

Norman Conquest of 1066; but all that survives from that period is part of the crypt, now known as the Chapel of the Pyx. [see BASILICA, CHURCH, LESENE, LONG AND SHORT WORK, PORTICUS, **102, 229**]

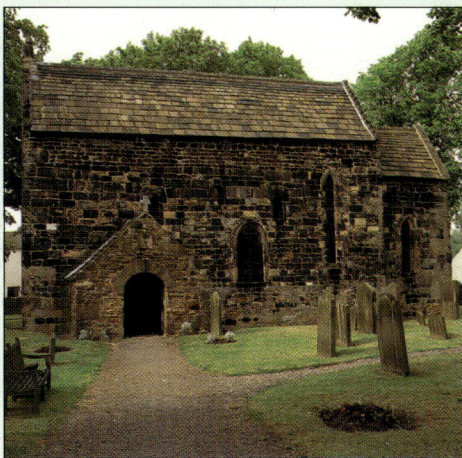

316 *St John the Evangelist, Escomb*, Durham, *is among the most intact of early Saxon churches.*

**317** *This statue niche or aedicule in Castle Howard, N Yorks, is the earliest revival of scagliola in Britain.*

**318** *The exterior of the Glasgow School of Art set new standards in the design of educational institutions.*

## SCAGLIOLA

Composite substance developed by the Romans to imitate marble, using gypsum, sand, lime, fragments of marble and cement. The compound could take a high degree of polish. Its use was revived in many Neo-Classical structures of the eighteenth century, notably in the great hall of **Castle Howard**, *N Yorks*, in 1712 by John Vanbrugh.

## SCALLOP

Classical ornament in the form of a shell, widely used in a variety of settings, from statue niches to door hoods. [see CONCH]

## SCARP

Also known as escarp, the inner sloping side of the ditch outside the rampart of a castle or earthwork. [see COUNTERSCARP]

## SCHOOL

Some of the earliest educational establishments were founded by individual benefactors, e.g. **Winchester College**, *Hants*, in 1382 by William of Wykeham; and the **Grammar School, Higham Ferrers**, *Northants*, refounded in 1422 by Henry Chichele, Archbishop of Canterbury. The medieval guilds were also active in the founding of grammar schools, e.g. at **Stratford-upon-Avon**, *Warw*, which was mentioned as early as 1295; and the old schoolroom where Shakespeare once studied is still in service as part of the **King's School**. The royal patronage of Henry VI was responsible for the founding in 1440 of **Eton College**, *Berks*. In the Tudor period, following the Dissolution of the Monasteries in the 1530s and 1540s, many schools were founded, notably the

319 *The interior of the Glasgow School of Art is still decidedly modern and contemporary in style.*

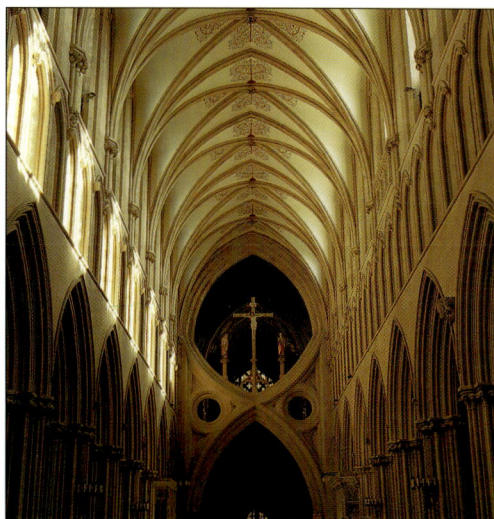

320 *The scissor arches at Wells Cathedral,* Somerset, *were a stylish solution to a structural problem.*

'Free Grammar Schools of King Edward VI' such as **Berkhamsted**, *Herts*, of 1549; **Sherborne**, *Dorset*, of 1550; and **Shrewsbury**, *Shrops*, of 1551. **Blundell's Old School** at **Tiverton**, *Devon*, of 1604 is now part of a much larger establishment. A fine schoolhouse of 1688 has survived in the **Bluecoat School** in **Westminster, London**.School building gathered pace during the eighteenth century, but the most spectacular achievements generally belong to the nineteenth century, e.g. the chapel of 1854 at **Lancing College**, *W Sussex*, which aspires to cathedral-like proportions. In Scotland, Charles Rennie Mackintosh (1868–1928) made architectural history with his visionary modern design for the **Glasgow School of Art** of 1896; and his work may be seen elsewhere in Glasgow at the **Scotland Street School** of 1904. [see **170**]

## SCISSOR ARCH
Type of strainer arch consisting of an inverted arch on top of a supporting arch.

Scissor arches were installed in 1338 at **Wells Cathedral**, *Somerset*, to withstand the pressure exerted by the central tower which had been raised to a greater height than originally planned.

## SCONCE
Subsidiary earthwork or fort to protect a castle gate.

## SCOTIA
Pronounced concave moulding. [see MOULDING]

## SCOTTISH BARONIAL [see BARONIAL]

## SCREEN, SCREENS PASSAGE
In a medieval hall a screen was generally installed at the end of the chamber away from the dais and high table in order to conceal the doors to the kitchen and pantry as well as to exclude draughts from the entrance. Such screens were often elaborately carved and continued in use into Tudor and Jacobean times, e.g. **Middle Temple Hall, London**, and

**Audley End**, *Essex*. When the screen is a fixed structure with a central opening, it is known as a spere. The space between the screen and the doors to the kitchen and pantry is known as the screens passage. [see PULPITUM, REREDOS, ROOD SCREEN]

## SCRIPTORIUM

Room of a monastery where manuscripts were copied and illuminated.

## SCROLL

Carved ornament resembling a scroll of paper. [see ROLL]

## SCULLERY

Room for washing dishes, pots and pans.

## SCULPTURE

Decorative carving in an architectural and monumental context has a long ancestry in the British Isles. The swirling spiral patterns on the kerbstone of the Neolithic passage grave at **Newgrange**, *Meath*, Ireland, show that great skills were already in evidence some five thousand years ago. The abstract artistic vision of the Iron Age Celts in Ireland may be seen in the sculptured stones at **Turoe**, *Galway*, and **Castlestrange**, *Roscommon*, dating to *c.* 300 BC. Figurative carving made an early and enigmatic appearance in the bizarre Janus heads on **Boa Island**, *Fermanagh*, N. Ireland, which probably belong to the very end of the Iron Age. In Scotland, the intriguing art of the Pictish cross slabs, e.g. at **Aberlemno**, *Tayside*, documents a nascent Christianity that was still absorbed with symbols of pagan memories. By contrast, the seventh-century **Ruthwell Cross**, *Dumfr & Gall*, Scotland, which ranks among the finest works of sculpture in Europe at that time, is thoroughly Christian in inspiration. Ireland in the tenth century

was the scene of a spectacular flowering of sculptural talent, of which many examples have survived. On **White Island** in **Lough Erne**, *Fermanagh*, there is a magnificent collection of small statues of clerics portrayed with a haunting otherworldliness; and at several locations, e.g. at **Monasterboice**, *Louth*, and at **Clonmacnoise**, *Offaly*, there are magnificent specimens of intricately carved high crosses, an art which the Irish monks also introduced to western Scotland, Wales and Cornwall.

Fine Saxon sculpture of the eleventh century may be seen in the porch of **Malmesbury Abbey**, *Wilts*, and inside **Chichester Cathedral**, *W Sussex*. The spread of Norman culture brought sculpture more firmly into the realm of architecture as beakheads and chevrons made

**321** *The sculptured shaft of the magnificent seventh-century cross at Ruthwell,* Dumfr & Gall, *Scotland.*

322 *Mysterious early Christian sculpture* (ABOVE) *on White Island,* Fermanagh, *N Ireland.*
323 *The west front* (BELOW) *of Exeter Cathedral,* Devon.

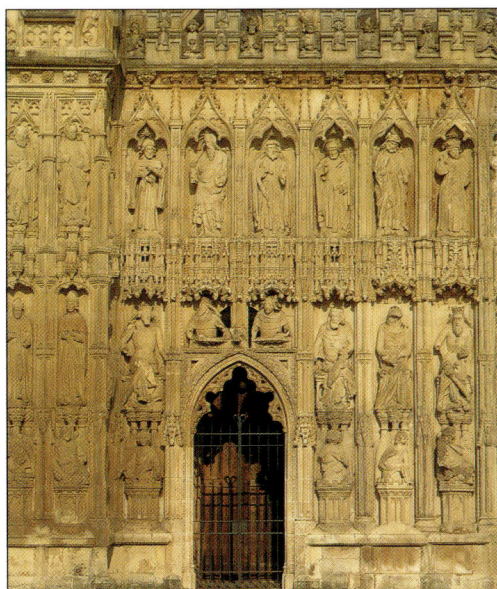

a dramatic appearance in church and cathedral; and doorways received lavish treatment, e.g. the **Prior's Doorway, Ely Cathedral**, *Cambs.* By the thirteenth and fourteenth centuries architecture was frequently used as a vast framework for sculpture, e.g. the west fronts of **Wells Cathedral**, *Somerset*, and **Exeter Cathedral**, *Devon*, which were conceived as external galleries filled with the statues of saints, apostles, bishops and kings. At **Jerpoint Abbey**, *Kilkenny*, Ireland, the once austere Cistercians created a cloister where the colonnade was decked out with a host of statues. Throughout the Middle Ages sculptural work abounded inside churches: on capitals, corbels and bosses as well as on bench ends, misericords, gargoyles, fonts and tombs. The bargeboards and timbers of medieval houses were likewise embellished with all manner of carving. Even external plasterwork

261

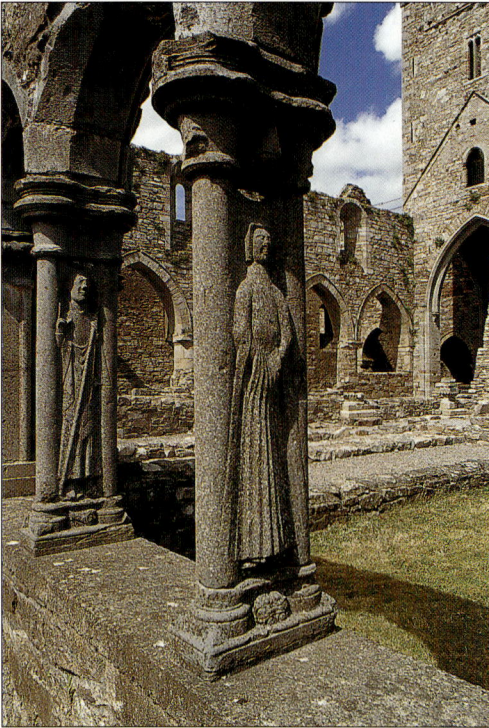

was moulded into sculptural shapes by the technique known as pargeting.

During the sixteenth and seventeenth centuries the enthusiasm for sculpture, except in the form of commemorative tomb effigies, languished. However, in the eighteenth century the Grand Tour brought a direct encounter with the original sculpture of Classical Antiquity and the Renaissance. The statues of Italy – whether copied or purchased – soon made an appearance in stately homes and gardens, and were often used to enliven a Neo-Classical façade or roofline. Monuments and tomb effigies in the Classical manner were produced in abundance. During the nineteenth century the Gothic Revival drew its inspiration from the works of the Middle Ages, and produced an astounding array of sculptural monuments which still adorn many a town square and public park. The Edwardian Baroque brought sculpture even more boldly into architecture on the

324 *Cloister at Jerpoint Abbey*, Kilkenny, *Ireland.*
325 *The Antique Passage at Castle Howard,* N Yorks.

grand scale, with its predilection for colossal figures emerging from the masonry of monumental buildings. After such exuberance, the 1920s and 1930s had a much reduced role for sculpture. The 1950s and 1960s witnessed a proliferation of both figurative and abstract sculpture, by artists such as Henry Moore and Barbara Hepworth, in prominent public places and occasionally applied to the façade of a building. Nowadays, there is much modern sculpture to be seen in shopping malls and city centres, e.g. the massive bronze **Broadgate Venus, Exchange Square, London**. [see ACROTERIA, BAS RELIEF, BEAKHEAD, BENCH END, CARYATID, COADE STONE, CROSS SLAB, FONT, GARGOYLE, HERM, HIGH CROSS, MISERICORD, MONUMENT, TOMB SCULPTURE, **229**]

## SEASIDE PIER

Piers at seaside resorts first developed as landing places for coastal steamers, e.g. at **Ryde, Isle of Wight**, in 1814; and at **Brighton**, *E Sussex*, in 1823. However, the public found them to be lively places to promenade; and with the boom of railway tourism from the 1840s, the notion of the pleasure pier became central to the popularity of a holiday resort. Possibly the first pleasure pier was that at

**326** *Palace Pier, Brighton,* E Sussex, *is a typical example of fanciful seaside architecture.*

**Southport**, *Mers*, of 1860, followed by that at **Worthing**, *W Sussex*, in 1861, the **North Pier, Blackpool**, *Lancs*, of 1863; and then the **West Pier, Brighton**, *E Sussex*, in 1866. The golden age of pier building was 1870–1900 when some fifty were constructed. The heyday of the seaside pier was the Edwardian era, when the exotic, fantasy architecture of domes and pavilions with elegant ironwork captured the fun-loving mood of the age. However, these structures have proved vulnerable to fire and constant pounding by the sea. As a result many have been destroyed or seriously damaged.

## SEDILIA

Seats for the clergy, usually recessed and canopied, set in the south chancel wall of a church.

## SEGMENTAL

Describes a curved element consisting of less than a semi-circle. [see PEDIMENT]

## SEMI-DETACHED

A pair of houses which share a party wall and usually a common pitched roof. Although the semi-detached was already a feature of Victorian and Edwardian urbanism, it came into its own in the 1920s and 1930s when vast new suburbs were added to major cities. [see RIBBON DEVELOPMENT]

## SEPULCHRE

Usually known as the Easter Sepulchre, this consists of a recess in the wall of a church and symbolizes Christ's tomb. Prior to the Reformation of the 1530s such sepulchres were ornately carved and contained a tomb chest. By tradition, the Easter Sepulchre is located in the north chancel wall close to the altar, e.g. at **St John Baptist, Stanton St John**, *Oxon*, and at **All Saints, Hawton**, *Notts*.

**SETT** [see COBBLESTONE]

**SHAFT, SHAFT RING**
In Classical architecture, the main part of a column between the base and capital. In Gothic architecture, a shaft is a slender column, of which several may be clustered round a pier and sometimes embellished by one or more shaft rings, also known as annulets. [see COLUMN, ORDER, PIER]

**SHAPED GABLE** [see GABLE]

**SHELL** [see CONCH, SCALLOP]

**SHELL-KEEP** [see CASTLE]

**SHINGLE**
Small piece of wood, traditionally oak, used in the manner of a tile for covering a roof or wall. Shingles were widespread in the Middle Ages, but they have since been superseded by the more durable and fire-resistant clay tiles and slates.

**SHOP**
Purpose-built premises for the sale of goods were a vital part of the medieval town, and the shopkeeper invariably resided over the shop. Security at night was provided by a wooden shutter which, during the day, could be turned on a pivot – built into the frame – to serve as counter giving directly on to the street, e.g. at **Abbey Cottages, Tewkesbury,** *Glos,* and the wine merchant's house in **French Street, Southampton,** *Hants.* **Gladstone's Land, Edinburgh,** Scotland, is a stone arcaded shop and house of the early seventeenth century. **London's Old Curiosity Shop** goes back to 1567, but the shopfront is more recent. It was during the eighteenth century that the glazed shopfront became the norm, e.g. the bow windows added to **Goodwin's Court, London**. Huge plate-glass windows

327 *The premises of a medieval wine merchant in Southampton,* Hants, *combined a shop and residence.*

328 *Late eighteenth-century bow window shopfronts in Goodwin's Court off St Martin's Lane, London.*

replaced the small panes and glazing bars of the Georgian era in the course of the nineteenth century, e.g. at **Asprey's** in **New Bond Street, London**. [see ARCADE, COVERED MARKET, DEPARTMENT STORE, GALLERIA, MARKET HALL]

# SHRINE

During the Middle Ages the shrines of the most popular saints were richly embellished tombs containing their much venerated mortal remains, or smaller receptacles known as reliquaries which held particular relics. Most important were the shrines of St Thomas at **Canterbury**, *Kent*; St Hugh at **Lincoln**, *Lincs*; St Swithun at **Winchester**, *Hants*; and St Cuthbert at **Durham**, *Durham*. These and many more fell victim in the post-Reformation era to Henry VIII who ordered their destruction on the pretext that 'symple people be moch deceaved

and brought into great supersticion'. Of the major shrines, only those with royal status had any chance of survival, e.g. those of Edward the Confessor at **Westminster Abbey, London**, and of Edward II at **Gloucester Cathedral**, *Glos*. Fragments of the shrine of St Frideswide have been rebuilt in **Christ Church Cathedral, Oxford**, *Oxon*. St Candida at **Whitchurch Canonicorum**, *Dorset*, is the only parish church in England which still possesses the relics of its founding saint in a medieval shrine. Several reliquaries remain to be seen, e.g. the **Bodmin Casket** in **Bodmin Priory**, *Cornwall*; and the **Shipley Reliquary** at **St Mary, Shipley**, *W Sussex*. The bones of St David and St Justinian are kept in a wooden casket in **St David's Cathedral**, *Dyfed*, Wales.

**329** *The tomb of Richard Beauchamp, Earl of Warwick, in the chantry chapel of St Mary, Warwick,* Warw, *has the style and splendour of a grand medieval shrine.*

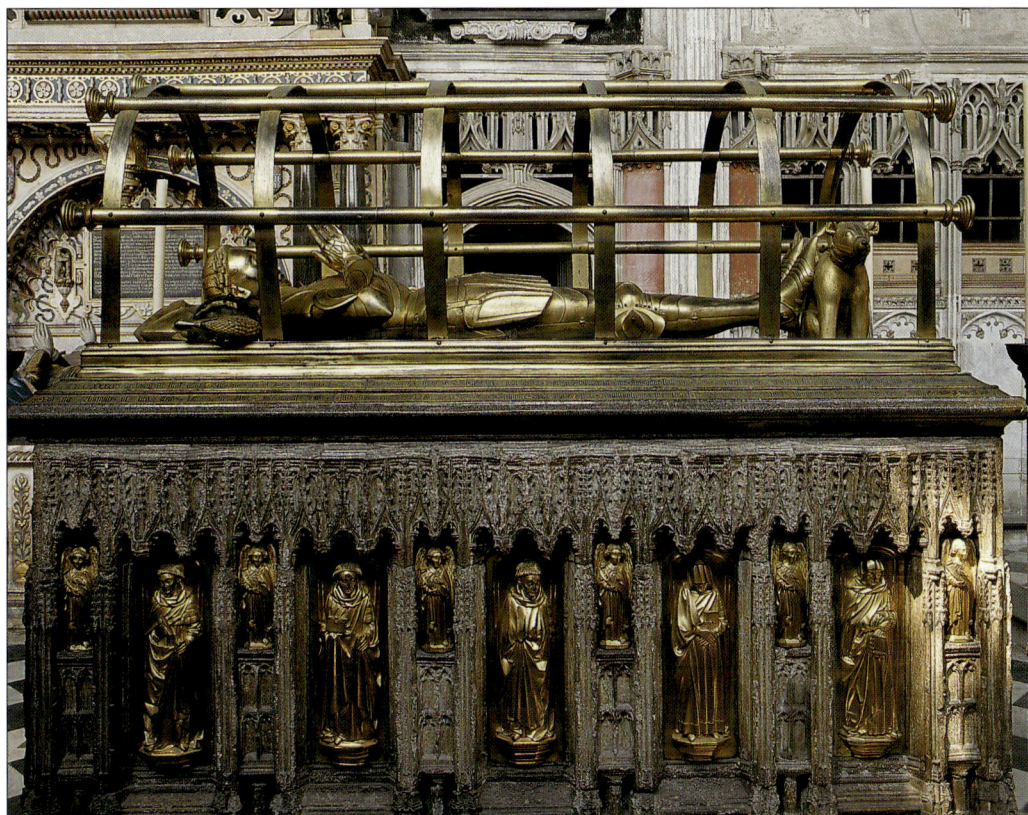

## SHUTTERING

Mould or framework, usually of timber, into which concrete is poured. The concrete when set bears the imprint of the shuttering. Also known as formwork. [see CONCRETE]

## SILL or CILL [see HALF-TIMBERING]

## SKEW [see KNEELER]

## SKIRTING

Wooden board protecting the base of an internal wall.

330 *The bright and airy solar at Old Soar Manor, Plaxtol,* Kent, *with a characteristic timber-trussed roof.*

## SKYLIGHT

Window set in a roof or ceiling.

## SLAB [see FLAGSTONE]

## SLATE

Deposits of this non-porous metamorphic rock occur in Wales, Scotland, Cumbria and Cornwall. The relative ease with which slate can be split into thin sheets has made it a convenient roofing material. The improved railway transport of the nineteenth century spread its use throughout Britain when it became the most common form of roofing. It is still in demand for quality work, but cheaper alternatives have priced it out of the mar-

ket. Slate can also be hung vertically on external walls to prevent penetration by damp. In thick slabs slate can be used for stairs, floors and even tombstones. Relics of the once thriving slate industry in Wales may be seen at **Llechwedd Slate Caverns** and the **Deep Mine,** near **Blaenau Ffestiniog**, *Gwynedd*. **Easdale Island**, *S'clyde*, Scotland, contains impressive remains of the local slate industry. At **Delabole**, *Cornwall*, slate extraction over a period of 400 years has created the largest open excavation in England. Some of the local houses are made entirely of slate, from the roofs and walls to the floors and lintels.

## SLEEPERS

Beams which support joists. The walls which carry sleepers are known as sleeper walls.

## SLYPE

Covered passage between the transept of a monastic church and the chapter house.

## SNUG [see PUBLIC HOUSE]

## SOFFIT

Underside of an arch, balcony or cornice. Also known as an intrados. [see ARCH]

## SOLAR

Private family chamber in a medieval house, usually located on an upper floor, e.g. at **Old Soar Manor, Plaxtol,** *Kent*. [see HALL]

## SOLOMONIC COLUMN [see BARLEY-SUGAR COLUMN]

## SOPRAPORTA

Decorative deployment of a painting above a doorway, whose frame forms a unified ensemble with that of the door.

## SOUNDING BOARD [see PULPIT]

## SOUTERRAIN [see FOGOU]

## SPANDREL

Triangular interspace between arches or between an arch and a square frame. Gothic spandrels were frequently ornamented, e.g. on the gatehouse of **St Osyth Priory**, *Essex*, where the spandrels portray St George and the dragon. **The Dragon Hall, Norwich,** *Norfolk*, is so called after a carved dragon motif on the spandrels of the wooden beams. [see **136**]

## SPERE [see SCREEN]

## SPIRAL STAIR

Winding staircase supported by a central post or newel. Also known as a newel stair, and in Scotland as a vice or turnpike. [see STAIR]

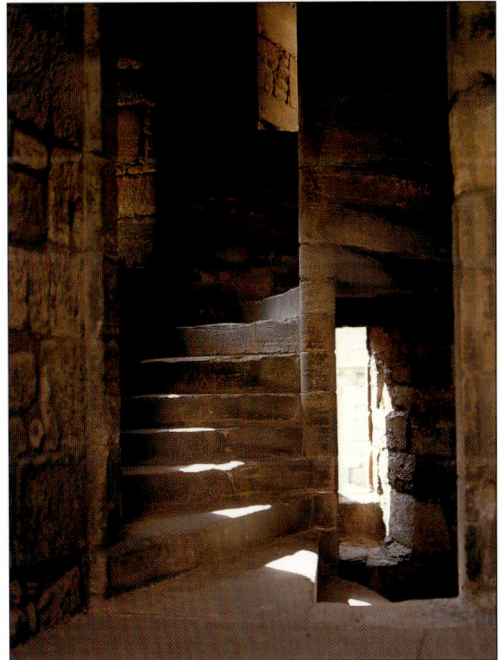

**331** *Spiral stair at Linlithgow Palace*, Lothian, *Scotland. The newel is an integral part of the steps.*

# SPIRE

Norman spires were squat pyramids, e.g. at **Southwell Minster**, *Notts*: the slender, elongated structures which taper to a lofty point and grace many a church tower were a later, Gothic refinement. Probably the best-known spire in Britain is that of **Salisbury Cathedral**, *Wilts*, which was added to the tower early in the fourteenth century. For the first 20 feet (6·1m) of the 180 feet (54·9m) high spire the stone is 2 feet (0·6m) thick. After this, the outer shell of the octagonal spire thins to just 8 inches (20cm); it is held in place by a cunningly contrived timber scaffold within, of which most of the wood goes back to the original construction.

A broach spire is octagonal on a square tower without a parapet; the weight of the masonry is contained by four wedges of masonry, known as broaches, at the base of the spire.

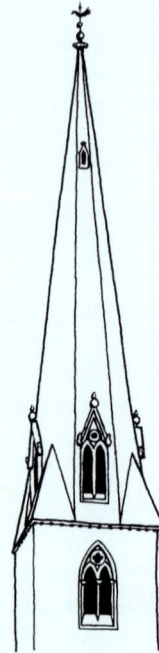

Broach

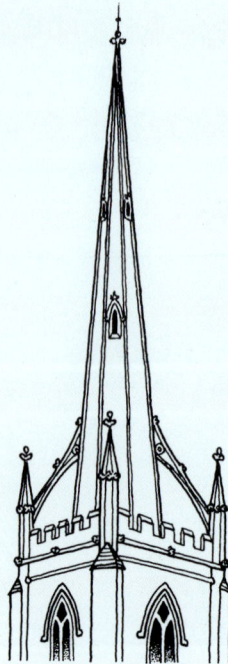

Crown spire            Needle spire

Parapet spire

A parapet spire is set on a tower and surrounded by a walkway with parapets; it may be supported by flying buttresses connected to piers with decorative pinnacles, e.g. at the church of **St James, Louth**, *Lincs*. A needle spire is very slender and usually rises from a square tower. A crown spire is in the form of an open crown composed of flying buttresses, e.g. at the **High Kirk of St Giles, Edinburgh**, Scotland, and **St Dunstan-in-the-East, London**. [see FLÈCHE, STEEPLE, 65]

**SPIRELET** [see FLÈCHE]

**SPLAY**
Diagonally cut angle, e.g. the jamb of a window in a thick stone wall.

**SPRINGER, SPRINGING LINE**
A springer is the bottom stone of an arch, i.e. the stone that rests on the impost. The springing line is the level at which an arch begins. [see ARCH]

**SPUR STONE**
Projecting stone set at the corner of a building to protect it from damage by wheeled traffic.

**SQUARE**
Formal open space of square or rectangular shape, which became the most popular single element of Georgian and Victorian urbanism, e.g. in **Dublin**, Ireland. The London squares of **Bloomsbury, Belgravia** and **Kensington** contained gardens which were accessible only to local residents; and many continue to be private enclaves. The square may also be a

**332** *Albert Gardens, London, is a modest Georgian square once typical of the urban plan in the East End.*

monumental space, designed to display prestigious buildings, e.g. **Trafalgar Square, London**; **George Square, Glasgow**, Scotland; **Donegall Square, Belfast**, N. Ireland. [see PIAZZA]

**SQUINCH**
Device used in masonry and brickwork to form a smooth transition from a square base to a round superstructure such as a dome. It consists of one or more arches spanning the right angle between two walls. [see PENDENTIVE]

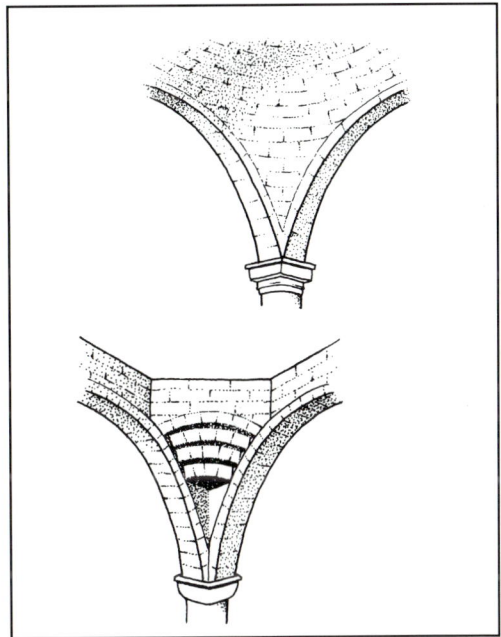

**SQUINT**
Also known as a hagioscope, an aperture cut through a wall or pier, usually in a church, to permit a view of the altar from a side aisle, e.g. at **St John Baptist, Burford**, and **St Mary the Virgin, Chipping Norton**, *Oxon*; also in the **Lord Mayor's Chapel, Bristol**, *Avon*. At **St Mary the Virgin, Bridgwater**, *Somerset*, a series of three squints opens up a line of sight from the porch to the high altar. The manor houses at **Great Chalfield,**

*Wilts*, and **Cotehele**, *Cornwall*, have squints in the hall and chapel respectively, which were designed for the master of the house to keep an eye on things.

## STABLE

Accommodation for horses, either in a basement or a separate block, was essentially utilitarian until Classical ideas required that the stables be orchestrated as part of the grand design of the country house. At **Seaton Delaval**, *Northum*, by John Vanbrugh in *c.* 1718 the stables reflect the noble style of the house itself. The Baroque stables at **Chatsworth**, *Derbys*, built by James Paine in 1758–63

333 *The stable at Strokestown Park*, Roscommon, *Ireland. Note the groin vault and Tuscan columns.*

for the 4th Duke of Devonshire, are treated as a grand work of architecture with columns adorned with rock-faced blocks. At **Strokestown Park**, *Roscommon*, Ireland, the stable block was linked in typical Palladian fashion to the main house in the 1730s by Richard Castle. Its vaulted interior, supported on Tuscan columns, has been aptly described as 'an equine cathedral'. So magnificent were the Orientalist stables of 1803–8 at **Brighton**, *E Sussex*, by William Porden that the Prince Regent complained that his horses enjoyed more princely accommodation than he did. [see MEWS]

## STADDLE STONES

Mushroom-shaped stones supporting granaries or barns in order to prevent incursions by mice and rats.

## STAINED GLASS

The technique of producing coloured glass by adding metallic oxides to the molten material is extremely ancient and may be traced back to the lands of the eastern Mediterranean. The earliest occurrence of stained glass in the British Isles in the post-Roman era has been attested at **St Paul's, Jarrow**, *Tyne & Wear*, where fragments of blue, orange and yellow glass from the late seventh century have been discovered.

Generally, however, stained glass is associated with the spectacular windows of the great Gothic cathedrals from the twelfth to the fifteenth centuries, e.g. at **Canterbury**, *Kent*; **Lincoln**, *Lincs*; **York Minster**, *N Yorks*, and **Wells**, *Somerset*. These vast compositions of coloured light were created by assembling small pieces of stained glass within a malleable and

334 OPPOSITE  *Stained-glass window dating from c. 1500 in the church of St Mary, Fairford*, Glos.

335 *Medieval stained glass in Canterbury Cathedral,* Kent, *showing pilgrims at Becket's shrine.*

watertight nexus of lead cames set in a larger framework. Such windows were not built for their aesthetic effect alone: their purpose was also didactic and inspirational. They amounted to picture books in glass which reminded the largely illiterate congregations of the stories narrated in the Bible.

Parish churches were also treasure houses of stained glass, and there are some splendid medieval survivals, e.g. at St Neot's, *Cornwall*; All Saints, North Street, York, *N Yorks*; St Peter Mancroft, Norwich, *Norfolk*; and St Mary the Virgin, Fairford, *Glos.* However, an incalculable quantity of medieval stained glass was destroyed during the sixteenth and seventeenth centuries; and new churches of the seventeenth and eighteenth centuries opted for bright interiors lit by large windows of clear glass as if to underline the triumph of modern rationalism over medieval mysticism. The Gothic Revival of the nineteenth century witnessed an enthusiastic return to the use of stained glass in churches, even to the extent that the Victorian restorers installed stained glass in churches that had been designed to have clear glass, e.g. Christopher Wren's parish churches in the City of London. The harsh colours and mechanical craftsmanship of Victorian stained glass make it stand out from medieval work. There are excellent examples of Victorian stained glass by Edward Burne-Jones at the church of St Deiniol, Hawarden, *Clwyd,* Wales, and in Christ Church Cathedral, Oxford, *Oxon.* The Victorian love of the medium extended to the domestic sphere; and many homes made use of stained glass in at least some windows, e.g. the Linley Sambourne House in Kensington, London. In the twentieth century modern art has revived the use of stained glass in churches with its bold abstract and figurative designs; e.g. John Piper's windows of the 1950s in the new Coventry Cathedral, *W Mids.* [see GLASS]

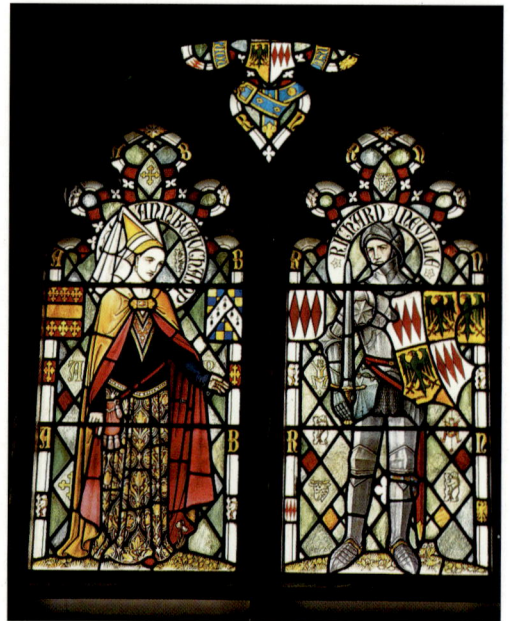

336 *Romantic Victorian medievalism in Cardiff Castle,* S Glam, *Wales, showing a knight and lady.*

# STAIR, STAIRCASE

Medieval staircases were generally utilitarian in concept, works of practical engineering rather than aesthetic design. Nevertheless, some grand effects were achieved, e.g. the stairway to the Chapter House in **Wells Cathedral**, *Somerset*; and the night stair in **Hexham Abbey**, *Northum*. Stairways in medieval castles could be spiral, e.g. at **Linlithgow Palace**, *Lothian*, Scotland; built into the thickness of a wall, e.g. at **Conisbrough**, *S Yorks*; or broad and solid, e.g. at **Castle Rising**, *Norfolk*. Early wooden stairs were of the ladder type, where the treads were fitted to the strings without risers. In Elizabethan buildings staircases became objects of prestige, and newel posts and banisters were ornately carved.

Greater inventiveness followed in the seventeenth century as Baroque

337 *The great staircase at Ham House,* Surrey, *with carved newel posts and Baroque trophies on the panels.*

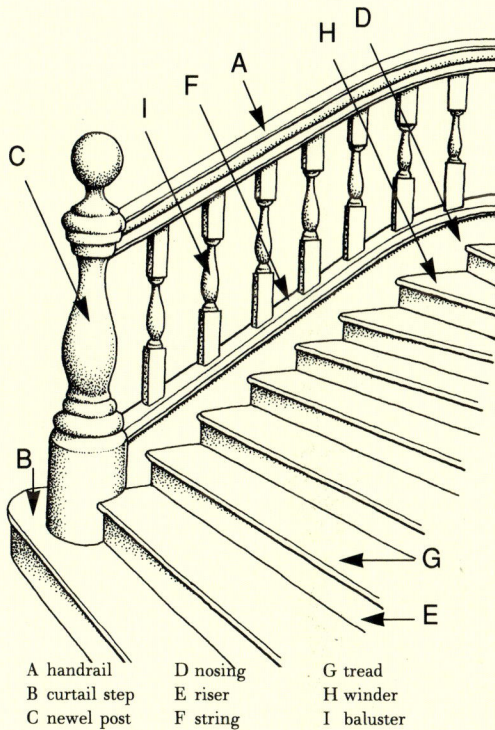

grandeur was added to Jacobean exuberance, e.g. at **Ham House**, *Surrey*, in the 1630s. Elegant wrought iron made an appearance at this time in the **Tulip Staircase** of the **Queen's House, Greenwich, London**. In the eighteenth century many noble staircases were restrained in their Classicism, but others achieved almost theatrical effect, e.g. at **44 Berkeley Square, London**, by William Kent. Such grand staircases had a strong appeal to the Victorians who often turned the staircase into a powerful architectural statement, whether in the context of a Norman Revival castle, e.g. **Penrhyn**, *Gwynedd*, Wales, or a municipal building, e.g. **Glasgow City Chambers**, Scotland. The twentieth century has witnessed a partial return to the relative simplicity of the staircase as an item of architectural engineering. [see BALUSTER, BANISTER, CURTAIL STEP, DOG-LEG STAIR, FLYING STAIR, NEWEL, NIGHT STAIR, NOSING, RISER, SPIRAL STAIR, STRING, TREAD, WALL STAIR, WINDER, **154**]

| | | |
|---|---|---|
| A handrail | D nosing | G tread |
| B curtail step | E riser | H winder |
| C newel post | F string | I baluster |

**338** *Spirited stone carving embellishes the stalls in the chapter-house of Southwell Minster, Notts.*

## STALLS

Continuous series of seats within individual compartments which are formed by arm rests and/or vertical partitions. Choir stalls in a church or cathedral are generally of wood, and are sometimes decorated on the underside with elaborately carved misericords. Stalls may also be of stone, e.g. in a chapter house such as those at **Southwell Minster**, *Notts*, and **York Minster**, *N Yorks*. [see MISERICORD, RETURN]

## STANCHION

A support consisting of a vertical iron bar positioned between the mullions of a window or one of a series of iron bars forming a railing. In modern usage, the stanchion is an upright structural element, usually made of steel.

## STANDING STONE

A widespread feature of Neolithic and Bronze Age culture in the British Isles, the erection of isolated monumental stones was a significant but now dimly understood prehistoric activity. The monoliths, as the standing stones are also called, were laboriously hauled to their positions and painfully levered and pulled until they stood vertically in their foundation pits. There is a majestic 23 feet (7m) high specimen at **Punchestown**, *Kildare*, Ireland; that at **Rudston**, *Humbs*, is 25 feet (7·6m) high and weighs 26 tons. The **Tristan Stone** near **Fowey**, *Cornwall*, has been tenuously linked to Arthurian legend. Standing stones are often found in complex configurations, e.g. at **Beaghmore**, *Tyrone*, N. Ireland. A parallel alignment of standing stones, the **West Kennet Avenue**, *Wilts*, once linked Avebury's stone circles with other sites of ritual significance in the vicinity, but many of the original stones are missing. [see AVENUE, STONE CIRCLE, TRILITHON]

## STARLING [see CUTWATER]

## STATELY HOME

Not a precise architectural term, but one which embraces the most palatial category of country houses, e.g. **Blenheim Palace**, *Oxon*; **Castle Howard**, *N Yorks*; **Chatsworth**, *Derbys*; **Woburn Abbey**, *Beds*. [see COUNTRY HOUSE, PALACE]

## STATION

The railway station was perhaps the most significant new building type of the nineteenth century, but the first ones were unpretentious affairs, e.g. **Liverpool Road Station, Manchester**, of 1830, the oldest in the world. Brunel's original **Temple Meads Station, Bristol**, *Avon*, of 1841 was built as the terminus of the Great Western Railway; its wooden roof was inspired by the hammerbeam structures of the Middle Ages and its exterior is in the historical style of the Tudor Revival, a curious choice for an enterprise that was in the vanguard of technology. Throughout the nineteenth century station design reflected the confu-

**339** *The original Brunel station at Temple Meads, Bristol, Avon. Note the hammerbeam-type wooden roof.*

sion which existed between architecture and engineering. While the façades of the station buildings remained wedded to traditional styles, the trainsheds behind were revolutionary concepts in the new materials of glass and iron. Nowhere is this ambivalence more apparent than at **St Pancras, London**, of 1868–74 where the station and hotel are pure Gothic Revival, whereas the trainshed set new engineering standards with its great span of 245 feet (74·7m). The excellence of the western trainshed of 1875 at **Liverpool Street Station** prompted the following comment in *Building News*:

Our metropolitan termini have been the leaders of the art-spirit of our times, however loath we may be to admit it, and despite our declaring them to be the works of engineers without artistic merit except of the lowest order.

Of the London termini, only **King's Cross** of 1850 expressed the engineering of the sheds in its external architecture. The London Underground pioneered a new breed of station architecture, especially on the Northern and Piccadilly lines in the 1930s, e.g. **Arnos Grove** and **Osterley**. [see **165, 188, 189**]

## STATUARY [see SCULPTURE]

## STEEL, STEEL-FRAME
Extremely tough but malleable alloy of iron and carbon, which was first used as a building material in the 1860s. By the

1890s steel had become sufficiently cheap and reliable for it to be employed as the essential structural component of the revolutionary high-rise buildings of the twentieth century. In these, the structure was supported not on load-bearing walls but on a steel-frame of horizontal and vertical girders. The **Ritz Hotel** of 1906 was the earliest steel-frame building in London; **Kodak House, Holborn, London**, of 1910 was another significant pioneer of this method of building.

## STEEPLE
Denotes the tower and spire of a church as a single entity. [see SPIRE, 169, 291]

**340** *The tiered steeple of St Bride, Fleet Street, London, was one of many inventive designs by Wren.*

## STELLAR VAULT
Vault in which the ribs, liernes and tiercerons form a star-shaped pattern. [see VAULT]

## STEREOBATE
In Classical architecture, the base of a wall or colonnade. [see STYLOBATE]

## STIFF-LEAF
Gothic ornament of sculptured foliage, used especially on capitals of the twelfth and thirteenth centuries. [see CAPITAL]

## STILE [see DOOR, PANELLING]

## STONE
[see ALABASTER, ASHLAR, CAEN STONE, CAPSTONE, CHALK, CHEQUER-WORK, CHERT, CLUNCH, COADE STONE, COBBLESTONE, CORNERSTONE, DOLMEN, DRESSINGS, DRIPSTONE, DRYSTONE, FLAGSTONE, FLINT, FLUSHWORK, FREESTONE, GALLETING, GRANITE, KEYSTONE, LIMESTONE, MARBLE, MASONRY, MASON'S MARK, MEGALITHIC, MONOLITH, MOORSTONE, ORTHOSTAT, PUDDING STONE, QUOIN, RAGSTONE, RUBBLESTONE, RUSTICATION, SANDSTONE, SARSEN, SCULPTURE, TERRAZZO, TRILITHON]

## STONE CIRCLE
The arrangement of standing stones in circular or elliptical shapes was one of the highest achievements of the Neolithic and Bronze Age peoples of the British Isles. In addition to solar and lunar orientations the stone circles also provided vast arenas for ritual gatherings. The **Merry Maidens**, *Cornwall*; **Drombeg**, *Cork*, Ireland; and **Castlerigg**, *Cumbria*, are of modest size but are impressively sited, using the landscape to form natural amphitheatres of great scenic effect. **Callanish** on the Hebridean island of Lewis, Scotland, is more complex, since the circle has radiating arms which cen-

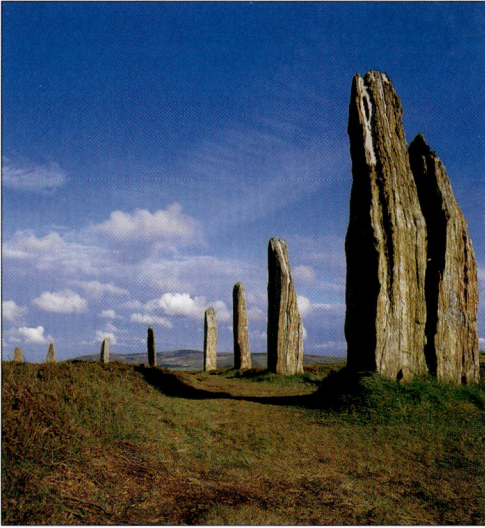

341 *The Ring of Brodgar, Orkney, Scotland: one of the most dramatic stone circles of prehistoric Britain.*

tre on a great monolith 16 feet (4·9m) high. Some of the most spectacular stone circles are contained within a henge, e.g. the **Ring of Brodgar, Orkney**, Scotland; **Avebury** and **Stonehenge**, *Wilts*. The monoliths at Stonehenge have been pounded with stone mauls to a smooth finish and fitted with stone lintels. [see HENGE, PREHISTORIC, SARSEN, STANDING STONE, TRILITHON]

## STOP
Termination, usually ornamental, to a chamfer, hood-mould or string course. When carved to represent a human face, it is known as a mask stop.

## STOUP
Container for holy water, usually a shallow dish set in a recess by the church door.

## STRAINER ARCH
Supplementary arch built across a nave or aisle to withstand a lateral strain. [see SCISSOR ARCH]

## STRAPWORK
Type of surface decoration, popular in the Elizabethan and Jacobean eras, consisting of broad, flat bands of interlacing pattern. Particularly in evidence in plaster ceilings, e.g. **Forty Hall, Enfield, London**. [see CEILING, JACOBEAN, PLASTERWORK]

342 *The strapwork ceiling of Forty Hall, Enfield, London, clearly demonstrates the features of its type.*

## STRAWBERRY HILL GOTHIC [see GOTHIC REVIVAL]

## STRETCHER [see BRICKWORK]

## STRING
Sloping edge of a staircase which supports the treads of the individual steps. [see STAIR, STAIRCASE]

## STRING COURSE
Horizontal band, e.g. of stone, which runs across a façade and usually projects from it. Its purpose is decorative. [see **78**]

## STRUT
Vertical or inclined timber located between a beam and a rafter. [see TIMBER-TRUSSED ROOF]

## STUART

Not the easiest of architectural labels, since the Stuart period falls into two parts: the reigns of James I and Charles I (1603–49) and those of Charles II and James II (1660–88) being separated by the Commonwealth. The term is usually applied to the later Stuart period but this may also be classified as Restoration or the Age of Wren, with its chief characteristic being the style of

English Baroque. Nevertheless, the term Stuart does conjure up a general image of a domestic version of Classicism with some Dutch Palladian features as practised by Hugh May (1621–84), Roger Pratt (1620–85) and John Webb (1611–72), e.g. May's **Eltham Lodge**, *Kent*, of 1664 and Pratt's **Coleshill House**, *Berks*, of 1650–62. [see BAROQUE, JACOBEAN, PALLADIANISM, RESTORATION]

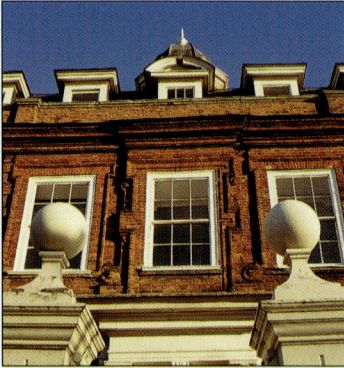

343 *Cromwell House, Highgate, London, of 1637–8.*

344 *The chequer-work floor and the grandiose chimneypiece are the stylistic clues to this Stuart interior at Ham House*, Surrey.

## STUCCO

Very fine but durable form of plaster invented in Italy in the fifteenth century. Its secret lay in the addition of powdered marble to lime and gypsum; but a variety of other ingredients were tried, e.g. milk and egg-white, in order to obtain a special finish. Some stucco recipes were patented, including that devised by the Adam brothers. A stucco suitable for external use was created by the addition of sand and brick dust, and eventually cement was added too. John Nash's favourite formula

for his Regency façades was Parker's Roman Cement. [see PLASTERWORK]

## STUD

Vertical wall timber in a half-timbered structure. As wood became scarce, so more space for infill was left between the studs. A closely studded building is generally of greater age. [see HALF-TIMBERING]

## STYLOBATE

Top step of the substructure of a colonnade. [see PODIUM, STEREOBATE]

345 *Typically Stuart exterior of Forty Hall, Enfield, London with its pleasing contrast of red brick and white cornice, porch and window frames. Note the hipped roof with prominent chimneystacks.*

## SUMMERHOUSE

Garden building, usually of light construction, to provide shade and shelter. [see BELEVEDERE, GAZEBO, ORANGERY, PAVILION, PERGOLA]

## SWAG

Decorative motif in the form of a draped cloth hanging over two supports. Similar to the festoon, it was a favourite device of the seventeenth and eighteenth centuries and features on both exteriors and interiors of buildings. [see FESTOON]

## SYNAGOGUE

Jewish place of worship. The **Spanish and Portuguese Synagogue** at **Bevis Marks, London**, dates back to 1700. It was constructed by a Quaker master builder, and it resembles the early meeting houses of the Nonconformists. The architecture of the **Dollis Hill Synagogue, London**, expresses the Modernist mood of 1930s. Synagogues are not generally such an immediately recognizable architectural type as are churches and mosques.

# T

## TABERNACLE
Recess, usually with an ornate canopy, designed to receive an image.

## TELAMONES [see ATLANTES]

## TELEPHONE BOX or KIOSK
The archetypal British telephone box is the cast iron Neo-Grecian creation, known as the K2, designed in 1924 by Giles Gilbert Scott in the guise of a miniature building. Despite its Classical lines and decorative detail, the K2 managed to express the modernity associated with telecommunications. Various attempts were subsequently made to update the K2 design, but none found favour until Scott came up with his 'Jubilee Design' of 1936, better known as the K6. This was essentially a slimmed-down version of the K2 with a modified fenestration. In recent decades several other short-lived designs have been tried, and many of Scott's K2s and K6s have disappeared in the process. As a result of some spirited campaigning, many of the remaining examples of Scott's distinctive work have been accorded the status of listed buildings.

## TEMPLATE
1) Mould or pattern, usually in the form of a metal plate or wooden board, from which the outline could be transferred by a mason or carpenter.

2) [see KNEELER]

## TEMPLE
Building of religious worship, generally of a non-Christian nature. The Romans built many temples in Britain, but scant traces remain above ground, e.g. the **Temple of Mithras** in the **City of London**. The Iron Age hillfort of **Maiden Castle**, *Dorset*, contains the exposed stone foundations of a small temple dating back to *c.* AD 380, a significant sign of Romano-British paganism at that time. A similar temple may be seen at **Jordan Hill,** near **Weymouth**, *Dorset*. In the eighteenth century Neo-Classical temples began to appear in the landscape gardens of the gentry, e.g. at **Stowe**, *Bucks*; and **Stourhead**, *Wilts*. Examples abound of Doric temples and copies of the Tower of the Winds in Athens. The temple architecture of the Greeks and Romans has also been widely imitated to provide many a country house, public building and even Christian church

**346** *The updated K6* (LEFT) *alongside its predecessor the K2, both designed by Giles Gilbert Scott.*

**347** OPPOSITE *Temple of the Winds at Mount Stewart,* Down, *N Ireland, reflects the mood of the Greek Revival.*

with a Neo-Classical portico and pediment. Recently, a number of Buddhist and Hindu temples have been built. [see GREEK REVIVAL, MONOPTERAL, PAGODA, PALLADIANISM, PERIPTERAL, ROMAN]

## TENEMENT

From Latin, meaning 'a holding or a plot of land', but the word has come to denote, and especially in Scotland, a type of urban housing consisting of a multi-storey dwelling with many apartments and access by a common stair. There was a prolific building of tenements in Glasgow, Scotland, in the late nineteenth and early twentieth centuries, forming complete streets of uniform terrace architecture. Overcrowding and poor maintenance earned the tenements a bad reputation; but in recent years that perception has changed and many of the surviving tenements have been modernized to provide comfortable urban homes. One tenement

**348** *A modest Georgian terrace in Torrington Square, Bloomsbury, London. Note the decorative balconies.*

of 1892 vintage in the **Garnethill** district of **Glasgow** has been acquired by the National Trust for Scotland as an example of the type. [see APARTMENT HOUSE, COUNCIL HOUSING, PEABODY BUILDINGS]

## TERM [see HERM]

## TERRACE

1) A flat promenade, usually in front of a building, but sometimes carved out of a hillside to provide a platform offering panoramic views, e.g. the **Rievaulx Terrace**, *N Yorks*, built by Thomas Duncombe in 1713 overlooking the ruins of Rievaulx Abbey in the valley below.

2) In the context of urban architecture, the terrace is a row of houses conceived as a continuous, unified ensemble. Before construction could commence, it was necessary to create a level piece of ground; this was the terrace which gave its name for the buildings themselves. Terrace architecture was taken up in earnest in the eighteenth century and endured throughout the nine-

teenth. The Georgian terraces of **Dublin**, Ireland; **Bath**, *Avon*; **Edinburgh**, Scotland; and **London** rank among the best productions of European urbanism. Some of the most spectacular were given a quasi-palatial treatment with pediments embracing many houses, e.g. **Cumberland Terrace, Regent's Park**, which forms the *pièce de résistance* of John Nash's 'Grand Design' for the West End of London. [see CIRCUS, CRESCENT, TENEMENT, **297, 298**]

## TERRACOTTA

Italian for 'baked earth', it denotes a clay used for earthenware which is both harder and less porous than brick. Terracotta was first used in England as a decorative material in the early sixteenth century in the guise of the Italianate medallions set into the courtyard walls of **Hampton Court Palace, London**, by Cardinal Wolsey. It was lavishly deployed on the façade of **Layer Marney Tower**, *Essex*, of 1520 and **Sutton Place**, *Surrey*, where the material was used for window and door surrounds, shafts, mullions and finials. Terracotta was then largely ignored until rediscovered by Victorian architects such as Charles Fitzroy Doll who used it for the entire façade of the **Hotel Russell, London**, of 1898 which has been likened to a 'François Premier Château'. In London, at the **Natural**

**349** *The façade of the Hotel Russell in Russell Square, London, is an extravaganza of terracotta.*

**History Museum**, terracotta creates a splendid effect; at the **Royal Albert Hall** it combines attractively with red brick, and the exterior of **Harrods** in **Knightsbridge** is entirely of terracotta. [see **244**]

## TERRAZZO

Composite material used for flooring and walls, made from chips of marble set in cement, then ground and polished to form a smooth, hard surface.

## TESSELLATED

Describes a mosaic pavement formed of small cubes of glass, stone or marble, known as tesserae. [see MOSAIC]

## TESSERAE [see TESSELLATED]

## TESTER

Canopy above a bed, throne or pulpit. [see PULPIT]

## TETRASTYLE

A portico with four columns on its front elevation.

## THACKSTONE [see FLAGSTONE]

## THATCH

Traditional roof covering composed of straw, heather or reeds, which is popularly associated with the essential image of the country cottage. The craft of thatching goes back at least to Saxon times and the basic techniques of the craft have an ancient lineage. Bundles of reeds or straw, known as yealms, are laid and fastened to the roof in several layers so that water cannot penetrate the thatch. A generous overhang ensures that any rain falls well clear of the house. A skilled thatcher can create quite elaborate patterns, especially along the ridge of a roof which may sometimes be adorned with figures similar to those encountered in topiary. The best-

350 *Thatch at Anne Hathaway's Cottage, Shottery, Warw.*

quality thatch is made of reed from Norfolk or Somerset. Thatch was once extremely common both in town and country, but its susceptibility to fire has restricted its use to rural locations. In recent years the demand for this most picturesque type of roofing has revived what appeared to be a dying craft. [see **81, 92**]

## THEATRE

In Roman Britannia the theatre for dramatic performances was a semicircular structure formed by tiers of seats facing the stage, e.g. at **St Albans**, *Herts*, the Verulamium of the second century AD. Thereafter, theatre building lapsed until Tudor times when a specialized structure was evolved which grew out of the galleried courtyards of the inns where itinerant groups of players staged their plays in the Middle Ages. The theatres of Shakespeare's day were galleried constructions of wood; the foundations of both the **Rose** and the **Globe** in **Southwark**, London, have recently been excavated. Under James I and Charles I the courtly masque was patronized as a dramatic allegory to celebrate the idea of monarchy; these costume charades were played in a great hall in the presence of the King who would sit on a throne in the centre of the dais. The **Banqueting House** in **Whitehall, London**, designed by Inigo Jones and inaugurated in 1622, also served as a 'masquing house' on many occasions. However, the elaborate stage sets and machinery had frequently to be dismantled and removed.

It was not until the late seventeenth and early eighteenth centuries that the modern idea of the theatre as a permanent, purpose-built and properly roofed structure came into being. Some notable early survivors include the **Theatre Royal, Bristol,** *Avon*, of 1766; the **Georgian Theatre Royal, Richmond**, *N Yorks*, of 1788; and the **Theatre Royal, Bury St Edmunds**, *Suffolk*, of 1819. None of London's eighteenth century theatres has survived intact; the oldest was the **Drury Lane Theatre** which was rebuilt in 1809, but the interior is much changed. So too is that of the **Theatre Royal, Haymarket**, of 1821, which was reconstructed in 1879. Many grand theatres and opera houses were built in the late Victorian and Edwardian eras as veritable palaces of entertainment in cities such as **Belfast**, N. Ireland; **Bradford**, *W Yorks*; **Cardiff**, Wales; **Glasgow**, Scotland; **Leeds**, *W Yorks*; **Nottingham**, *Notts*, and **Sheffield**, *S Yorks*. The most prolific of theatre architects was Frank Matcham (1854–1920), whose main works in London were the **Hippodrome** of 1900 and the **Coliseum** of 1904. Thereafter, theatre design lost much of its glamour: the **Royal Shakespeare Memorial Theatre** of 1932 at **Stratford-upon-Avon**, *Warw*, has affinities with the brick monumentalism of **Battersea Power Station, London**. The long-awaited **National Theatre** in **London** of the 1970s has been described by HRH the Prince of Wales as 'more like a bunker than a palace'. As if in direct opposition to the trend of the twentieth century, the **Minack Theatre** of 1929 near **Porthcurno**, *Cornwall*, reverted to the prototype of ancient Greece for its open-air arena

perched on a rugged clifftop with the sea as a backdrop. A novel modern theatre is the **Royal Exchange, Manchester**, of 1976, a capsule built inside its Edwardian parent building. [see AMPHITHEATRE]

## TIE BEAM
Main horizontal timber laid transversely, supporting the feet of the principal rafters. [see TIMBER-TRUSSED ROOF]

## TIERCERON
Subsidiary rib in a vault connecting a point on the ridge-rib with one of the main springers, e.g. in the nave vault of **Exeter Cathedral**, *Devon*. [see VAULT, 157]

## TILE
Tiles are tablets of an earthenware material which are fired in a kiln, but are much thinner than bricks as well as harder, smoother and less porous. Roman bricks are sometimes referred to as tiles, since they were much flatter than their Tudor and modern successors. Tile-making was a flourishing industry during the Middle Ages, and a number of floors with

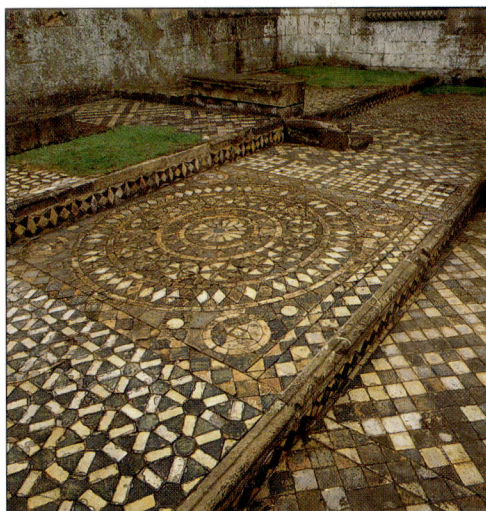

**351** *A floor of medieval tiles still in situ at Byland Abbey*, N Yorks.

352 *Detail of the Victorian tiled exterior of the Crown Liquor Saloon, Belfast, N Ireland.*

medieval tiles have survived, e.g. the chapter house at **Westminster Abbey, London**, the retro-choir of **Winchester Cathedral**, *Hants*, and at **Byland Abbey**, *N Yorks*. Patterns were created by inserting white clay into a background of red clay and covering the surface with a metallic glaze prior to firing. Tiles of this kind are known as encaustic tiles.

The practice of tile-hanging began in the seventeenth century as an attractive and weatherproof form of cladding. At the same time, roof tiles increasingly replaced thatch and shingles in towns and cities on account of their resistance to fire. The decorative use of tiles was revived by the Victorians both in churches and in commercial premises such as public houses, e.g. the **Crown Liquor Saloon, Belfast**, N. Ireland. The Food Halls of **Harrods** in **Knightsbridge, London**, represent a most lavish use of ornamental tiles. The **London Underground** was an enthusiastic user of coloured tiles, in particular for the station façades in their distinctive livery of ox-blood red. [see BONNET TILE, MATHEMATICAL TILE, TERRACOTTA, PANTILE, **118**]

## TIMBER-TRUSSED ROOF

Wooden roof of a type evolved in the Middle Ages, in which a tight structure of timbers, known as the truss, created a framework capable of enduring the stresses and strains put on it over hundreds of years. The ingenuity of the medieval carpenters, notably Hugh Herland who, from 1395 to 1402, rebuilt the roof of **Westminster Hall, London**, enabled ever wider spaces to be spanned. The exposed beams and rafters were often carved and painted to enhance their effect. Subtle structural variations were devised e.g. the trussed-rafter, the tie-beam, the collar-braced, the hammerbeam and the wagon or barrel roof. In addition to the many medieval timber-trussed roofs to have survived in parish churches, e.g. **St John Baptist, Bere Regis**, *Dorset*, there are notable specimens in the secular domain, e.g. at **Oakham Castle**, *Leics*; **Rufford Old Hall**, *Lancs*; **Eltham Palace, Crosby Hall**, and **Westminster Hall, London**; the **Merchant Adventurers Hall, York**, *N Yorks*, and **Fiddleford Manor**, *Dorset*. [see ANGEL ROOF, HAMMERBEAM, WAGON ROOF, **330**]

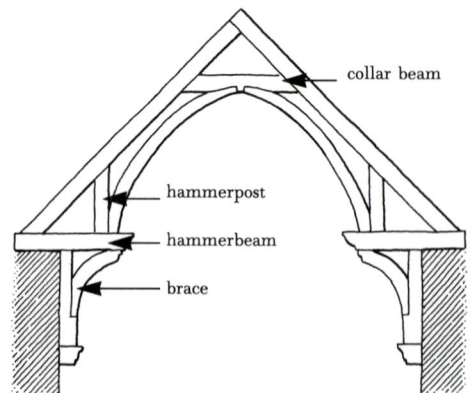

Hammerbeam roof

collar beam

hammerpost

hammerbeam

brace

## King-post roof

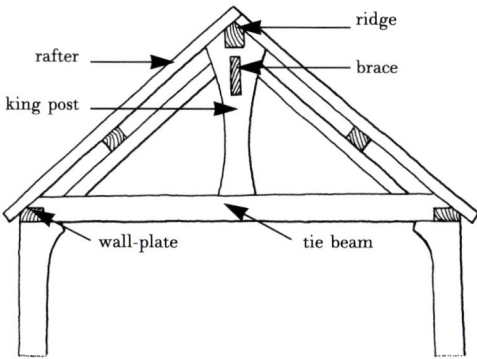

ridge

rafter

brace

king post

wall-plate

tie beam

## Crown post roof

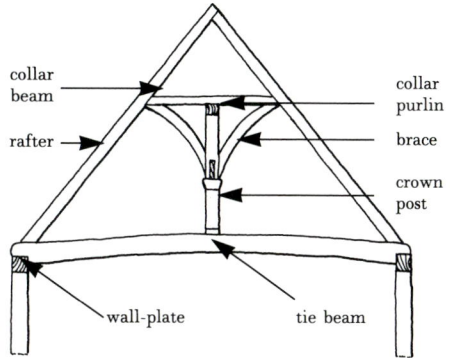

collar beam

collar purlin

rafter

brace

crown post

wall-plate

tie beam

353 The colourful timber-trussed roof of the church of St John Baptist, Bere Regis, Dorset.

## TIMBER-FRAMING [see HALF-TIMBERING]

## TITHE BARN [see BARN]

## TOLBOOTH
Old Scottish term for a town hall, often comprising a gaol e.g. at **Crail**, *Fife*, Scotland.

## TOLLHOUSE
Roadside dwelling built to accommodate the toll collector at bridges and by the side of turnpike roads, e.g. at **Keswick**, *Cumbria*; at **Mythe Bridge, Tewkesbury**, *Glos*, and at **Ironbridge**, *Shrops*.

## TOMB, TOMB SCULPTURE
The custom of building statues of the deceased as tomb memorials was introduced to Britain by the Romans, e.g. the carving of the centurion Marcus Favorius Facilis, now in the **Colchester & Essex Museum, Colchester**, *Essex*. But the native art of sculpting tomb effigies only began in earnest several centuries later.

355 *Alabaster effigies of the Neville tomb in St Mary the Virgin, Staindrop, Durham.*

354 *Grave slabs of Hebridean chieftains at Kilmory Knap, S'clyde, Scotland.*

Among the most dramatic figures are those portraying crusading knights in battle gear, e.g. in the **Temple Church, London**. A magnificent example in **Dorchester Abbey**, *Oxon*, is shown in a cross-legged posture, caught in the act of drawing his sword from its scabbard. Throughout the Middle Ages it was the fashion for the gentry to invest in elegant tombs crowned with idealized effigies, and these were given prominent positions in many a parish church, e.g. **St Mary the Virgin, Staindrop**, *Durham*; **St James, Spilsby**, *Lincs*; and **St Mary the Virgin, Ewelme**, *Oxon*. Grander productions were possible in the larger churches and abbeys, e.g. the Despenser and de Brien tombs in **Tewkesbury Abbey**, *Glos*, and the splendid tomb of the Earl of Warwick in the **Beauchamp Chapel of St Mary, Warwick**, *Warw*. The tomb of Edward II in **Gloucester Cathedral**, *Glos*, amounts to a work of architecture in miniature; and the magnificent royal tombs in **Westminster Abbey, London**, seem to indicate that rank and title might even be

356 OPPOSITE *Fettiplace tomb sculptures in the church of St Mary the Virgin, Swinbrook, Oxon.*

357 *Monument in Southwark Cathedral, London, to the pillmaker Lockyer who died in 1672.*

358 *The tomb of Lady Milton in Milton Abbey, Dorset, is a poignant Georgian monument.*

carried beyond the grave. However, some medieval tombs portrayed the grim reality of death in effigies of naked and rotting cadavers to remind the onlooker that dying meant physical decomposition as well as spiritual transformation.

In Scotland, a distinctive school of tomb sculpture evolved around the Hebridean chieftains known as the Lords of the Isles. Their grave slabs present a precious record of these seafaring warlords of Norse and Celtic ancestry. The deceased are carved in relief with helmet, sword and armour, and in the background may be seen the occasional Viking-style long ship with furled sails, a poignant symbol of voyages across the seas. Fine collections of these grave slabs may be seen at **Kilmory Knap** and **Saddell Abbey**, *S'clyde*, Scotland. Medieval Ireland imported the current fashion for recumbent effigies from England, but added its own artistry to the embellishment of the tomb chests.

In the sixteenth and seventeenth centuries tomb sculpture became more ani-

mated; and the effigies were given various life-like postures from semi-recumbent to kneeling, e.g. the Fettiplace monuments at **St Mary the Virgin, Swinbrook**, *Oxon*, and in Ireland those of the Earl of Cork at **St Mary, Youghal**, *Cork*, and of Arthur Chichester at **St Nicholas, Carrickfergus**, *Antrim*. Humour features occasionally in the elaborate epitaphs, e.g. that on the tomb of the pillmaker Lockyer in **Southwark Cathedral, London**, which makes merry with the fact that the apothecary was unable to cure himself. A more sombre mood was to permeate the tombs of the eighteenth and nineteenth centuries, e.g. that of Lady Milton in **Milton Abbey**, *Dorset*, whose recumbent body is watched over by an effigy of her grieving husband. Increasing use was made of Classical motifs such as funerary urns and broken columns to symbolize the abrupt termination of life. The Victorian desire for novel forms of tomb resulted in many eccentric productions such as the tomb of the Arabian explorer Richard Burton (1821–90) in the **Roman Catholic**

**Cemetery** at **Mortlake, London**, which was designed as a concrete replica of an oriental tent. Victorian cemeteries abound in fascinating examples. Most modern tombs are in the form of simple headstones. [see ALTAR TOMB, BARROW, BRASSES, CAIRN, CHAMBERED TOMB, CEMETERY, CENOTAPH, CIST, MAUSOLEUM, MEMORIAL, MONUMENT, URN, WAR MEMORIAL, **128**, **299**, **329**, **371**]

## TORUS

Prominent convex moulding, semicircular in profile, e.g. on the base of a column. [see MOULDING]

## TOWER

Tall structure, either freestanding or part of a larger building. Towers were built as strongpoints to defend a castle or town wall. The **Tower of London** acquired its name from the original Norman keep, known as the **White Tower,** which once dominated London. The most frequent type of tower is that of the parish church, which evolved from the squat, square form of the Norman style to the lofty and ornate versions of Perpendicular Gothic, which are a distinctive feature of the Somerset landscape, e.g. at **St Mary Magdalene, Taunton**, *Somerset*. In the eighteenth century the building of towers as follies on country estates became fashionable, e.g. **Broadway Tower** by the Countess of Coventry in 1797, which surveys the borders of Gloucestershire and Worcestershire. In 1827 the millionaire eccentric William Beckford built himself a stately tower on the crown of **Lansdown Hill** outside **Bath**, *Avon*, in the guise of an Italian campanile. Nowadays, towers are generally for a practical purpose, e.g. the **Telecom Tower, London**, of 1964. [see BELFRY, MARTELLO TOWER, MONUMENT, PELE TOWER, ROUND TOWER, TOWER HOUSE, WATER TOWER, **78**]

## TOWER HOUSE

Fortified residence, built particularly in Scotland and Ireland, consisting of a single tall block, usually within an enclosure known as a barmkin or bawn. The tower house was essentially a vertical version of the hall house: a stone barrel-vaulted basement supporting the principal chamber, with the laird's solar on the storey above. Within the thickness of the walls a spiral stair gave access to the various levels. Many of Scotland's oldest tower houses have been engulfed by later buildings, but that of the late thirteenth century at **Drum Castle**, *Grampian*, is fairly intact. The fourteenth-century **Loch Leven Castle**, *Tayside*, is a model of austerity; **Borthwick Castle**, *Lothian*, of 1430 is of a more sophisticated type. The tower house tradition in Scotland continued well into the seventeenth century, although some of the later designs, e.g. **Craigievar**, *Grampian*, of 1626, were more concerned with elegance than

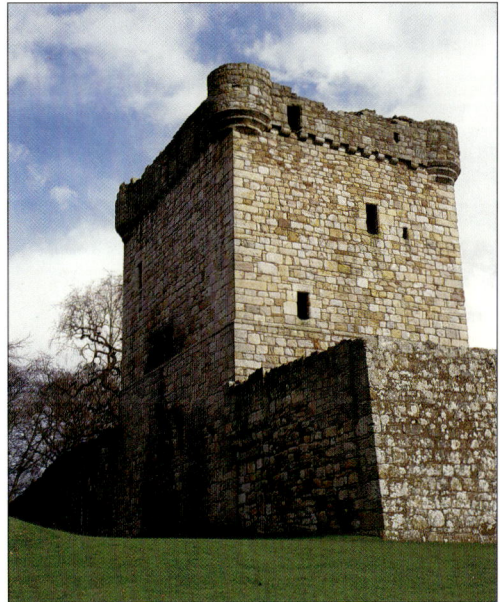

**359** *Loch Leven Castle*, Tayside, *Scotland: an austere tower house with its barmkin wall intact.*

**360** *Craigievar Castle*, Grampian, *Scotland, exudes grace rather than martial strength.*

defence. In 1677 the Earl of Strathmore, referring to his own tower house of **Glamis**, *Tayside*, wrote: 'Such houses truly are quite out of fashion, as feuds are ... the country being generally more civilized than it was of ancient times.' [see PELE TOWER, PLANTATION CASTLE]

**TOWN HALL** [see MUNICIPAL BUILDINGS]

**TOWN HOUSE**
Usually a house with a narrow frontage which forms part of a terrace in an urban context. In Scotland, the term can signify a town hall, e.g. the **Town House, Aberdeen**, *Grampian.* [see 34]

**TRABEATED**
Describes the post-and-lintel principle of construction, i.e. one which uses only vertical and horizontal structural elements. [see ARCUATED]

**TRACERY**

The ornamental division of a Gothic window by means of stone elements arranged in a variety of patterns. Changes in tracery accompanied and defined each phase of Gothic style. The earliest and simplest was plate tracery, essentially a foiled shape carved out of the stone spandrel between two lancet windows. Slimmer, more elegant tracery evolved in the second half of the thirteenth century: this is termed geometrical or bar tracery since the stonework was reduced to supporting bars. As windows became larger, so tracery patterns of increasing intricacy were devised. Intersecting tracery continues the curves of the lancets to create a series of lozenges. Reticulated tracery consists of ogee-shaped forms resembling the mesh of a fishing net. Curvilinear, sometimes known as flowing or undulating tracery, creates more sinuous patterns. The most imaginative use of tracery belonged to the Decorated period. In Perpendicular Gothic there was a proliferation of vertical lines, known as rectilinear or panel tracery. A regional variant, Kentish tracery, consists of foils with barbs in a circle. [see FOIL, GOTHIC, JESSE WINDOW, 85]

Plate tracery

trefoil

cusp

quatrefoil

cinquefoil

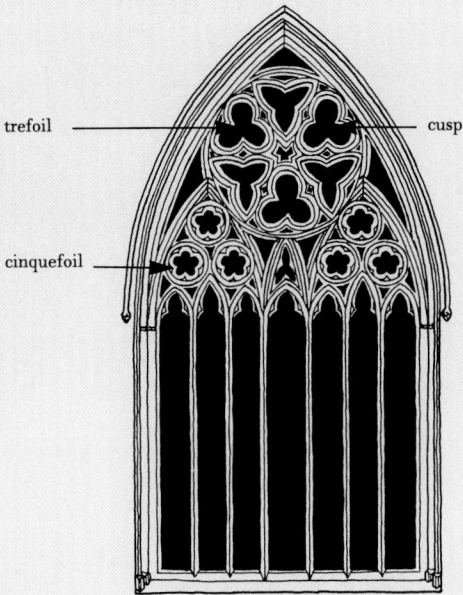

Geometrical tracery

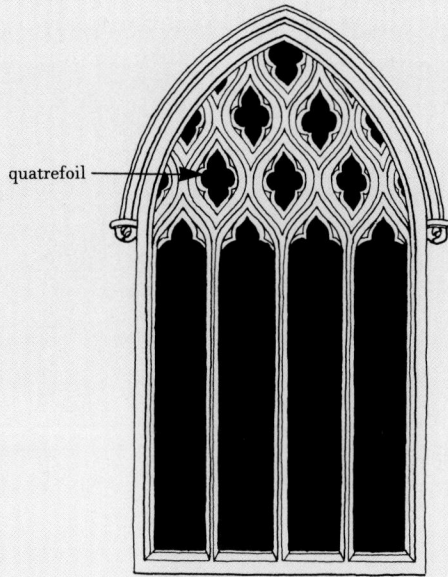

Reticulated tracery

Intersecting tracery

Panel tracery

## TRANSEPT

Transverse arm of a cruciform church. The north and south transepts generally meet at the junction of the nave and chancel to form the crossing. **Beverley Minster**, *Humbs*, is exceptional in having two sets of transepts. [see CRUCIFORM]

## TRANSITIONAL [see GOTHIC]

## TRANSOM

Horizontal element of wood or stone which divides a window. [see MULLION]

## TREAD

Horizontal, upper surface of a step. [see STAIR]

## TREFOIL [see FOIL]

## TRIBUNE

Originally, the presiding seat in the apse of a basilica. The term later came to be applied to the rostrum or raised platform on which that seat was placed. It also denotes the gallery of a church. [see DAIS, GALLERY]

## TRIFORIUM

Arcaded wall passage in a church located above the nave arcade but below the clerestory. The triforium may be represented by blank arcading and be called a blindstory. The triforium was increasingly dispensed with during the late Middle Ages.

## TRIGLYPH

Grooved block between the metopes of a Doric frieze. [see **170**]

## TRILITHON

Megalithic monument of prehistory consisting of a massive lintel resting on two upright monoliths, e.g. at **Stonehenge**, *Wilts*, where the trilithons form a circle.

**361** *Surviving trilithon at Stonehenge*, Wilts.

[see HENGE, STONE CIRCLE]

## TROMPE L'OEIL

Art of illusionist mural painting which imitates views and architectural features. The term is French, meaning 'deceives the eye'. The art derives ultimately from Italy, and it became fashionable in the late seventeenth century in Baroque interiors. One of the most prolific practitioners was James Thornhill (1675–1734), whose spectacular works may be seen at **Hampton Court, London**; **Chatsworth**, *Derbys*; **Blenheim Palace**, *Oxon*; **Moor Park**, *Herts*; and inside the dome of **St Paul's Cathedral, London**. There are fine examples of eighteenth-century *trompe l'oeil* at **Dyrham Park**, *Avon*, and **Kensington Palace, London**; and a creation of 1969–83 by Graham Rust at **Ragley Hall**, *Warw*. The painting of architectural tableaux is also known by the Italian '*quadratura*'. [see MURAL]

## TROPHY

Decorative Baroque motif consisting of an arrangement of arms and military equipment. [see ACHIEVEMENT, **337**]

## TRUSS

Framework of timbers to bridge a space in a timber-trussed roof. [see TIMBER-TRUSSED ROOF]

## TUDOR

The Tudor monarchs ruled from the accession of Henry VII in 1485 until the death of Elizabeth I in 1603. In terms of architectural development the Tudor period thus contained the terminal decline of Gothic as symbolized by the flattened four-centred arch, but it also witnessed the first influx and gradual absorption of Renaissance ideas. This was a slow transition in which traditional, medieval concepts of planning combined in a novel and unique fashion with the emerging 'modern' taste of the times for Classical ornamentation. The sixteenth century was a time of frenetic

363 *Tudor manor house at Sandford Orcas,* Dorset.

building activity in the secular domain as economic resources accrued to the Tudor gentry in the aftermath of the Dissolution of the Monasteries. Fine new residences were constructed in all parts of the land, ranging from the prodigy houses of the flamboyant courtiers to the half-timbered homes of the rural yeomanry. The pace of change quickened to a marked extent during the reign of Elizabeth I (1558–1603), so that the Tudor period may be usefully considered in two broad divisions, i.e. early Tudor and Elizabethan. [see ARCH, BRICKWORK, COUNTRY HOUSE, ELIZABETHAN, FAN VAULT, FORT, LODGE, PRODIGY HOUSE, PALACE, RENAISSANCE, SCHOOL, TOMB SCULPTURE]

362 *Tudor-style gate to Lincoln's Inn, London.*

## TUDOR ARCH [see ARCH]

## TUDOR FLOWER

Formalized leaf motif characteristic of late Gothic and Tudor architecture.

## TUMULUS [see BARROW]

## TUNNEL

One of the major engineering achieve-ments of the canal and railway eras of the late eighteenth and nineteenth centuries was the digging of long tunnels through the hills. The tunnel entrances were sometimes adorned with grandiose architectural porticos, e.g. at **Box Hill** on the Great Western Railway just outside **Corsham**, *Wilts*. Canal tunnels were of smaller calibre e.g. **Sapperton Tunnel**, *Glos*, of which the eastern entrance is a fine example of architectural ambition on the canals.

## TUNNEL VAULT
Simple form of continuous vault which may be pointed or round in outline. The latter variant is known as a barrel or wagon vault. [see GROIN VAULT, VAULT]

## TURNPIKE [see SPIRAL STAIR]

## TURRET
Small subsidiary tower of a castle.

**364** *Christ in majesty occupies the tympanum of the Norman church of St Nicholas, Barfreston,* Kent.

## TUSCAN ORDER [see ORDER]

## TWISTED COLUMN [see BARLEY-SUGAR COLUMN]

## TYMPANUM
Space between the lintel of a doorway and the arch enclosing it above, a prominent decorative feature especially of Norman churches, e.g. at **St Nicholas, Barfreston,** *Kent*; **St Swithin's, Quenington,** *Glos*; and the famous **Prior's Doorway** of **Ely Cathedral,** *Cambs*. In Classical architecture, the tympanum is the triangular space within the pediment.

# U

## UNDERCROFT

Vaulted structure, sometimes below ground level, supporting an upper chamber such as a hall. The undercroft is generally the best-preserved feature of a medieval building, e.g. at **Battle Abbey**, *E Sussex*; **Fountains Abbey**, *N Yorks*; **Lanercost Priory**, *Cumbria*; and **Burton**

**365** *This undercroft at Battle Abbey, E Sussex, is a noble vault with prominent ribs.*

**Agnes Manor House**, *Humbs*. The undercroft at **Glasgow University**, Scotland, is a fine example of the Gothic Revival. A church undercroft is usually known as a crypt. [see CRYPT, 230]

## UNDERPASS

The idea of the subterranean walkway was devised by the Victorians to provide safe and convenient passage for pedestrians at busy junctions, usually in connection with stations, e.g. at the old **Crystal Palace, High Level Station, London**, where a magnificent brickwork vault resting on massive octagonal pillars was built by a team of Italian bricklayers. [see **192**]

**UNDULATING TRACERY** [see TRACERY]

**UNIVALLATE** [see HILLFORT]

## UNIVERSITY

The medieval universities, e.g. those of **Cambridge**, *Cambs*; **Durham**, *Durham*; **Oxford**, *Oxon*, and **St Andrews**, *Fife*, Scotland, evolved by a gradual accretion of individual colleges. Their Gothic buildings set the style of university architecture for centuries to come, e.g. when **Glasgow University** moved from its original site in the city centre to the suburb of Gilmorehill in the latter half of the nineteenth century, it commissioned a full-blooded Gothic Revival design from George Gilbert Scott, completed by his son John Oldrid Scott. **Bristol University**, *Avon*, opted for Perpendicular Gothic as late as 1915; but by the time its great tower was completed in 1925 the style was decidedly anachronistic. The first stirrings of a modern approach to university architecture may be seen in the **Senate House** of the **University of London** by Charles Holden in the 1930s; but it was not until the 1960s that several entirely new universities were built in a modern style, e.g. the **University of Sussex** at **Brighton**, *E Sussex*, by Basil Spence. Its combination of brickwork with massive segmental arches of concrete was novel, but the structural layout with courtyards drew on traditional values. Nowadays, a university is generally a much looser collection of buildings, scattered about a campus rather than orchestrated within a grand design, e.g. the **University of East Anglia, Norwich**, *Norfolk*. [see COLLEGE]

## URBANISM

[see ALLEY, APARTMENT HOUSE, AVENUE, BURGH, BURH, CIRCUS, COUNCIL HOUSING, CRESCENT, GARDEN CITY, MEWS, MUNICIPAL BUILDINGS, NEW TOWN, PEABODY BUILDINGS, PIAZZA, PLANNED VILLAGE, PLANTATION TOWN, RIBBON DEVELOPMENT, SEMI-DETACHED, SQUARE, TENEMENT, TERRACE, TOWN HOUSE, UNDERPASS]

## URN

Decorative element, especially in Neo-Classical architecture, used to ornament balustrades, niches and garden terraces as well as funerary monuments. [see **246**]

**366** *The Senate House of the University of London strikes a modern note in Georgian Bloomsbury.*

**367** *Graceful garden urn at Saltram House*, Devon. *Note the Neo-Classical statues in their niches.*

# V

contrivance goes back to the early Middle Ages. It often represents the form of a cock, and hence it may be called a weathercock. Also known as weathervane.

## VANE

Rooftop finial which can revolve in order to indicate the direction of the wind. This

## VENETIAN DOOR or WINDOW

Tripartite arrangement in which the central door or light rises to a semicircular

## VAULT

Arched roof or ceiling which may be round or pointed in section. The form of the vault was an ever-changing feature of medieval architecture, evolving from the simple barrel and groin vaults of the Norman era to the various pointed rib vaults of Gothic, which culminated in the fan vaults of the Perpendicular

phase. [see ARCH, BOSS, CRYPT, FAN VAULT, GOTHIC, GROIN VAULT, LIERNE, RIB, STELLAR VAULT, TIERCERON, TUNNEL VAULT, UNDERCROFT, 157]

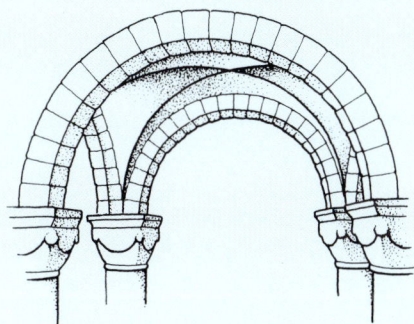

Groin vault

Barrel vault

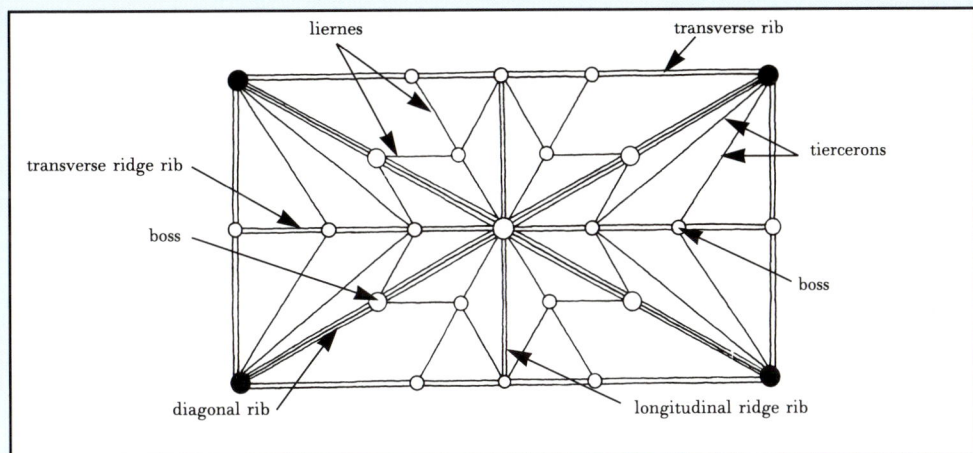

liernes
transverse rib
transverse ridge rib
tiercerons
boss
boss
diagonal rib
longitudinal ridge rib

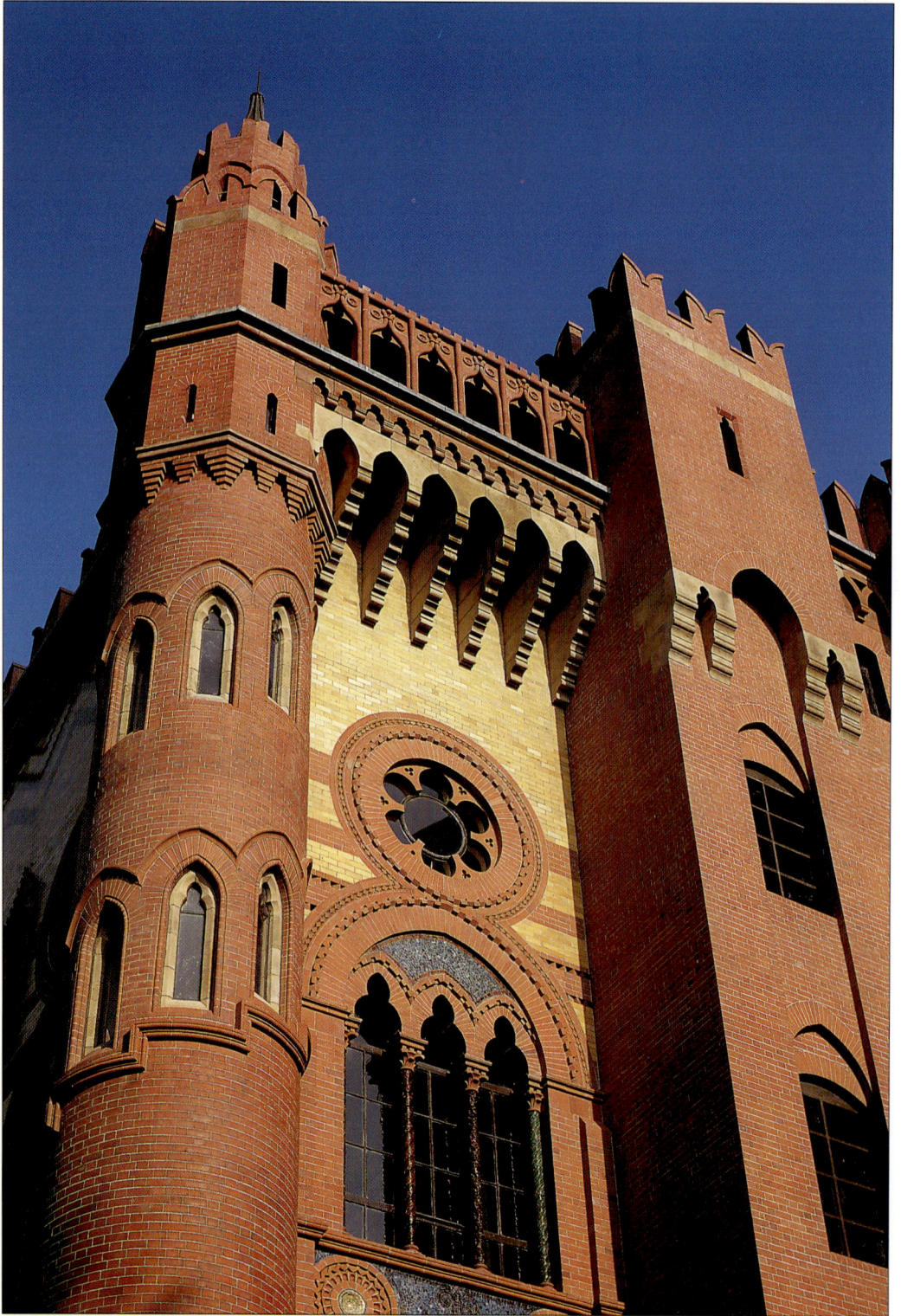

arch, and is flanked by two square-headed lights of lesser height. Venetian doors and windows were favourite features of Palladianism.

Venetian window

## VENETIAN GOTHIC

The attractive patterns and striking colours of the buildings of Venice were energetically promoted in nineteenth century Britain by John Ruskin. Venetian Gothic became one of the most exotic historical styles of the Victorian era, e.g. the resplendent polychromatic brickwork at **Templeton's Carpet Factory, Glasgow**, Scotland, of 1888–90. [see POLYCHROME, RUSKINIAN]

## VERANDA

External balcony or gallery, roofed over and usually built with light metal or wood uprights. Verandas were a popular feature of Regency and Edwardian houses. [see BALCONY]

## VERMICULATION

Surface decoration of dressed stones con-

sisting of a profusion of short, curved, shallow channels in a worm-like pattern. [see RUSTICATION]

## VESTIARY [see VESTRY]

## VESTIBULE

Lobby or antechamber adjacent to the outer door of a building. [see 5]

## VESTRY

Chamber attached to a church where the robes of the priests and choir are hung and the communion vessels are kept. Also known as vestiary or sacristy.

## VIADUCT

Structure carrying an elevated road or railway on a series of arches over a valley or marshy terrain. The railway engineers of the nineteenth century built the most spectacular viaducts, e.g. the **Balcombe Viaduct**, *W Sussex*, of 1841 over the River Ouse, a noble structure of brick piers and arches crowned by a Classical

**368** OPPOSITE *The Venetian Gothic of Templeton's Carpet Factory, Glasgow, Scotland. Note the polychromy.*

**369** *Holborn Viaduct, London, is surprisingly ornate for a utilitarian structure.*

balustrade carved from Caen limestone. Also of note is the spectacular 24-arch **Ribblehead Viaduct**, *N Yorks* of 1875. The **Glenfinnan Viaduct** of 1898 on the West Highland Railway, Scotland, was built of concrete. Although roads can cope with much steeper gradients than railways, the **Holborn Viaduct, London**, of 1869 was built to spare the horses the strenuous descent and ascent of the Fleet Valley. This structure is a fine piece of urban engineering made of cast iron and rampant with allegorical statuary. [see AQUEDUCT, BRIDGE]

## VICE OR VYSE [see SPIRAL STAIR]

## VILLA

In Roman times, a farmstead or the country home of a landowner. Their mosaic floors are the most interesting visual feature to have survived at several sites in Britain. In the eighteenth century the Renaissance-style villas of Andrea Palladio

## VICTORIAN

The reign of Queen Victoria (1837–1901) coincided neatly with one of the most architecturally productive epochs ever known. By contrast to the homogeneous Classical character of the preceding Georgian age, the architecture of the Victorians delighted in diversity. The label 'Victorian' thus conjures up many images rather than a unified picture. The Gothic Revival was certainly the most distinctive and prolific feature of the period, which amounted to a deliberate attempt to counteract the Classical transformation of Britain that had been accomplished by the Georgians. Classicism, however, was not abandoned: some of the grandest productions of the Greek Revival were Victorian in date, and the start of the Victorian era was dominated by the debate between Classicism and Gothic, known familiarly as 'The Battle of the Styles'.

The underlying common denominator of almost all Victorian architecture was its blatant historicism. In spite of the revolutionary progress made with glass and iron, there was hardly a stirring of a progressive, forward-looking school of thought in matters of style; the new building technology

**370** *The Buxton Memorial Fountain, London, is a miniature gem of the Gothic Revival.*

in northern Italy caught the imagination of the arbiters of fashion, and many imitations were built, e.g. Lord Burlington's **Chiswick House, London**, of 1725–9 and Colen Campbell's **Mereworth Castle**, *Kent*, of 1723. In the nineteenth century, 'villa' came to mean a suburban house. [see MOSAIC, PALLADIANISM, **193**]

## VITRIFIED FORT
A hillfort in which the firing of the timber superstructure caused the stone to fuse or vitrify in the intense heat of the flames, e.g. **Finavon**, *Tayside*, Scotland. [see HILLFORT]

## VOLUTE
Spiral or scroll-like motif, e.g. on the capitals of the Ionic, Corinthian and Composite orders. [see ORDER, **82**]

## VOUSSOIR
One of the wedge-shaped stones forming an arch. [see ARCH]

371 *The tomb sculpture in Highgate Cemetery, London, exudes a quintessentially Victorian atmosphere.*

and often overpowering treatment. Georgian reticence and architectural understatement were replaced by bombast and display. Deceit and sham became common currency: factories and pumping stations were dressed up as palaces, and railway stations as Gothic castles or Classical temples. But this excessive eclecticism, as the purists may see it, was largely due to the material success and overconfidence of the Victorians. They had the means to achieve their dreams, and to stamp their own vision on what they considered to be a drab and monotonous Georgian inheritance. [see ARTS & CRAFTS, BARONIAL, BATTLE OF THE STYLES, BYZANTINE REVIVAL, CEMETERY, FACTORY, GLASS, GOTHIC REVIVAL, GREEK REVIVAL, MUNICIPAL BUILDINGS, PEABODY BUILDINGS, PUBLIC HOUSE, QUEEN ANNE, RUSKINIAN, STATION, TENEMENT, TUNNEL, VENETIAN GOTHIC, VIADUCT, WAREHOUSE]

was usually dressed up or concealed behind traditional façades. The historical styles ranged from Greek, Roman, Byzantine and Gothic to Jacobethan, Queen Anne, Venetian, Norman and Egyptian. Perhaps the unifying element of all these styles was their lavish

# W

## WAGON ROOF

Type of arched ceiling resembling the shape of a covered wagon. The structure is created by closely set rafters and arched braces. The interspaces between the timbers may be panelled or plastered. The wagon roof was a speciality of West Country churches, e.g. **St Peter & St Paul, Shepton Mallet**, *Somerset*, and **St Andrew, Cullompton**, *Devon*. Also known as a cradle-roof or barrel roof. [see CELURE]

## WAGON VAULT [see TUNNEL VAULT, VAULT]

## WAINSCOT [see PANELLING]

## WALL

The wall as an architectural feature in its own right may be seen at its most spectacular in the Roman fortification of **Hadrian's Wall** of AD 122–30 which extended 72 miles (115 km) from Newcastle, *Tyne & Wear*, to Carlisle, *Cumbria*, and has survived in impressive stretches. By contrast, the **Antonine Wall** in Scotland of AD 143–5 was an earthwork and has suffered from the forces of erosion to a greater degree. Defensive walls were an important feature of medieval castles and towns. Many city walls have been demolished in the course of subsequent urban expansion, but those of **York**, *N Yorks*, and **Chester**, *Cheshire*, are still largely intact, though much restored. Long high walls were built in the eighteenth and nineteenth centuries to mark the boundaries of country estates;

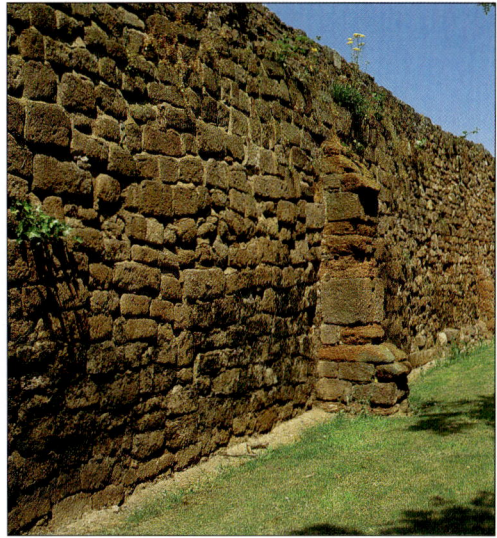

373 *The Roman wall of Exeter, Devon, was rebuilt in the Middle Ages. Note the coarse masonry.*

and extremely high brick walls were built around the docks and warehouses at that time, e.g. in London, to prevent theft. [see CRINKLE-CRANKLE, CURTAIN WALL, **204**]

## WALL-PLATE

Timber laid lengthways along the top of a wall into which the ends of the rafters are fitted. [see TIMBER-TRUSSED ROOF]

## WALL-STAIR

Staircase built into the thickness of a wall, usually of a castle. [see STAIR]

## WALL-WALK [see ALURE]

## WAR MEMORIAL

A monument specifically to commemorate those who died in battle is a relatively recent phenomenon. One of the first was the **Guards Crimea Memorial** in **Waterloo Place, London**, built in remembrance of the 2162 men of the three regiments of foot guards who died during the Crimean War of 1854–6. The heavy casualties of the First World War

372 OPPOSITE *Wagon roof in the church of St Andrew, Cullompton, Devon. Note the angels with spread wings.*

**374** *The impressive war memorial to the Royal Regiment of Artillery at Hyde Park Corner, London.*

(1914–18) prompted the building of numerous memorials, e.g. that to the **Royal Regiment of Artillery** at **Hyde Park Corner, London**. Many more memorials followed the Second World War (1939–45). [see CENOTAPH]

**WARD** [see BAILEY]

**WAREHOUSE**

Large building evolved in the eighteenth century, for the storage of goods, especially at dockside for handling ships' cargo. In **London** and **Liverpool**, *Mers*, many of the nineteenth-century warehouses have been converted for other purposes. Textile warehouses remain prominent features of industrial cities such as **Bradford**, *W Yorks*, and **Manchester**. [see FACTORY]

375 *Waterfront warehouse at Butler's Wharf, London, of a type once commonplace in London Docklands.*

376 *Watermill used in the process of linen manufacture at Wellbrook, Tyrone, N Ireland.*

## WATERGATE
Gateway providing access by boat to a building of consequence, e.g. the **Tower of London**. The **York House Watergate** of *c.* 1626 has been left stranded as a result of land reclamation in the **Embankment Gardens, London**.

## WATER-LEAF
Gothic ornamentation, e.g. on capitals, of scroll-like leaf shapes. [see CAPITAL]

## WATERMILL, WATERWHEEL
Mills powered by water were used by the Saxons on a massive scale: the Domesday Book records that more than 7500 were in service in the 1080s. The natural force of flowing water was directed on to a wheel by the digging of narrow channels known as leats. Watermills were originally used for grinding corn. That at **Mortimer's Cross**, *Heref & Worcs*, dates back to the

eighteenth century. The textile industry in the pre-industrial era was dependent on watermill power: the **Wellbrook Beetling Mill,** *Tyrone*, N. Ireland, of 1768, operated a hammering device which gave unbleached linen its sheen. The largest waterwheel in the world is the Lady Isabella at **Laxey** on the **Isle of Man**, 72 ft (22m) in diameter, which was built in 1854 to pump out the local lead mines.

## WATER TOWER
Tower built to support a water tank at a height providing sufficient pressure for distribution to outlets in the vicinity, e.g. the 303ft (92·4m) high imitation of Siena's Torre del Mangia of 1851 by the docks at **Grimsby**, *Humbs*. Equally fantastic is the **House-in-the-Clouds** at **Thorpeness**, *Suffolk*, which carries a 30,000-gallon water tank, built in 1923, disguised as a weatherboarded house

perched on a five-storey pedestal complete with fake windows and a front door.

## WATTLE AND DAUB

Type of wall construction consisting of a loose structure of branches (wattles) covered with mud or clay (daub) and mixed with straw. Wattle and daub could be used as infill in a half-timbered house or on its own for a primitive and flimsy sort of cabin that was common in the Middle Ages.

377 *Alfriston Clergy House*, E Sussex *is a fourteenth-century wealden house. Note the jettied bay.*

## WAVE

Moulding consisting of a convex curve between two concave curves, typical of Decorated Gothic.

## WEALDEN HOUSE

Medieval half-timbered house with a central hall open to the roof and bays at each end jettied out at the front. A pitched roof spans the entire house, including the recess between the bays. The type is particularly associated with Kent and Sussex, e.g. the fine specimen at the **Weald & Downland Open Air Museum**, *W Sussex*. [see HALF-TIMBERING]

## WEATHERBOARD

External cladding composed of overlapping horizontal wooden boards. The boards are thinner at the top, thereby permitting them to hang as close to the vertical as possible. Many examples occur in south-east England, and elsewhere. Also known as clapboard. [see **379**]

## WEATHERCOCK, WEATHERVANE [see VANE]

## WEATHER-TILE [see MATHEMATICAL TILE]

## WEDGE-TOMB [see CHAMBERED TOMB]

## WEEM [see FOGOU]

## WELL HOUSE

During the Middle Ages small structures were often built to provide a roofed shrine

**378** *The medieval well house at Dupath, Cornwall, is built of stone, including the roof.*

at a holy well, e.g. at **Dupath** and **St Cleer**, *Cornwall*. The buildings at the **Struell Wells**, *Down*, N. Ireland, date back to the seventeenth century. [see SHRINE]

## WHEELHOUSE

Circular building of drystone masonry in which the partition walls extend like spokes from the open space in the centre to the outer wall. The wheelhouse was a speciality of prehistoric Scotland, e.g. at **Jarlshof, Shetland.**

## WHEEL WINDOW

Circular window with radiating segments resembling the spokes of a wheel, e.g. in **Christ Church Cathedral, Oxford,** *Oxon.* [see ROSE WINDOW]

## WICKET

A small door which forms part of a larger one. It enables pedestrians to pass freely without the inconvenience of opening and shutting the larger door. Often found in medieval gateways.

## WINDER

Individual step of a staircase which is wider at the outside edge. A succession of winders creates a spiral or geometric stair. Several winders form a right-angled turn on a straight staircase. [see STAIRCASE]

## WINDMILL

Structure designed for grinding corn between millstones driven by rotating sails which are turned by the wind. With constant variations in wind direction, ingenious ways were devised to bring the sails into the wind. The earliest British windmills, of the twelfth century, were of the post-mill type, in which the entire superstructure could be turned around a central post supported by four sturdy oak beams mounted on

**379** *1680s windmill of the post-mill type at Brill,* Bucks. *The cladding is known as clapboard or weatherboard.*

stone or brick piers. None of the original medieval post-mills has survived; and the oldest is probably **Pitstone Mill**, *Bucks*, of 1627. That at **Saxtead Green**, *Suffolk*, goes back to *c.* 1700. The next major development was the tower-mill, in which only the cap containing the windshaft and sails was turned to catch the wind. The rest of the structure consisted of a solidly built tower, e.g. **Sibsey Trader**, *Lincs*, of 1877. A variant of the tower-mill was the smock-mill, a timber polygonal structure clad with weatherboarding, which suggested the profile of a man in a peasant's smock. Windmills were less reliable than watermills, and

they did not figure in an industrial context. However, the windmill is now being used as an environmentally clean method of generating electricity. **Orkney**, Scotland, has one of the first and the largest of these wind turbines, 246 ft (75m) high, which generates 3000 kilowatts.

## WINDOW

The openings in the walls of a building for the admittance of light and ventilation have long been the subjects of architectural embellishment; and they thus document stylistic changes from age to age. In modest medieval houses the windows were unglazed and protected by wooden shutters. Castle windows were usually narrow for reasons of defence and often splayed on the inside to make the most of the available light. Glazing was not generally

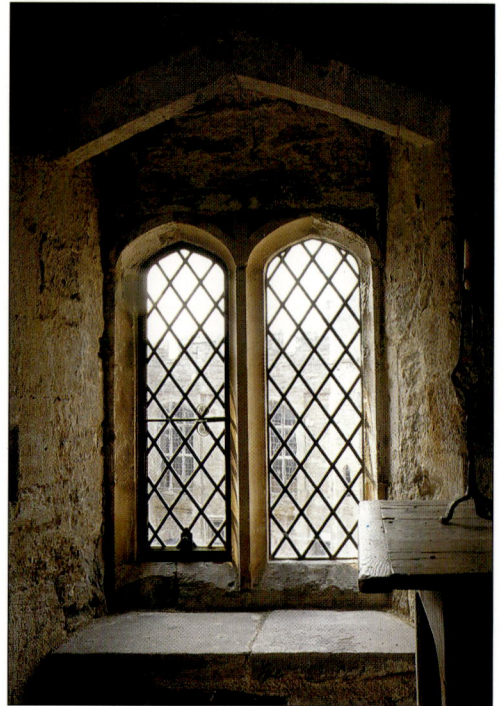

**380** *A pair of leaded lights at Berkeley Castle,* Glos. *Note the lattice pattern of the cames.*

affordable until the fifteenth century; before that a variety of substitutes were tried such as horn, alabaster, linen and parchment. Stained glass was fitted in church windows from early medieval times. The shapes of the windows followed the transition from the round arch of the Normans to the pointed arch of Gothic and tracked every subsequent phase from Early English to Decorated and Perpendicular. Domestic architecture was less adventurous, though the great halls of castles and manor houses did not eschew elaborate, squareheaded, mullioned and transomed windows. These were often stately and imposing, e.g. in the ruined fifteenth-century banqueting hall at **Sudeley Castle**, *Glos*; and at **Gainsborough Old Hall**, *Lincs*, of the same era, a lofty bay window maximizes the natural light. In Elizabethan times, the prodigy houses, e.g.

**Hardwick Hall**, *Derbys*, incorporated vast expanses of glazing in broad windows. From the seventeenth century the Classical style introduced tall, rectangular sash windows with slim glazing bars of wood. Elegant bow windows were a feature of the Regency period. The Victorians did much damage to Georgian windows by replacing the glazing bars and inserting large expanses of plate glass. In this way the appearance of most house façades was radically altered. [see ANGEL LIGHT, BAY WINDOW, BOW WINDOW, BULL'S EYE WINDOW, CAME, CASEMENT, DORMER, FANLIGHT, FENESTRATION, FRENCH WINDOW, GLASS, GLAZING BAR, JESSE WINDOW, LACED WINDOWS, LANCET, LEADED LIGHT, LOWSIDE WINDOW, LUCARNE, MULLION, OCULUS, ORIEL, QUARRY, ROSE WINDOW, SASH WINDOW, STAINED GLASS, TRACERY, TRANSOM, VENETIAN WINDOW, WHEEL WINDOW]

**381** *Painted glass set in a decorative window at Sudeley Castle*, Glos.

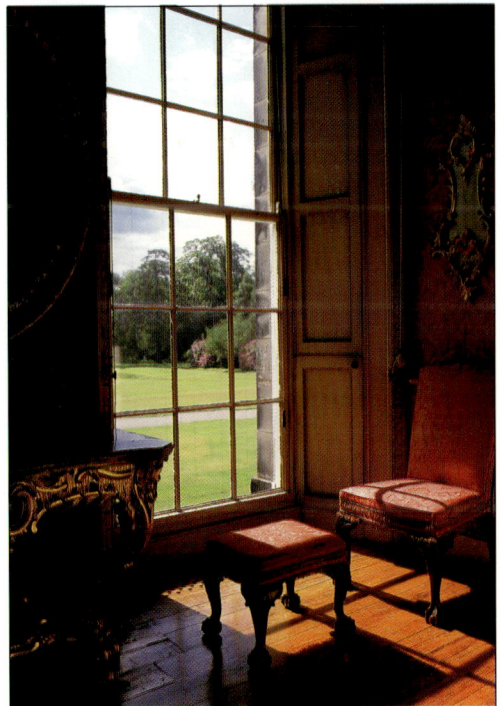

**382** *This huge sash window at Hopetoun House,* Lothian, *Scotland, reaches almost from floor to ceiling.*

**383** opposite *Holy Trinity, Long Melford, Suffolk, is one of the outstanding wool churches of East Anglia. Note the long aisle parallel to the nave and above it the range of clerestory windows.*

# Y

## Wing
Flanking extension to a large house.

## Wool church
Not a specific type or style, the term refers to churches which were largely financed through the profits of the wool and cloth trade. These were generally parish churches in the Perpendicular mode of the fifteenth century, e.g. **Holy Trinity, Long Melford**, *Suffolk*, and **St Peter & St Paul, Northleach**, *Glos.*

## Wrought iron [see IRONWORK]

## Yealm [see THATCH]

## Yett
Defensive door in a Scottish castle, consisting of an iron grille, e.g. at **Mingarry Castle**, *Highland*, Scotland. [see PORTCULLIS]

# Z

## Zig-zag [see CHEVRON]

## Acknowledgments

The material for this book has been gathered in the course of research and photography over a period of several years. The people whose help and co-operation have made it all possible are now too many to mention individually, so I would simply like to restate my indebtedness to them all as expressed in acknowledgments in previous books. This present publication is my sixth in what has been a series of illustrated books on the British Isles; and I count myself truly fortunate to have enjoyed the commitment of a single publisher. I would like to record my appreciation of the efforts of all concerned at Michael Joseph, most especially Susan Watt, Jenny Dereham and my editor, Anne Askwith. It has been at times an arduous enterprise, and I would like to thank my wife for her encouragement and understanding as I have pursued my researches from one end of the country to other. Finally, I would like to thank Shell U.K. Limited for their generous support in making possible this ambitious publication.

# Index of Buildings

Numbers in italics refer to the page numbers of illustrations

# Index of Architects

# List of County Abbreviations